VIENNESE APPLE PA[...]
MIDNIGHT ONION S[...]
SEAFOOD NEWBURG • HAM QUICHE •
CREAMY SCALLOPED POTATOES •
STRAWBERRIES ROMANOFF • POT AU FEU •

From appetizer to soup to entree to dessert; from breakfast to dinner; from snacks to banquets; from cooking for one to preparing food children will enjoy, *The Tappan Creative Cookbook for Microwave Ovens and Ranges* provides the most complete array of recipes for both microwave and conventional stoves. This remarkably versatile book offers over 400 savory dishes to suit anyone's taste, budget, and lifestyle. So turn on your oven, mix the ingredients, and then sit back and enjoy a mouth-watering meal courtesy of

THE TAPPAN CREATIVE COOKBOOK FOR MICROWAVE OVENS AND RANGES

"Recipes you never dreamed could be made on a microwave."—THE PHOENIX GAZETTE

"Features recipes that cannot be found in any other book."—THE FLINT JOURNAL

SYLVIA SCHUR, a noted food consultant and former food editor of *Look* Magazine, is currently the director of Creative Food Service.

Creative Cookery from SIGNET

☐ **THE LOS ANGELES TIMES NATURAL FOODS COOKBOOK** by Jeanne Voltz, Food Editor, Woman's Day Magazine. Discover the joys of cooking and eating naturally with this book of over 600 savory, simple-to-follow recipes. Whether you are concerned with taste or nutrition, these delicious and healthy recipes—high in fiber content—will delight everyone from the gourmet chef to the dedicated dieter.
(#E9038—$2.95)

☐ **THE JEWISH LOW-CHOLESTEROL COOKBOOK** by Roberta Leviton, with an Introduction by Rabbi Meyer J. Strassfeld. This modern, health-conscious cookbook offers over 200 taste-tempting recipes from around the world to help you cut your cholesterol and lose weight without sacrificing any of those traditional favorites. Replete with tables, charts, and tips for easy preparation, here is your passport to a kitchen full of healthy nourishment. (#E8623—$2.50)

☐ **DR. ATKINS' SUPER ENERGY COOKBOOK** by Fran Gare and Helen Monica, with an Introduction by Dr. Robert C. Atkins. The authorized cookbook for the #1 new diet discovery! It contains 3 high-energy diets and over 300 rejuvenating recipes that conquer fatigue and depression while helping you control your weight. (#E7942—$2.25)*

☐ **BAKE YOUR OWN BREAD** and Be Healthier by Floss and Stan Dworkin. Dozens of easy, delicious recipes for breads that are healthier and cheaper than "store bought" and free of harmful additives. This illustrated, step-by-step guide will take you through each stage of preparation for making and storing a whole breadbasket full of old favorites and new variations. It's a simple process, easily mastered—try it!
(#J9424—$1.95)

* Price slightly higher in Canada

THE TAPPAN CREATIVE COOKBOOK FOR MICROWAVE OVENS AND RANGES

RECIPES COMPILED, DEVELOPED AND TESTED BY
SYLVIA SCHUR

A SIGNET BOOK

NEW AMERICAN LIBRARY

TIMES MIRROR

SIGNET TRADEMARK REG. U.S. PAT. OFF. AND FOREIGN COUNTRIES
REGISTERED TRADEMARK—MARCA REGISTRADA
HECHO EN CHICAGO, U.S.A.

SIGNET, SIGNET CLASSICS, MENTOR, PLUME, MERIDIAN AND NAL BOOKS
are published by The New American Library, Inc.,
1633 Broadway, New York, New York 10019.

First Signet Printing, April, 1981

1 2 3 4 5 6 7 8 9

PRINTED IN THE UNITED STATES OF AMERICA

CONTENTS

FOREWORD

Most cookbooks today are divided according to appetizers, entrées and desserts, with side trips to sauces and other recipes.

At Tappan where we make appliances to suit the way people live (we make one kind of range for apartment life, another for homes, still another for vacation houses or mobile homes) we thought it about time that someone created a recipe book that understood our eating differences. Some people cook for adults only, others for little children with small appetites, some for people who love to eat fancy, and some for people who want plain cooking.

We commissioned Sylvia Schur, director of Creative Food Service, to work with Margaret Kelly of Tappan. Our goal was to develop new and interesting recipes that include ingredients to be found in most supermarkets and to provide instructions that give satisfactory results for the effort involved. But most of all we wanted recipes that fit the kind of life real people live. We wanted to recognize the fact that in a society where almost half the married women work, there must be a simple way to eat at home. To help provide that simple way we developed the microwave oven for home use over 20 years ago. But no one knows better than I that not all recipes will be prepared with microwave, so we have included instructions for both microwave and conventional cooking throughout the book.

There are easy, comfortable ways to eat at home. We don't think you have to spend your life eating hamburgers in your car at a fast food operation. We don't think take-out pizza is the same as live-in cooking. And we also believe that no one should spend unnecessary time in the kitchen.

The idea of this book, then, is to present recipes that fit the way you live ... recipes that are easy to prepare and fun to eat, and that add pleasure to the way you live.

Mansfield, Ohio

W. R. Tappan

THE IMPORTANT
FACTS ABOUT
MICROWAVE COOKERY

A microwave oven, like all other appliances, should be understood before it is used. There are a lot of myths about microwave cookery, so before you begin to cook with a microwave oven be sure you understand not only how to operate the oven but how to get the most out of it.

What are microwaves? Microwaves are small waves similar to radio waves. They are produced by a magnetron tube which is the heart of a microwave oven. This magnetron tube generates many microwaves when the microwave oven door is closed and latched, the timer dial set and a cook button pushed. Microwaves are similar to light waves that are produced when a light switch is turned on. Just as there is no more light in a room when the light is switched off, there are no more microwaves in the oven when the microwave oven is turned off, the door is opened or the timer dial reaches the end of a set time.

What are the advantages of microwave cooking? The most obvious advantage is speed. As you will see from the recipes in this book, cooking time with microwave can be cut as much as 75%. And since the oven does not require preheating, even more time is saved.

The use of microwave cookery is economical and vital in conserving energy. Generally, because of shorter cooking times, less energy is used and electric bills are reduced.

Clean-up time is also cut, because microwave cooking does not require pots and pans. You can cook foods in the dish that goes to the table. In other words, you can cook and eat from the same plate.

Because of the unique way in which microwave energy is released, the oven does not generate heat, so the kitchen remains cool and comfortable.

Microwave ovens are easy to clean. The oven walls are cool even immediately following cooking, and any spatters or spillovers will not burn. A simple wiping with a damp cloth is all that is needed.

What can I cook in the microwave oven? You can cook almost everything in the microwave oven. You can cook meat, poultry and fish. You can prepare vegetables. The microwave oven can poach, bake and steam. The only thing it cannot do is broil.

The microwave oven is not only ideal for cooking foods from the raw state, but it is excellent when used to defrost frozen meats or heat frozen cooked foods.

Does microwave cookery affect the nutritive value of foods? No, except for vegetables. Generally vegetables are cooked in a microwave oven without the water required for conventional cooking. As a result, there is less vitamin loss.

Do I need special pots and pans for microwave cookery? No, because you can use ordinary china or pottery. No metal utensils are to be used in the microwave oven because they reflect the microwaves and prevent penetration of the food. Do not use any dishes with metal trim, they can damage the oven. And do not use a meat thermometer unless it is specially made for a microwave!

Recommended for use are glass and ceramic dishes (including casseroles, utility dishes, cake dishes and pie plates); pottery, paper (but not paper plates with wax coatings or designs . . . plates should be white); china; plastic (if it's safe for the dishwasher, it's safe for the microwave oven); wood and straw (yes, you can use your baskets to heat dinner rolls).

Aluminum foil in small amounts may be used to prevent over-cooking of certain portions of poultry or meats. For example, poultry wing tips and leg ends are covered with foil to prevent over-cooking, but the foil should not touch the walls or top of the oven. Metal skewers may be used if they are placed carefully in large amounts of food (do not allow the skewers to touch, nor should they come in contact with the metal sides, back, or door of the oven). Or, use wooden picks rather than metal.

To check a utensil for microwave usage, place a glass measuring cup with water inside the utensil. Set in the oven and put the timer at 30 seconds. If the utensil feels warm at the end of that time, do not use it for microwave cookery. If the water is warm and the utensil cool, then go ahead and use the utensil.

How should foods be arranged in the oven when more than one item is cooked? Arrangement of food is important because objects or other foods shield the microwaves and prevent them from reaching all foods at the same time.

Recommended procedure in baking potatoes, apples, cupcakes or eggs in custard cups is to place all items in a circle. The objects in the circle would shield an item placed in the center and slow the cooking.

Because of shielding it is sometimes necessary, for more even cooking, to stir foods, turn them, or change position in the oven during the cooking process.

When placing foods on a platter, put thicker pieces or those that absorb heat more slowly (because of composition or size) at the edge of the plate. Put foods that cook fast in the center and the heating of the plate of food will be more even.

What shape dishes should be used for cooking? Foods cook more evenly in round dishes than in square. In square dishes the energy may cause overcooking in the corners.

Are foods ready for serving as soon as they come out of the oven? In many recipes a standing time is given at the end of the cooking time. This is important. Remember that the heat energy is quickly absorbed into food. To make certain that the food is evenly cooked, it is necessary to allow a standing or heat-equalizing time. Thus, if roasts are to be rare (internal temperature of 140°), they are removed from the oven when the internal temperature is 120°. For medium roasts, the internal temperature after standing should be 160°; well done, 170°. To assure proper temperature, remove roasts when the interior temperature is about 20° less than the cooked temperature needed. Cover the roasts with foil after removing from the oven so the surface will be warm. Allow a standing time of about 30 minutes. The same procedure should be followed for poultry.

With vegetables it is recommended that following cooking, the vegetables stand 2 to 4 minutes with the lid in place. Cooking will continue from the heat that is absorbed by the food, and this heat will spread evenly throughout the vegetables.

What are some everyday shortcuts I can take with the microwave? The best thing about a microwave oven is its versatility. It can be used in both cooking and baking to shorten times for:

Melting butter, margarine or chocolate: Place the ingredients in a dish and heat until melted.

Heating or boiling water: Just put the container of water in the oven. One glass measuring cup of water will take about 2½ to 3 minutes.

Baking or stewing fruits: Most fruits must stand for five minutes after cooking. Baked apples may seem slightly hard after cooking but will be soft after the standing time. To retain heat be sure to cover the fruit during the standing time.

Preventing excess charring of grilled meats: Precook chicken, ham or roasts in the microwave oven until three-quarters cooked. Then finish on a rotisserie or charcoal grill.

Heating dinner rolls and/or stale breads to oven freshness: Place in basket lined with a cloth or paper napkin. Set in microwave oven with a cup of hot water, and cook until only slightly warm. Do not overcook, or rolls will become tough and rubbery.

What are some of the shortcuts for gourmet cooks using a microwave oven?

Making white roux without scorching or darkening: Use the microwave to replace a double boiler or low heat control in preparing scalded milk, custard desserts, delicate sauces.

Thickening liquids in the microwave: Add the required amount of *beurre manié* (equal amounts of softened butter and flour combined). You can keep a quantity of *beurre manié* in a tightly covered jar in the refrigerator, or you can divide *beurre manié* into one-tablespoon packages, wrap in freezer paper and freeze up to six months. To use, add three tablespoons *beurre manié* for the thickening power of two tablespoons flour or one tablespoon cornstarch.

Preparing beef, chicken or vegetables stocks: The microwave cuts time considerably.

Preparing Duxelles (see page 166): This mushroom paste can be cooked quickly in the microwave and used to enrich gravies and sauces for meat and poultry.

Heating liqueurs for flaming: Heat for 20 to 30 seconds. Do not ignite the liqueur in the microwave oven.

Preparing Melba toast: Arrange thin slices of stale bread (crusts removed) on paper towels. Cook about two minutes, let stand five minutes, turn over and cook about two minutes longer. Repeat procedure until toast is very crisp and evenly colored. For herb Melba, spread individual portions with butter, sprinkle with dried herbs and heat in microwave one minute until hot.

Is microwave cookery safe? All microwave ovens sold in the United States meet the safety standards set for microwave ovens by the Department of Health, Education and Welfare, the Federal Communications Commission and the Underwriters Laboratory.

Microwave cookery emits fewer microwaves than a transistor radio. Like all appliances, however, the microwave oven must be used correctly, according to manufacturer's directions.

What else should I know before I start cooking with microwave? You should always read the owner's manual before using any appliance the first time. There are some general tips, however, that work no matter what brand of microwave oven you own:

Remember that when you increase or decrease the amount of food (two or three baked potatoes instead of one), the cooking times change.

Frozen foods (particularly meats) should be defrosted in the oven, removed and allowed to stand for five minutes before cooking proceeds.

Frozen prepared foods should be removed from metal containers before they are heated in the microwave oven.

Frozen foods in pouches can be placed directly in the microwave oven, but the pouch should be punctured with a fork to allow steam to escape. Potato skins should be punctured for the same reason.

The most important thing to know, before cooking with microwaves, is that your cooking time is going to be shortened . . . but you'll never shortchange the people who eat your food because microwave cookery is a family experience. We say everyone can be a happy microwave cook—and here are recipes to prove it!

IMPORTANT: Times may vary slightly from one microwave oven to another. The recipes in this book were developed for use in a 600-watt microwave oven. If the wattage is higher, required cooking times will be shorter. If wattage is lower, allow more cooking time than is indicated. It should be noted also that times may vary slightly from one 600-watt unit to another.

BREAKFASTS
(HOT AND COLD ... BIG AND LITTLE)

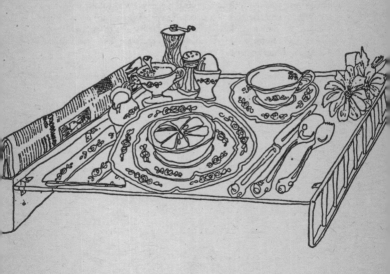

Breakfast is the most misunderstood meal in America. A good breakfast is a good start, but a good breakfast need not be elaborate. It can be quick and nutritious, hot and delicious, and just plain easy to fix.

Because so many of us tend to make breakfast an eat-and-run meal, we have some nutritious suggestions on doing just that. And where time is important, nothing works better for you than a microwave oven.

When cooking eggs in a microwave oven you can poach, scramble, froach (yes, froach) or make omelets of them. For plain hard or soft-cooked eggs in the shell, conventional cooking should be used.

When you cook eggs with microwave, be sure to undercook them slightly because cooking continues after the eggs are removed from the oven. Always pierce the yolk of a poached or fried (froached) egg with the tines of the fork during cooking in order to allow steam to escape.

When you scramble eggs you must open the oven door frequently and stir the eggs in order to get better texture.

In this section, as in all sections of the book, directions are given for both conventional and microwave cooking.

BREAKFASTS

FOR FAMILIES WITH CHILDREN WHO EAT AND EAT

HEATING CHART FOR FRESH ROLLS, PASTRIES AND BREADS

FOR
THE ONE
OF YOU

HOT GRAPEFRUIT

½ grapefruit, seeded and cored
1 teaspoon honey or brown sugar
¼ cup cottage cheese
1 tablespoon wheat germ

With a sharp knife separate grapefruit sections from skin. Sweeten fruit with honey or sugar

Range

Preheat oven to hot 450°F or set broiler at very low heat. Place grapefruit on square of heavy-duty foil or in small pan. Bake or broil 10 minutes until heated through.

Microwave

Place grapefruit on serving plate. Cook 2½ minutes until heated through.

Cooking Time Saved: 7½ minutes

Top hot grapefruit with cottage cheese and wheat germ. Breakfast on the half shell!

POACHED EGG

1 egg
Water
Salt
Pepper or parsley

Range

Fill small skillet with water. Add seasoning. Bring water to a boil, reduce heat. Break egg into cup, slip egg into simmering water. Cover, cook until white is opaque (3 to 5 minutes). Remove with slotted spoon.

Microwave

Pour ¼ cup water in small, deep bowl. Add seasoning, break egg into water. Cover bowl with wax paper, cook 45 seconds. If white is not opaque cook another 30 seconds. Drain off water.

Serve poached egg on toast, if desired.

EGG IN A HOLE

1 slice bread
2 teaspoons butter or margarine
1 egg
Salt, pepper

Cut 2" hole out of center of bread. Butter bread for range, if desired.

Range

Preheat butter or margarine in small skillet. Set bread in pan. Break egg into hole, season with salt and pepper. Cook about 8 to 10 minutes, or longer, to desired doneness. (Toast "hole," if desired.)

Microwave

Toast bread, put on plate, break egg into hole, season with salt and pepper. Cover with wax paper. Cook 45 seconds, or until egg sets. Uncover, cook 15 to 30 seconds, or until desired doneness. (Heat "hole," if desired.)

Cooking Time Saved: 6 to 8 minutes

Variations: Spread bread lightly with mustard before cooking; top with strips of ham or cheese, then add egg.

12

FROACHED EGGS

1 egg
1 teaspoon butter or margarine
Salt, pepper

Place 1 teaspoon butter or margarine in individual glass custard cup.

Range

Preheat oven to 325°F. Heat cups until butter melts, about 4 minutes. Break egg into each heated cup, season with salt and pepper, and bake about 15 minutes or until set.

Microwave

Melt butter for 20 seconds. Break egg into cup, season with salt and pepper. Cook about 45 seconds or until set.

Cooking Time Saved: 18 minutes

BREAKFAST SOUPER EGG

1 cup broth
1 egg
Toast

Range

Bring prepared soup or instant broth to boil in small pan. Break egg into soup. Simmer 3 to 5 minutes, until egg is set. Pour egg and soup over toast in bowl, cover, let toast soak 1 minute.

Microwave

Place in bowl: toast, soup and egg. Cover with wax paper, cook 2 minutes, or until egg is set.

INSTANT COFFEE OR TEA OR COCOA

1 teaspoon instant coffee or tea or cocoa mix
Water

Range

Bring water to boil, pour boiling over instant coffee, tea or cocoa in cup, stir.

Microwave

Stir coffee or tea or cocoa in cup with water. Cook until steam rises, about 1 minute. Better flavor than ever!

MOCHA

1 cup coffee
1 teaspoon chocolate pieces
1 dash of cinnamon
Cream

Range	Microwave
Heat coffee in small pan. Add chocolate pieces and cinnamon, stir over low heat until chocolate melts, about 4 minutes. Pour into cup.	Pour coffee over chocolate pieces in cup. Cook 1 minute. Stir. Add cinnamon.

Add cream, if desired.

COCOA

2 teaspoons cocoa
2 teaspoons sugar
Dash salt
¼ cup water
½ cup milk

Range	Microwave
Stir cocoa, sugar, salt and water in small pan over moderate heat until boiling. Add milk, heat until foaming, stirring constantly.	Combine cocoa, sugar, salt and water in mug. Cook 30 seconds. Stir in milk, heat one minute longer.

HOT TOASTED BREAKFAST

Toast or toasted English muffin   Tomato slice
Butter or margarine   Salt, pepper
Slice cooked ham   Cheese slice

*Spread toasted bread or English muffin with butter or margarine.
Top with ham, tomato, seasoning, cheese.*

Range	Microwave
Place toast or muffin on pan or foil and broil under low heat about 3 to 5 minutes, until bubbling and heated through. Remove to serving plate.	Place toast or muffin on serving plate or wax paper; heat about 45 seconds.

CEREAL IN THE BOWL

1 cup water	Butter or margarine
¼ teaspoon salt	Sweetener
½ cup oatmeal	

Range

In small saucepan, bring water and salt to boil. Stir in cereal, cook 1 to 15 minutes, or according to directions, stirring constantly. Spoon into serving bowl.

Microwave

In 2½ cup bowl, combine water, salt and cereal. Cover bowl with wax paper, cook 1 minute. Stir, cook 30 seconds.

Cooking Time Saved: 14 minutes

For rich flavor, just before finish, stir in butter, sweetener to taste.

Topping Options

Top each cooked serving to taste with a choice or mix of raisins, cheese or coconut shreds, sliced bananas, berries, applesauce, milk or cream.

Egg Option

Range

Prepare cereal as above. Break egg into cereal about ½ minute before cereal is cooked, stirring constantly until set. Egg will scramble in cereal.

Microwave

Break egg into cooked microwave cereal. Do not stir. Cook another minute. Egg will remain whole and poach in the cereal.

FOR
THE TWO
OF YOU

TROUT BREAKFAST

2 frozen trout (1 package, about 10 ounces)
2 tablespoons butter or margarine
¼ sweet pepper, in strips
Salt, pepper

¼ cup water
Juice of 1 lemon
1 yellow summer squash or
10 asparagus spears
Hollandaise Sauce (optional, page 207)

Range

Place rinsed trout on buttered shallow baking pan. Arrange pepper strips on fish, season with salt and pepper, dot with butter or margarine. Add water to pan, squeeze lemon juice over fish. Bake at 425°F until fish is opaque and white to the bone when pierced with a fork, about 18 to 20 minutes. Meanwhile, clean and cut squash or trim asparagus spears. Steam squash or asparagus in pan or range until tender. Serve with Hollandaise Sauce, if desired.

Microwave

Place rinsed trout on buttered individual plates. Arrange pepper strips on fish, season with salt and pepper, dot with butter or margarine. Add water to plates, squeeze lemon juice over fish. Clean and cut squash or trim asparagus spears. Arrange alongside fish, season. Cover with wax paper, cook 5 minutes. Rotate plates, turn vegetables if necessary, cook 2 minutes longer, until vegetables are tender and fish is opaque and white to the bone when pierced with a fork. Serve with Hollandaise Sauce, if desired.

Cooking Time Saved: 12 minutes

APPLE AND ORANGE RINGS

    1 medium apple
    1 seedless orange
    2 tablespoons butter or margarine
    2 tablespoons brown sugar

Core apple and cut into rings.
Peel orange, cut into wheels.

Range

Preheat broiler. Arrange fruit in one layer on buttered pan, dot with butter or margarine, sprinkle with brown sugar. Broil 3 to 4 minutes, until hot and slightly caramelized, turning once. Arrange overlapping slices on each plate. Sprinkle with pan syrup.

Microwave

Arrange overlapping slices of fruit on two individual plates, dot with butter or margarine, sprinkle with brown sugar. Cook about 3 minutes. Cool slightly before serving.

SOUFFLÉ OMELET

    3 eggs, separated
    3 tablespoons sour cream or milk
    Salt, pepper, dash cayenne
    2 tablespoons butter or margarine

Beat egg yolks with cream or milk and seasonings. Beat whites frothy,
add pinch of salt, beat until stiff. Fold whites into yolk mixture.

Range

Heat 2 tablespoons butter or margarine in skillet. Pour in egg mixture. Cook, pulling edges back as they set, until bottom is browned. Place under broiler a few minutes until top puffs.

Microwave

Melt 1 tablespoon butter in each of 2 rounded dishes or soup plates. Add egg mixture. Cook 45 seconds, rotate dish, cook 45 seconds longer until set.

Variations: Top omelet before finish with applesauce and cinnamon,
shredded cheese or preserves to your taste.

17

SUNNYSIDES

2 to 4 eggs
2 tablespoons butter or margarine, or
1 cup tomato sauce or 1 cup Spanish sauce (below)
Salt, pepper

Range

Heat butter or margarine or sauce in 8-inch skillet. Break eggs into hot base, season with salt and pepper, cook over moderate heat to desired doneness, about 10 minutes. Or bake the mixture in preheated moderate oven (325°F) about 15 minutes.

Microwave

Heat butter, margarine or sauce in individual serving dish about 1 minute. Break 1 or 2 eggs into each dish. Cook 1 minute. Rotate dish. Cook 1 minute longer until eggs are set.

Cooking Time Saved: 8 to 13 minutes

SPANISH SAUCE

1 small onion or shallot, chopped
2 tablespoons oil
¼ green pepper, diced
2 canned or seeded ripe tomatoes, chopped

Salt, pepper
2 fresh or 1 dry basil leaf
1 mushroom chopped (optional)

Range

Cook onion or shallot in oil until translucent, but not browned, about 3 minutes. Add green pepper, tomatoes, seasoning and mushrooms. Cook about 10 minutes, or until sauce thickens. Remove leaf before serving.

Microwave

Cook onion or shallot in oil until translucent, about 1 minute. Add ingredients, cook until sauce thickens, about 2½ minutes. Remove leaf before serving.

Cooking Time Saved: About 10 minutes

HOT 'N' HIGH TOASTED BREAKFASTS

2 eggs
.¼ cup slivered ham
(or tuna or chicken)
2 tablespoons diced green pepper
1 tablespoon chopped onion

Salt, pepper, seasonings to taste
2 slices toasted bread or
English muffin halves
2 teaspoons butter or margarine

Beat eggs, add ham, green pepper, chopped onion and seasonings.

Range

Arrange bread on greased baking
sheet or heavy foil, cover with egg
mixture. Bake at 400°F until hot
and bubbly, about 7 to 8 minutes.

Microwave

Place toast on serving plates, cover
with egg mixture. Cook about 3
minutes, or until puffed and set.

FOR FAMILIES WITH LITTLE CHILDREN WHO DON'T EAT MUCH

These recipes are developed in two stages.
The first stage makes it possible to take care of small children
and the second stage is for the family's heavier eaters.

TOAST SPECIALS

Lightly toasted bread
or English muffin halves
Butter or margarine
Cinnamon-sugar
Cheese strips
Preserves

*Cut toast into strips for small children. Spread bread or muffins with
butter or margarine. Top to taste with cinnamon-sugar or cheese
for grown ups, cinnamon-sugar or preserves for children.*

Range
Place on cookie sheet or foil in a hot
oven (400°F) and heat briefly.

Microwave
Place on wax paper or paper plate
and heat briefly, about 15 seconds.
Seconds are ready in seconds!

SCRAMBLED EGGS

3 eggs
3 tablespoons water or milk
Salt, pepper

Beat eggs with water or milk and seasonings.
Cook as directed below.

CHILD'S BACON AND SCRAMBLED EGG

1 slice cooked bacon (see page 22)
3 tablespoons beaten egg mixture (above)

Place bacon on child's tray for pick-up nibbling.
Pour egg mixture into buttered custard cup.

Range	Microwave
Place cup in simmering water in small pan, cook and stir until set, about 4 minutes.	Place cup in microwave, cook 30 seconds. Stir. Cook 15 seconds longer if necessary, until set.

ADULT'S BACON AND SCRAMBLED EGGS

3 slices cooked bacon (see page 22)
Butter or margarine
Remaining egg mixture

Range	Microwave
Place bacon pieces in skillet, heat. Add butter or margarine, if desired. Pour egg mixture into skillet. Cook, stirring with a fork, until set, about 2 minutes. Turn onto serving plate.	Place bacon pieces on each plate. Heat 45 seconds, with small amount of butter or margarine, if desired. Pour egg mixture onto buttered plate, cook 45 seconds. Stir, cook 30 seconds longer, or to taste.

READY-BACON

3 bacon strips, standard thickness

Cut bacon in two-inch pieces.

Range

Place bacon in cold skillet or in baking pan. Cook over low heat, turning pieces and draining fat, or in moderate oven (350°F) without turning, until crisp and browned. This takes about 5 minutes top range; 10 minutes in oven. Drain on paper towels.

Microwave

Place bacon pieces on triple thickness of paper towels (or paper plate); cover with paper towel. Cook about 2 minutes. If necessary, or for crisp bacon, cook 45 seconds longer.

FRENCH TOAST AND SCRAMBLED EGGS

3 eggs	**1 white or whole wheat bread slice**
½ teaspoon salt	Butter or margarine
¼ cup milk	Syrup or cinnamon-sugar

Break eggs into shallow dish. Beat with fork, adding salt and milk. Dip bread slice into mixture, turn just until coated. Reserve remaining egg mixture to scramble plain or with bacon pieces.

Range

Heat butter or margarine in small skillet until bubbling, about 2 minutes. Brown French toast on both sides, about 6 minutes. Remove to plate, add syrup or cinnamon-sugar, cut into small pieces for children.

Microwave

Heat butter or margarine in serving plate for 30 seconds. Place bread on plate, cook 40 seconds. Turn, top with syrup or cinnamon-sugar, cook 15 seconds. Cut into small pieces for children.

Make scrambled eggs with remaining mixture, or use to make additional French toast.

22

OMELETS IN THREE SIZES AND TASTES

4 eggs	Butter or margarine
4 tablespoons milk	1 tablespoon minced parsley or chives
Salt, pepper	2 tablespoons shredded cheese

Place eggs in shallow bowl with milk, salt and pepper.
Beat with fork until light. Use to make 3 omelets.

Range

For Child: Heat about 1 teaspoon butter in omelet pan. Add about 3 tablespoons egg mixture, tilt pan to spread. As it sets, roll up like a crepe and roll onto child's plate. Cut into "pick-up pieces." Wipe pan clean.

Microwave

For Child: Heat ½ teaspoon butter on 6-inch plate about 10 seconds. Add 3 tablespoons egg mixture, cook 30 seconds, until set. Cut into "pick-up pieces," cool a minute before serving.

Range

For Hearty Appetite: Heat about 1 tablespoon butter in omelet pan, pour in ⅔ of remaining egg mixture. Pull edges back with fork as egg sets, letting uncooked portion run to bottom. When center is almost set, sprinkle with ½ of herbs and all the cheese. Roll omelet onto serving plate. Wipe pan clean.

Microwave

For Hearty Appetite: Heat 1 tablespoon butter in shallow soup bowl, about 30 seconds. Pour in ⅔ of remaining egg mixture, sprinkle with ½ of herbs and all of cheese. Cook 30 seconds, rotate plate, cook 30 seconds longer, until set.

Range

For Lighter Appetite: Heat rounded teaspoon of butter in omelet pan. Beat remaining herb into remaining egg mixture and pour into pan. Cook as above, until top is set, omitting cheese. Roll onto serving plate.

Microwave

For Lighter Appetite: Add remaining herb to remaining egg mixture. Heat 1 teaspoon butter in 8-inch plate, 10 seconds. Add egg, cook 35 seconds, until set.

SHORT-CUT MILK DRINKS

Range
Heat 1 pint milk to scalding in small pan and pour into serving pitcher.

Microwave
Heat 1 pint of milk in serving pitcher until steamy, about 3 minutes.

Cocoa: Spoon instant cocoa mix into cup, top with hot milk and stir until frothy. Use small cups for small children.

Café au Lait: Pour hot milk over 1 teaspoon instant coffee in cup, stir until frothy.

FOR FAMILIES
WITH CHILDREN WHO
EAT AND EAT

BREAKFAST BUNS

Large rolls	Cooked Bacon
Butter	Jelly
Cheese	Sliced chicken or turkey
Sliced boiled ham	Cranberry Sauce
Mustard	Deviled ham
Peanut Butter	Poached or fried eggs

Split rolls, butter if desired. Fill with sliced cheese and ham, spread lightly with mustard. Or spread with peanut butter, top with cooked bacon, spread jelly on other side and close. Or fill roll with sliced chicken or turkey, cranberry sauce. Or spread a roll with deviled ham, top with fried or poached egg.

Range	Microwave
Wrap rolls in foil, place on pan, bake at 375°F about 15 minutes, until hot through.	Place on paper towel or serving plate. Heat through about 45 seconds to 1 minute each.

Cooking Time Saved: 14 minutes

SHAGGY BREAKFAST ROLLS

1 package unbaked refrigerator rolls (10)
Butter or margarine
½ cup granola cereal
Honey or syrup (cinnamon optional)

Separate rolls, flatten, spread with butter or margarine.
Sprinkle with granola. Roll up.

Range

Place filled rolls in buttered muffin pans, drizzle a little honey or syrup over each. Bake at 425°F about 10 minutes until puffed and golden. Sprinkle with cinnamon, if desired.

Microwave

Place filled rolls in buttered custard cups or paper cups. Cook, five at a time, until puffed (about 2 minutes). Pour honey or syrup over hot rolls. Sprinkle with cinnamon, if desired.

Cooking Time Saved: about 10 minutes

HASH AND EGGS

1 can (16 ounces) corned beef hash
4 slices canned or fresh pineapple (optional)

4 small eggs
Salt, pepper
Butter, margarine (for range only)

Open and remove top and bottom of can of hash, remove cylinder of hash.
Cut into 4 slices, set each on a pineapple slice, if desired.
Make a deep indentation in each with back of a tablespoon.

Range

Place hash nests on buttered baking sheet. Drop egg into each nest. Season with salt and pepper. Bake at 350°F for about 25 minutes, until hash is hot and eggs are set.

Microwave

Place hash nests on serving plates or 8-inch pie plate. Drop egg into each nest. Season with salt and pepper. Cook each 1 minute. Turn, cook another minute, or until eggs are set.

Cooking Time Saved: 20 minutes

PANCAKES IN MANY LANGUAGES

2 cups whole wheat flour or
enriched flour or a combination
4 teaspoons baking powder
1 teaspoon salt
2 tablespoons sugar

2 eggs
¼ cup salad oil
2 cups milk
½ cup ready-to-eat cereal flakes
or uncooked oatmeal

*Combine flour, baking powder, salt and sugar. Add eggs, oil and milk,
stir just to blend. Fold in cereal flakes or oatmeal.*

Range

Preheat griddle until very hot, grease
lightly if desired. Pour on ¼ cup
batter per pancake. Cook until
bubbles appear on the surface and
break. Turn and brown on other
side. Serve 2 to 3 pancakes to a
portion, topping as desired. Makes
16 pancakes.

Microwave

Butter 8-inch serving plate. Pour on
⅓ cup batter. Cook each 1½ minutes,
or until bubbles appear on surface
and break. Turn dish ¼ turn half way
through cooking time. Top as desired
(see below). Heat 30 seconds. Makes
about 12 hearty pancakes.

Serving Suggestions

Egg Pancakes: Top with poached or fried egg.

Pancake Fun: Just before pancake is finished cooking,
spell a name or a birthday greeting on it
with cheese, raisins or chocolate or dark
syrup. Complete cooking briefly.

American Berries: Top with blueberries and sugar, or
cranberry sauce.

Viennese Apple: Top with poached apple sections or
applesauce, sprinkle with cinnamon-sugar,
serve with whipped cream.

Banana: Top with banana slices, butter and honey.

Cheese: Top with slivered American cheese.

Meaty: Add to batter before cooking, 2
frankfurters, cut into thin slices, or ½
pound crumbled hamburger meat. Cook
slightly longer if necessary.

Sausage: Top pancakes with hot sausage and
applesauce.

Tex-Mex: Top with chili.

*Tip: Wrap and freeze any leftover pancakes, reheat in microwave,
about 45 seconds per pancake; or in oven at 350°F about 8
minutes.*

Other Breakfast Ideas

Fruit: Small boxes of raisins, orange sections to nibble, pitcher of orange juice in refrigerator, or bananas or berries.

Cereal: Instant oatmeal (assorted flavors), prepared cereals with fruit flavored gelatin to sprinkle on, wheat germ and yogurt.

Beverage: Non-fat dry milk combined with instant cocoa mix—add water or milk heated in pan or microwave.

Frozen pancakes or waffles:

Range

Place on foil or pan. Heat at 375°F, or as directed on package, for about 8 minutes, until heated through. Heat with toppings, if desired.

Microwave

Place on serving plate, heat each pancake or waffle 45 seconds, or until heated through. Heat with toppings, if desired.

Cooking Time Saved: 7 minutes

Bagels:

Frozen bagels make the once specialty rolls available in many areas. Set out with cream cheese, preserves, canned kipper slices for a do-it-yourself spread. This roll with a hole in the middle heats most effectively in the microwave.

Range

Place bagels on foil or pan, heat at 375°F until piping hot, about 6 minutes.

Microwave

Place bagel on paper towel. Heat about 15 seconds for one, 30 to 35 seconds if frozen.

HEATING CHART
FOR FRESH ROLLS,
PASTRIES AND BREADS

	425°F Oven	Microwave
Hard roll (one)	3 to 5 minutes	15 to 20 seconds
Blueberry or other muffin (one)	3 to 5 minutes	10 to 15 seconds
Cinnamon roll (one 3" diameter)	3 to 5 minutes	10 to 15 seconds
Danish pastry (one 3" diameter)	3 to 5 minutes	15 to 20 seconds
Coffee cake (one 3" square)	3 to 5 minutes	15 to 20 seconds
Small loaf white bread, unsliced (7 ounces)	5 minutes	45 to 50 seconds
Small loaf whole wheat bread, unsliced (7 ounces)	5 minutes	45 to 50 seconds
Apple pie (one 4-ounce piece)	5 minutes	15 to 20 seconds
Plain doughnut (one)	3 to 5 minutes	10 to 15 seconds
Frozen bagel (one)	5 minutes	30 to 35 seconds

EASY EATING

(IDEAS THAT WORK
NO MATTER WHEN YOU EAT)

In some families, nobody eats at the same time.

The children eat dinner while their parents are still at work, and parents eat dinner while children watch TV.

Although this is often stand-up eating or hurry-up kind of food, you can still do more than open a can of tuna fish or warm a TV dinner.

Easy eating, whether it's alone or with others, can be pleasant. It can also be simple, which is what makes it pleasant.

You will notice that when you use a microwave oven cooking times are shortened.

In this EASY EATING section we have also included some instant recipes for entertaining. After all, if you can make a fondue in five minutes in your microwave oven, or chicken yakitori in three minutes, why not entertain at home?

And if you want, you can prepare foods early in the day, refrigerate them, and then heat them in minutes (sometimes seconds) in your microwave oven.

In this section, as in all sections of the book, directions are given for both conventional and microwave cooking.

EASY EATING

FOR FAMILIES

FOR GUESTS

FOR
THE ONE
OF YOU

BAKED SWEET POTATO BOATS

1 medium sweet potato, scrubbed
1 tablespoon butter or margarine, optional

Range	Microwave
Bake potato at 350°F for 45 minutes, until fork-tender.	Cook potato about 4 minutes. Remove. Allow to stand 3 minutes. Potato should be fork-tender

Cooking Time Saved: 40 minutes

*Split potato without separating the halves,
to make a pocket. Dot with butter or margarine,
if desired, or add filling and finish cooking as below.*

Other Serving Suggestions:

Ham Boat: Fill baked sweet potato pocket with one slice chopped boiled ham, sprinkle with brown sugar, and heat 10 minutes in 350°F oven, 1 minute in microwave.

Chicken Boat: Fill potato pocket with ½ cup cooked or canned chicken and ¼ cup drained pineapple chunks, and heat 10 minutes in 350°F oven, 1 minute in microwave.

Sausage Boat: Fill potato pocket with two brown-and-serve sausages (pre-cook for range, uncooked for microwave), top with ¼ cup applesauce, and heat 10 minutes in 350°F oven, 2 minutes in microwave.

BAKED POTATO BOATS

1 medium potato, scrubbed
Salt, pepper
1 tablespoon butter or margarine

Range
Bake potato at 350°F for 45 minutes, or until fork-tender.

Microwave
Cook potato about 5 to 6 minutes, turning once. After removing from the oven allow to stand for 3 minutes. Potato should be fork-tender.

Cooking Time Saved: 40 minutes

*Split without separating the halves, to make a pocket.
Season with salt and pepper. Dot with butter or margarine.
If desired, add filling, heat as below.*

Other Serving Suggestions:

Bacon Baker: Fill baked potato pocket with two strips of crumbled, cooked bacon.

Tuna Baker: Fill baked potato pocket with a 3 to 4 ounce can of tuna to which ⅛ tablespoon of mayonnaise has been added. Sprinkle with pepper, and heat 10 minutes in 350°F oven, 1 minute in microwave.

TUNA-SPINACH SUPPER

1 can (3-4 ounces) tuna, drained
1 small onion, sliced
Dash garlic powder

Salt, pepper to taste
¼ pound fresh spinach leaves, washed
1 tablespoon oil (range only)

Range
Heat 1 tablespoon oil in a skillet, add tuna and onion, season with garlic powder, salt and pepper to taste. Stir over moderate heat 3 minutes. Add spinach, cover the pan, cook 4 minutes longer, until spinach wilts. Transfer to serving dish.

Microwave
Arrange tuna and onion on serving dish, sprinkle with garlic powder, salt and pepper to taste. Top with spinach. Cover with wax paper, cook 2 minutes, until spinach wilts.

CHICKEN IN WRAP

1 whole breast of a broiler-fryer split in half
1 small onion, sliced
1 carrot, sliced thin
½ green pepper, slivered
½ cup tomato sauce

1 tablespoon butter or margarine
Salt, pepper
Two 12-inch squares of aluminum foil (for range)
Two 12-inch squares of wax or freezer paper (for microwave)

Lay a piece of chicken on the square, place ingredients on chicken in order given. Wrap tightly, folding edges over twice to seal. Cook one, store one in freezer for later use.

Range

Thawed: Bake foil-wrapped chicken packet at 325°F for 45 minutes.

Frozen: Bake frozen packet about 50 minutes, until heated through.

Microwave

Thawed: Cook one freezer-paper wrapped chicken packet about 7 minutes, turn half way through cooking time, let stand 5 minutes.

Cooking Time Saved: 33 minutes

Frozen: Cook one frozen packet about 12 minutes, let stand 5 minutes before serving.

Cooking Time Saved: 33 minutes

SAUSAGE AND APPLE MIX

2 brown-and-serve sausages
1 tart apple, cored and sliced
½ cup drained sauerkraut
2 teaspoons brown sugar
1 teaspoon lemon juice

Range

Combine ingredients in a small skillet. Cook over low heat about 8 minutes until apple is soft and sausages are browned. Stir occasionally. Transfer to serving dish.

Microwave

Combine all ingredients on a plate. Cook about 2 minutes or until apple and sausages are hot.

SEAWORTHY PACKETS

12 ounces frozen or fresh fish fillets
1 small onion, sliced
1 cup frozen peas
2 tablespoons lemon juice
½ teaspoon thyme

Salt, pepper
Two 12-inch squares of aluminum foil (for range)
Two 12-inch squares of wax or freezer paper (for microwave)

Divide fish fillets onto squares, divide remaining ingredients on fish in order given. Wrap tightly, folding edges over twice to seal. Cook one, store one in freezer for later use.

Range

Thawed: Bake foil-wrapped fish packet at 325°F, about 30 minutes.

Frozen: Bake frozen packet at 400°F, about 25 minutes, until heated through.

Microwave

Thawed: Cook one freezer paper-wrapped fish packet 3 minutes, turn, cook 3 minutes longer. Remove, let stand 5 minutes to finish cooking.

Cooking Time Saved: 14 minutes

Frozen: Cook one frozen packet 8 minutes. Remove and let stand 5 minutes to finish cooking.

Cooking Time Saved: 12 minutes

BANANA AND HAM ROLL-UPS

2 thin slices boiled ham
Mustard, mayonnaise
1 large banana, not very ripe

2 thin slices Cheddar cheese
Marmalade
A pinch of powdered cloves

Spread ham with mustard and mayonnaise. Peel banana and split lengthwise, fill with cheese. Cut into quarters, wrap each quarter in ½ ham slice. Spread top of ham with marmalade seasoned with powdered cloves.

Range

Place ham-banana rolls on greased baking dish. Bake at 375°F, 12 minutes, until ham is lightly glazed, banana heated through, and cheese is melting. Transfer to serving dish.

Microwave

Place ham-banana rolls on serving dish, seam side down. Cook 2 minutes.

Cooking Time Saved: 10 minutes

CHINESE VEGETABLE SALAD

1 small zucchini
1 stalk celery
½ green pepper, cored and seeded
1 stalk scallion or 1 small onion
1 small tomato

Lettuce leaves
1 tablespoon oil
1 tablespoon soy sauce
Pepper

*Cut zucchini, celery, green pepper and scallion into thin diagonal slices.
Cut tomato into wedges. Tear lettuce leaves into bite-sized pieces.*

Range

Heat oil in a skillet over high heat. Add zucchini, celery, green pepper, scallion, tomato, soy sauce and pepper to taste. Cover skillet, cook 4 minutes, stirring occasionally. Add lettuce, cover, cook about 3 minutes longer.

Microwave

Place zucchini, celery, green pepper, scallion and tomato in a large serving plate. Sprinkle with oil, soy sauce and pepper to taste. Cover with an inverted glass pie plate, cook 2 minutes. Add lettuce, stir, cover, cook 1 minute more.

Vegetables should be crisp.

APPLE CHEESEWICH

2 apple slices, cored
1 English muffin, split and toasted
¼ cup grated Cheddar or crumbled blue cheese

Range

Cover English muffin halves with apple slices, sprinkle with cheese. Broil 3 to 4 minutes or until cheese is melted and apples are heated through.

Microwave

Top muffin halves with apple slices, sprinkle with cheese. Cook on serving plate about 2 minutes or until cheese melts.

IN A
SOUP
BOWL

BEANS AND FRANKS SOUP

1 can (8 ounces) baked beans with tomato sauce
1 can (10½ ounces) undiluted condensed tomato soup
1 teaspoon prepared mustard
1 tablespoon brown sugar

2 tablespoons instant minced onion
¼ cup water
2 frankfurters, sliced
Salt

Range
Combine all ingredients in a saucepan, bring to a boil, simmer 5 minutes, stirring often. Ladle into 2 serving bowls.

Microwave
Divide ingredients into 2 serving bowls, stir. Cook 5 minutes, until steaming hot, serve.

Makes 2 servings.

QUICK VEGETABLE SOUP

1 cup tomato juice
2 tablespoons fine egg noodles
¼ cup cooked or canned vegetables
Sour cream garnish (optional)

Range
Bring tomato juice to a boil in saucepan, add noodles, cook about 8 minutes, until noodles are tender. Add vegetables, heat through.

Microwave
Combine all ingredients in a large soup bowl or divide into 2 mugs. Cook about 5 to 6 minutes or until noodles are tender.

Cooking Time Saved: 10 minutes

Top with a dollop of sour cream, if desired. Makes 1 or 2 servings.

QUICK POTATO SOUP

1 teaspoon instant chicken bouillon
1 teaspoon butter or margarine
½ cup water
⅓ cup milk
⅓ cup instant mashed potato flakes

Range
Bring bouillon and butter or margarine and water to boil in saucepan. Stir in milk and potato flakes. Heat to serving temperature, ladle into bowl.

Microwave
Combine bouillon and butter or margarine and water in a soup bowl. Cook 1 minute, stir in milk and potato flakes. Heat about 1 minute longer or until at correct serving temperature.

Serve hot or cold. Makes 1 serving.

ALBONDIGA SOUP (Meatball Soup)

¼ pound chopped beef	Flour
¼ teaspoon minced onion	Butter or margarine for
½ slice bread, crumbled	frying (Range only)
2 tablespoons milk	1 cup water
¼ teaspoon salt	1 beef bouillon cube
Dash pepper	Grated Parmesan cheese

Mix meat, onion, bread, milk and seasonings.
Shape into 4 balls, coat with flour.

Range
Brown meatballs on all sides in hot butter or margarine in skillet. Add water and bouillon cube, stir to dissolve. Simmer 5 minutes. Pour into soup bowl.

Microwave
Cook meatballs in soup bowl 1 minute, turn over, cook 30 seconds longer. Add water and bouillon cube, cook about 3 minutes, stir to dissolve cube.

Sprinkle with grated Parmesan cheese. Makes 1 serving.

ITALIAN SOUP

1 can (15 ounces) spaghetti
with tomato sauce
1 can (8 ounces) tomato sauce
1 cup beef broth

¼ pound peperoni or
salami, in bite-sized pieces
¼ teaspoon oregano
2 tablespoons grated Parmesan cheese

Range

Combine spaghetti, tomato sauce, broth, peperoni and oregano in saucepan. Stir, bring slowly to a boil, simmer about 5 minutes, stirring often. Ladle into serving bowls.

Microwave

Divide spaghetti into 4 soup bowls, add remaining ingredients except cheese, stir. Cook until steaming, about 10 minutes. Rearrange bowls half way through the cooking time.

Sprinkle with grated cheese, serve. Makes 4 servings.

CANNED SOUPS

Range

Stir any canned condensed soup and 1 can water together in a saucepan. Bring slowly to a boil, stirring now and then. Simmer 5 minutes.

Microwave

Divide canned condensed soup evenly into 2 or 3 bowls. Fill can with water, divide into bowls. Stir, cover bowls with wax paper, cook 3 to 5 minutes, until steaming hot.

Makes 2 or 3 servings.

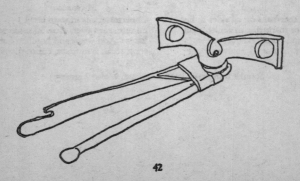

FOR THE TWO OF YOU

~

EGGPLANT SANDWICHES

1 small eggplant (about 6 ounces)
1 egg, beaten
Fresh bread crumbs
Salt, pepper

2 tablespoons butter or margarine
8 slices mozzarella cheese, ¼-inch thick
Oregano

Peel eggplant, slice into 8 rounds. Dip eggplant slices into beaten egg, then into bread crumbs seasoned with salt and pepper, to coat both sides.

Range

Melt butter or margarine in large skillet. Add eggplant, brown lightly on both sides. Top the eggplant slices with mozzarella cheese, sprinkle with oregano. Place under broiler until eggplant is tender and cheese is melted. Transfer to serving platter.

Microwave

Melt butter or margarine in shallow platter. Add eggplant slices, cover with wax paper, cook 4 minutes. Top eggplant slices with mozzarella cheese, sprinkle with oregano. Cook 3 minutes until eggplant is tender and cheese is melted.

Makes 4 sandwiches.

CHEESE ANCHOVY APPETIZERS

1 large tomato
6 flat anchovy fillets
2 thick slices Swiss or Gruyère cheese
Oregano

Cut off blossom and stem ends of tomato; slice tomato in half crosswise.
Top with anchovy fillets and cheese, sprinkle with oregano.

Range

Place tomato halves in small greased casserole. Bake at 350°F for 12 minutes, until cheese is melted and tomato is hot. Transfer to serving plate.

Microwave

Place each tomato half on individual serving plate. Cook 2 minutes until cheese is melted and tomato is hot.

Cooking Time Saved: 8 minutes

CREAMY TUNA SUPPER

3 tablespoons butter or margarine
3 tablespoons flour
1½ cups milk
1 can (7 ounces) flaked tuna, drained

¼ pound fresh mushrooms, thinly sliced
Salt, pepper
2 slices toast or 1 English muffin, split and toasted
Pimiento strips for garnish

Range

Melt butter or margarine in skillet, stir in flour. Add milk, stirring constantly over low heat until sauce is thick and smooth. Add tuna and mushrooms, cook until hot and bubbly, stirring occasionally.

Microwave

Blend butter or margarine and flour to make a paste. Heat milk in a 1 quart casserole until warm, about 1 minute. Stir in flour mixture, cook 5 minutes until sauce boils and is thick and smooth. Stir occasionally. Stir in tuna and mushrooms, heat 2 minutes or until hot and bubbly.

Season with salt and pepper to taste. Serve over toast or toasted
English muffin halves, garnish with pimiento strips.

FISH DISH FOR TWO (AND THEN SOME)

1 pound frozen fish fillets
⅔ cup quick cooking rice
1 can (10½ ounces) onion soup
¼ cup milk
½ tomato, thinly sliced

Thaw fish slightly at room temperature to separate fillets, or thaw in microwave 2 minutes. Put rice into shallow 2-quart oven casserole. Add onion soup, milk, fish and tomato slices.

Range | Microwave
Bake casserole at 350°F for 25 minutes or until fish flakes easily. | Cook casserole 4 minutes, rotate dish, cook 4 minutes longer.

Cooking Time Saved: 17 minutes

Bonus: Use 1 cup or more of leftover Fish Dish for fish chowder (below).

FISH CHOWDER

1 cup leftover Fish Dish (above)
1 tablespoon flour
1 cup + 2 tablespoons milk

Break fish into small chunks. Make a paste of flour and 2 tablespoons milk. Add 1 cup milk and stir smooth. Add fish and remaining sauce.

Range | Microwave
Bring chowder to a boil in a saucepan, reduce heat, simmer, covered, 5 minutes. | Cook chowder in covered 1-quart casserole about 4 minutes or until hot.

Makes 2 hearty servings.

LICKETY-SPLIT DIVAN

1 package (10 ounces) frozen broccoli
4 thick slices cooked chicken
1 can (10½ ounces) condensed cream soup
(celery, chicken, or mushroom)
⅓ cup milk or sour cream
2 tablespoons grated Parmesan cheese

Range

Thaw broccoli at room temperature or plunge into boiling water until it can be separated into spears.
Arrange broccoli in buttered shallow baking dish. Top with chicken slices. Blend soup and milk or cream. Pour over chicken. Sprinkle with grated cheese. Bake at 350°F for 30 minutes or until broccoli is tender and sauce is bubbly.

Microwave

Thaw broccoli about 3 minutes in package in microwave. Arrange broccoli in shallow baking dish. Top with chicken slices. Blend soup and milk or cream, pour over chicken. Sprinkle with grated cheese. Cook 5 minutes, or until broccoli is tender and sauce is hot.

Cooking Time Saved: 25 minutes

Makes 4 servings. Wrap the extra servings in freezer wrap, and freeze for future use.

Range

To reheat, remove freezer wrap, turn into buttered casserole. Preheat oven to 350°F. Bake about 25 minutes.

Microwave

To reheat, turn onto serving plate, heat 5 minutes.

Cooking Time Saved: 20 minutes

Divine Divan Variations:

Fresh or frozen vegetables:	Asparagus, green peas, string beans, corn kernels, sliced carrots, zucchini, yellow squash.
Meat or fish:	Cooked turkey, boiled ham, cooked pork, lamb or veal; canned tuna or salmon.
Soups into sauces:	Condensed cream of tomato, onion, Cheddar cheese.
Seasonings:	Try a pinch of curry, nutmeg or cayenne; a splash of Worcestershire, hot pepper or soy sauce.
Cheese:	Top with grated Parmesan, Monterey Jack, American, Swiss, Cheddar, Gruyère.

GOLDEN CHICKEN AND FRIES

2 chicken legs (drum stick and thigh)
2 tablespoons mayonnaise
¼ cup seasoned fine dry bread crumbs
6 ounces frozen French fried potatoes
Salt
Paprika (optional)

Brush chicken with mayonnaise, coat with bread crumbs.

Range

Place chicken parts, skin side up, in buttered baking dish. Bake at 350°F for 45 minutes, until tender. Heat frozen French fries according to package directions, sprinkle with salt and with paprika, if desired.

Microwave

Place chicken parts, skin side up, on a double layer of paper towels. Cook 4 minutes, turn. Place French fries in center of oven with chicken, cook 5 minutes longer, or until chicken is done and French fries are heated through. Sprinkle with salt and with paprika, if desired.

Cooking Time Saved: 33 minutes

SALISBURY STEAK AND SLICED POTATOES

¾ pound lean ground beef
1 small onion, diced
1 slice bread, cubed
½ cup canned stewed tomatoes

Salt, pepper
1 large potato, thinly sliced
1 tablespoon butter or margarine

Combine beef, onion, bread cubes, half the stewed tomatoes and seasonings to taste. Shape into 2 oval patties.

Range

Arrange potato slices in a greased pie plate, dot with butter. Arrange meat patties in an oven casserole. Place potatoes and meat in oven and bake at 350°F. for 20 minutes. Pour remaining tomatoes over meat patties, continue baking until meat is done to taste and potatoes are tender, about 10 minutes.

Microwave

Arrange sliced potatoes on serving plate, dot with butter. Cover with wax paper, cook 3 minutes. Meanwhile, form meat patties. Push potatoes to edge and center meat on plate. Cook in oven 5 minutes. Turn potatoes and patties, top with remaining tomatoes, rotate platter. Cook about 2 minutes longer, until done to taste. Add seasonings.

Cooking Time Saved: 20 minutes

THE OMELET GUIDE

One of the all-time easy recipes is for the omelet.

The omelet is both delicious and inventive, and to help you expand your own omelet creativity, here is an omelet guide. We call these Peasant Omelets because each makes a hearty meal, while making use of leftover meats, fish, chicken or vegetables.

Prepare your choice of omelet by beating egg(s) or equivalent with liquid and seasonings, just until foamy. Cook egg mixture slightly as directed below, sprinkle with remaining additions, and complete cooking as directed.

Of course, you can mix and match your own omelet ideas, but here's a start. The recipes given are for one serving, but they can be expanded to match a guest list.

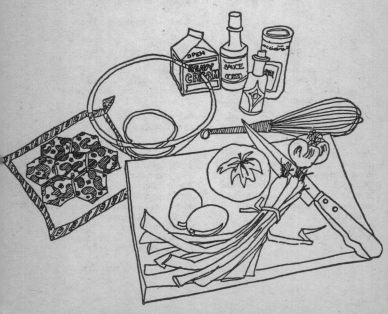

OMELET CHART

Eggs	Liquid	Seasoning	Hearty Addition	Meaty Addition	Garnish
As Suggested Below	2-3 Tbs.	to taste	all diced—2 Tbs.	all diced or slivered—2 Tbs.	all diced—1 Tbs.
2-3 eggs	milk	salt, pepper	cooked potato	cooked ham or bacon	green pepper
1 duck egg	sour cream	herbs, fresh or dry, chopped	cooked rice	cooked chicken or liver	seeded chopped tomato
packaged egg substitute	yogurt	sesame seeds	bread cubes	canned tuna	mushrooms
Low Cholesterol: 2 egg whites, 1 Tbs. skim milk solids, 2 Tbs. oil	do not add liquid to egg white mixture	curry or clove (easy on these)	cooked carrots	shrimp	green olives
packaged omelet mix	broth	onion, shallots	macaroni	beef or pork	cheese
1 egg	water	soy sauce	Chinese vegetables	crabmeat	water chestnuts, celery

Beat eggs or substitute with liquid and seasonings.

Range

Heat 1 tablespoon butter in omelet pan until bubbling. Pour in egg mixture, cook over high heat, stirring constantly, about 1 minute. Sprinkle with "additions", reduce heat and cook until set, shaking pan occasionally, about 3 minutes. Roll onto serving plate, garnish to taste.

Microwave

Melt 1 tablespoon butter in wide soup dish, about 30 seconds. Pour in egg mixture. Cook 1 minute. Sprinkle with "additions". Rotate bowl and cook 30 to 45 seconds longer, until omelet is set. Garnish to taste. Serve in plate.

Makes 1 serving.

FOR FAMILIES

CHEESE PUFF

8 slices white bread, crusts removed
Butter or margarine
4 slices American cheese

4 eggs, beaten
2 cups milk
Salt, pepper, paprika

Spread bread with butter or margarine. Make 4 sandwiches with bread and cheese. Blend eggs with milk, seasonings to taste.

Range

Arrange sandwiches in greased baking dish. Cover with milk and eggs. Let stand 15 minutes or longer before baking. Sprinkle with paprika. Bake puff at 375°F for about 45 minutes, until custard is set and lightly browned.

Microwave

Divide sandwiches in four ungreased individual casseroles or deep pie dishes. Cover with milk and eggs. Let stand 15 minutes or longer. Sprinkle with paprika. Cook in microwave, two dishes at a time, 5 to 6 minutes. Rearrange dishes half way through the cooking time.

Cooking Time Saved: about 30 minutes

Makes 4 servings.

Variations on this theme: Add sliced chicken, turkey or ham to the sandwiches, or a slice of tomato. Use Swiss cheese or grated Cheddar, or a sprinkling of blue cheese in place of American cheese.

CHEESY POTATO FRANKS

4 frankfurters
4 slices American Cheese,
cut in thin strips

1 tablespoon mustard
1 cup seasoned, mashed potatoes
(fresh cooked or instant)

Split franks without separating the halves, to make pockets.
Brush with mustard, fill with mashed potatoes, top with cheese.

Range	Microwave
Arrange franks on broiler pan, broil until cheese is melted and franks are hot.	Arrange franks on serving plates. Cook 4 minutes, until cheese is melted and franks are hot.

Makes 4 servings.

MAC 'N FRANK MEAL

2 cups cooked macaroni
1 tablespoon butter or margarine
1 can (8 ounces) cut green beans, drained

2 franks, sliced into ½-inch pieces
½ cup grated American cheese
Salt, pepper

Range	Microwave
Combine ingredients in a greased 1½-quart casserole. Cover, bake at 350°F for 25 minutes, until piping hot.	Combine ingredients in an ungreased 1½-quart casserole. Cover casserole. Cook 3 minutes, until piping hot. Let stand covered about 5 minutes before serving.

Cooking Time Saved: 22 minutes

Makes 3 servings.

STEW ON A PLATE

2 cups cubed cooked beef or other meat
1 can (10¾ ounces) condensed vegetable soup

Range	Microwave
Mix meat and soup in saucepan. Cook over moderate heat, stirring constantly, 5 minutes, until piping hot. Transfer to 2 serving plates.	Divide meat in 2 soup plates, add soup, stir. Cook until hot, about 3 minutes.

Makes 2 servings.

FISH STICK STACKS

5 thin slices whole grain bread
1 package (10 ounces) cooked frozen fish sticks
1 large tomato, sliced thin
2 tablespoons sweet pickle relish
⅓ cup mayonnaise

Cover each slice of bread with fish sticks, tomato slices, pickle relish.

Range
Place fish stick stacks on cookie sheet. Bake at 350°F for 20 minutes until heated through. Transfer to serving plates.

Microwave
Cook sandwiches on individual plates about 3 to 4 minutes, or until heated through.

Top with mayonnaise. Makes 5 sandwiches.

HOT DOGS

Range
Heat frankfurter in boiling water. Or heat frank in hot skillet, turning often, until lightly browned on all sides; or brown under preheated broiler. Toast or heat roll in oven, put frank in roll, spread with mustard.

Microwave
Put frankfurter in roll, spread with mustard if desired, wrap in a paper towel. One hot dog will cook in microwave in 30 seconds, or follow chart below:

Amount	Cooking Time
1 hot dog	30 sec.
2 hot dogs	45 sec.
3 hot dogs	1 min.
4 hot dogs	1½ min.
5 hot dogs	1 min., 45 sec.
6 hot dogs	2 min.
7 hot dogs	2 min., 15 sec.
8 hot dogs	2½ min.
9 hot dogs	2 min., 45 sec.
10 hot dogs	3 min.

Note:
If cooking more than 4, rearrange halfway through cooking time. Exact time will depend on size of frankfurter.

FRANKS IN BEANS AND SAUCE

1 can (16 ounces) pork and beans   ¼ cup ketchup
4 frankfurters   1 teaspoon prepared mustard
1 tablespoon molasses   Salt, pepper

Pour pork and beans into shallow 1 quart casserole. Arrange frankfurters on beans.
Combine molasses, ketchup and mustard, spoon over frankfurters.
Sprinkle with salt and pepper to taste.

Range
Bake casserole at 350°F for 25
minutes, until bubbling hot.

Microwave
Cover casserole with wax paper.
Cook in microwave 3½ minutes,
until hot.

Cooking Time Saved: 20 minutes

Makes 4 servings.

GLAZED CHICKEN WINGS

1 pound chicken wings, without tips
1 cup prepared barbecue sauce

Split wings and brush generously with barbecue sauce.
Reserve remaining sauce for dip.

Range
Arrange wings on shallow baking
pan. Bake at 375°F for about 40
minutes or until browned and crisp.
Transfer to serving platter.
Meanwhile, heat remaining sauce,
transfer to small bowl.

Microwave
Arrange wings on long serving
platter. Cover with wax paper. Cook
5 minutes. Rearrange wings on
platter. Cover again with wax paper.
Cook 5 minutes longer or until done.
Heat remaining sauce in a small
serving bowl 1 minute. Serve sauce
with wings.

Cooking Time Saved: 30 minutes

Serve wings with sauce as dip. Makes 3 servings.

MEXICAN ARABS

4 pita breads (flat Arab breads)
1 can chili con carne with beans
Shredded lettuce

Split pita breads to make a pocket, fill with chili con carne.

Range	Microwave
Bake sandwiches at 400°F on baking sheet 5 minutes, until filling is piping hot. Sprinkle with lettuce, transfer to serving plates.	Cook sandwiches on individual paper plates for about 1 minute. Sprinkle filling with lettuce, serve.

Makes 4 servings.

MACARONI AND CHEESE

1 cup elbow macaroni (uncooked)
1 cup water
⅓ cup nonfat dry milk
1 tablespoon butter or margarine

½ cup grated cheese (2 ounces)
1 tablespoon flour
1 egg, beaten
Salt, pepper

Range	Microwave
Cook 1 cup macaroni in salted water according to directions on package. Drain. Transfer cooked macaroni to a greased baking dish. Add 1 cup water mixed with nonfat dry milk, stir. Add butter or margarine. Toss cheese with flour, add. Add egg and seasonings, stir. Bake macaroni at 400°F until brown and set, about 30 minutes.	Combine macaroni in a 2-quart baking dish with ½ teaspoon salt and 1 cup water. Partly cover dish, cook 10 minutes. Drain cooking water, measure, add water to make 1 cup. Mix with nonfat dry milk, add to macaroni with butter or margarine. Toss cheese with flour, add. Add egg and seasonings, stir. Cook 5 minutes, stir.

Cooking Time Saved: 25 minutes

Makes 4 servings.

TASTY BURGERS

1 pound ground meat	¼ cup seedless raisins
1 carrot, grated	Salt, pepper
¼ cup ketchup	4 hamburger rolls

Combine ground meat, carrot, ketchup, raisins, salt and pepper to taste. Shape into patties.

Range

Broil meat on aluminum foil or broiler pan 3 to 4 inches from heat, 3 minutes. Turn, broil 3 to 4 minutes longer for medium. Toast rolls on broiler rack. Put patties into rolls to serve.

Microwave

Arrange patties on long, shallow baking dish. Cover with wax paper. Cook 5 minutes. Put patties into rolls. Cook on individual plates 1½ minutes longer.

Makes 4 servings.

VEGETABLE ROLLS

3 crusty rolls
4 ounces cream cheese
1 medium cucumber, peeled, sliced thin
1 sweet onion, sliced into thin rings
1 tomato, sliced thin

Split rolls in half.

Range

Soften cream cheese at room temperature, spread both halves of rolls. Fill with cucumber, onion and tomato. Bake at 450°F on baking sheet until hot and crisp, about 5 minutes.

Microwave

Soften cream cheese in microwave 15 seconds, spread both halves of rolls. Fill with cucumber, onion and tomato. Arrange on serving plates, cook until hot and crisp, about 1 minute.

Makes 3 servings.

HAMBURGERS

1 pound ground beef	½ teaspoon pepper
1 teaspoon salt	4 hamburger rolls, split and toasted

Mix ground beef with salt and pepper. Shape into 4 patties.

Range

Broil patties 3 to 4 inches from heat, on aluminum foil or in a shallow baking pan, until well browned, about 3 minutes. Turn, broil second side, 5 minutes in all for medium done. Toast hamburger rolls on broiler rack. Place patties in hamburger rolls, transfer to serving plates.

Microwave

Arrange patties on 8- by 12-inch shallow baking dish. Cover dish with wax paper, cook patties about 4 minutes for rare. Cook about 2 minutes longer for medium. Place patties in hamburger rolls on serving plates.

Burger Toppings

Cheese and Tomato Burgers: Slices of tomato and crumbled blue cheese, or spoonfuls of spaghetti sauce and grated mozzarella cheese.

Chili or Baked Bean Burgers: Spoonfuls of canned chili or baked beans and grated American cheese. (Sprinkle with canned french fried onion rings, optional).

Vegetable Burgers: Thinly sliced onion, tomatoes, green pepper, zucchini or chopped pickles.

Barbecued Burgers: Spoonfuls of prepared barbecue sauce, chili sauce, hot pepper sauce or ketchup.

Sauerkraut Burgers: Spoonfuls of sauerkraut mixed with caraway seeds.

Fruited Burgers: Chunks of canned, drained pineapple or fresh orange wedges.

Range

Mix, shape and broil patties as above. Cover with choice of topping, broil 2 to 3 minutes longer until topping is piping hot. Serve on hamburger rolls, toasted on broiler rack.

Microwave

Mix and shape patties as above. Cover with wax paper, cook on shallow baking dish about 4 to 6 minutes. Place patties in rolls on serving plates, top to taste, cook about 2 minutes longer.

RED RABBIT

2 eggs, beaten
1 can (10½ ounces) condensed
cream of tomato soup
½ cup milk or half-and-half

½ pound Swiss cheese, shredded
Paprika
French or Italian bread,
sliced and toasted

Range

Combine eggs, soup and milk in a
saucepan. Cook over low, stirring
constantly, until mixture begins to
bubble. Add cheese, stir until cheese
melts. Sprinkle with paprika.
Arrange bread slices side by side on
a pan, bake at 350°F for 5 minutes,
until hot. Transfer Rabbit to heated
serving bowl. Remove bread to
serving plates.

Microwave

Combine eggs, soup, milk and cheese
in serving bowl. Cook 5 minutes, stir,
cook 2 minutes longer. Beat well with
whisk. Heat bread slices 1 minute on
serving plates.

Spoon Rabbit onto bread. Sprinkle with paprika. Makes 2 cups, 4 servings.

SPEEDY SPIEDINI

1 loaf Italian bread
¼ cup butter
1 teaspoon prepared mustard
½ pound mozzarella cheese, sliced
¼ pound salami, thinly sliced

*Cut bread in half. Slice each half down to but not through the bottom crust,
at half-inch intervals.*

Range

Soften butter at room temperature,
cream with mustard. Spread cut
bread surfaces. Fill with slices of
mozzarella and salami. Bake on foil
at 450°F for 10 minutes until cheese
is melted.

Microwave

Soften butter in microwave, 30 to 40
seconds. Add mustard, spread cut
bread surfaces. Fill with mozzarella
and salami. Heat about 1 minute and
15 seconds or until cheese melts.

Cooking Time Saved: 8½ minutes

Makes 5 servings.

REUBEN REUBEN SANDWICH

¼ pound thinly sliced pastrami (or ham, bologna, corned beef)
⅓ cup drained sauerkraut
4 slices crusty pumpernickel or rye bread

1 tablespoon mayonnaise
1 teaspoon pickle relish, drained
1 teaspoon chili sauce
2 slices Swiss cheese

Divide the pastrami and sauerkraut on 2 slices of bread. Mix mayonnaise, pickle relish and chili sauce, spread on sauerkraut. Top with a slice of Swiss cheese, cover with bread.

Range
Arrange sandwiches on baking pan. Bake at 450°F, about 5 minutes until cheese melts. Transfer to serving dishes.

Microwave
Arrange on individual plates, cook about 2 minutes.

Makes 2 servings.

BARBECUE SUBMARINE

2 crusty hero rolls
4 ounces thinly sliced leftover pork, beef or lamb
2 tablespoons prepared barbecue sauce
2 slices Cheddar cheese

Split rolls, cover bottom half with meat, barbecue sauce and cheese. Cover with top half.

Range
Bake sandwiches at 400°F on baking sheet for about 5 minutes, until cheese melts. Transfer to serving plates.

Microwave
Arrange sandwiches on individual paper plates, heat 2 minutes.

Makes 2 servings.

FOR GUESTS

CHINESE BARBECUED CHICKEN

1 rotisseried chicken,
about 2½ pounds
3 tablespoons soy sauce
3 tablespoons vinegar

¼ cup honey
1 clove garlic, mashed
½ cup chicken broth
2 tablespoons sherry (optional)

*Leave chicken whole, or cut it into serving portions.
Arrange chicken in 13- by 9-inch baking dish. Blend remaining
ingredients to make a basting sauce. Brush chicken with sauce.*

Range	Microwave
Bake at 350°F for about 30 minutes, until hot and well glazed, brushing often with sauce.	Cover chicken with wax paper, cook 8 minutes, until hot and glazed.
	Cooking Time Saved: about 20 minutes

Serve remaining sauce over glazed chicken. Makes 4 servings.

YAKITORI

½ pound raw chicken
breast meat, sliced thin
2 tablespoons soy sauce
3 tablespoons sherry

1 tablespoon brown sugar
¼ teaspoon ginger
2 tablespoons oil (range only)

Marinate chicken in mixed soy, sherry, sugar and ginger for 20 minutes.
Thread on 6 wooden skewers.

Range
Brush chicken with oil. Broil
chicken, turning often, until cooked
through, about 10 minutes. Transfer
to serving plate.

Microwave
Arrange skewers on serving plate.
Cover with wax paper, cook 2
minutes. Turn skewers, cook 1
minute longer.

Cooking Time Saved: 7 minutes

Makes 6 appetizer servings.

BUTANIKU

Substitute ½ pound lean pork, cut into ¾ inch cubes, for chicken in
recipe for Yakitori above. Omit oil. Prepare as directed.

Range
Broil about 20 to 25 minutes,
turning often, until pork is cooked
through. Transfer to serving plate.

Microwave
Arrange skewers on serving plate.
Cover with wax paper, cook 3
minutes, turn, cook 2 minutes longer,
until pork is cooked through.

Cooking Time Saved: 15 to 20
minutes

Makes 6 appetizer servings.

TERIYAKI

Substitute ½ pound tender beef, cut into small cubes, for chicken in
recipe for Yakitori, above. Prepare as directed.

Range
Brush meat with oil, broil about 6
minutes, turning often, until done
to taste. Transfer to serving plate.

Microwave
Arrange skewers on serving plate,
cover with wax paper, cook 2
minutes, turn, cook 1 minute longer,
to taste.

Makes 6 appetizer servings.

SAVORY TOAST HORS D'OEUVRES

¼ cup butter or margarine
1 teaspoon or more anchovy paste

6 slices toast, cut into fingers, or
18 salted crackers

Range

Soften butter or margarine about an hour at room temperature. Cream with anchovy paste. Spread butter on toast fingers or crackers, arrange on baking sheet, bake at 350°F for 8 minutes, until hot and crisp. Serve on tray.

Microwave

Soften butter or margarine in microwave, 10 seconds, cream with anchovy paste. Spread on toast fingers or crackers. Arrange on serving tray, cook 1 minute or until hot and crisp.

SAVORY BUTTERS

SMOKED SALMON BUTTER
¼ cup butter or margarine
1 tablespoon finely mashed smoked salmon

MUSTARD BUTTER
¼ cup butter or margarine
1 teaspoon prepared mustard

DEVILED BUTTER
¼ cup butter or margarine
1 teaspoon dry mustard
1 teaspoon Worcestershire sauce
Hot pepper sauce to taste

HERB BUTTER
¼ cup butter or margarine
1 tablespoon chopped mixed fresh herbs
(parsley, chives, tarragon, dill)
Cayenne pepper to taste

Soften butter and mix as above. Use for savory toasts. Or, use savory butter as a canapé spread, or as a sauce to top fish, meat or vegetables.

RACLETTE

1-pound piece Swiss or Gruyère cheese
½ teaspoon caraway seeds
Pepper
Boiled potatoes, small onions, sour pickles

Cut cheese block into 4 pieces, 4- by 4- by ½-inch

Range

Arrange cheese pieces on 4 flame-proof serving plates. Broil 4 to 6 inches from heat, about 8 to 10 minutes, until cheese is hot and bubbly.

Microwave

Arrange cheese pieces on 4 serving plates. Cook 2 minutes, until cheese is hot and bubbly.

Cooking Time Saved: 6 to 8 minutes

Sprinkle with caraway seeds and pepper. Serve with potatoes, onions and pickles. Makes 4 servings.

SWISS FONDUE

1 pound Swiss cheese, cubed
1 tablespoon flour
1 clove garlic, cut in half
1 teaspoon dry mustard

1 cup dry white wine
3 tablespoons kirsch
Cubes of French bread, with crust

Toss cheese with flour and mustard.
Rub a heavy quart casserole or fondue pot with garlic.

Range

Add wine to pot, bring to a boil over low heat or over a table cooker. Add cheese, a little at a time, stirring until mixture is smooth and creamy, about 12 minutes.

Microwave

Add wine to casserole, bring to a boil in microwave. Stir in cheese. Cook about 5 minutes, stir until mixture is smooth and creamy.

Add kirsch. Serve with cubes of bread and long-handled forks for dipping. Makes 4 servings.

TOASTED SOYBEANS

Soak 1 cup soybeans overnight in a generous amount of salted water.

Range

Bring soybeans to a boil in the soaking water, cook 1 hour. Drain. Spread beans on a shallow baking sheet. Bake at 350°F for 40 to 60 minutes, until beans are brown and crisp.

Microwave

Drain soybeans. Spread beans on a double thickness of paper towels. Cook 20 to 30 minutes, stirring every 5 minutes, until beans are crisp. If paper toweling should begin to brown, replace with a new piece.

Cooking Time Saved: 1 hour, 20 minutes.

Makes 1 cup soybean snacks.

QUICK PIZZA SNACKS

Using packaged pizza mix, prepare dough according to directions on box. Divide dough into 10 equal pieces, shape each into a 4-inch round with upturned rim.

Range

Spread rounds with pizza sauce from package, sprinkle with Italian seasoning or oregano, top with cheese from package. Place on greased aluminum foil or greased baking sheet, bake at 425°F for 15 minutes, until brown.

Microwave

Place dough rounds on wax paper, cook 5 at a time, 3 minutes, turning over halfway through cooking. When ready to serve, spread with sauce from package, sprinkle with Italian seasoning or oregano, top with cheese from package. Place on baking sheet, brown under browning unit or in 425°F oven.

Makes 10 snacks.

SOUP'S ON
(HOT SOUPS, COLD SOUPS,
SUMMER SOUPS, WINTER SOUPS)

Gone are the days of the six-course dinner.

For many of us a hearty soup, some cheese and wine make a good dinner. Others prefer soup and a favorite dessert.

Soup is no longer simply the start of a meal.

Soup is a first course, a main course, or the only course . . . providing, of course, it's a good soup.

Homemade soups are especially good cooked in the microwave oven. Vegetable soups taste fresh from the garden because this quick method of cooking helps retain both flavor and vitamins.

In using canned soups, you can put the soup (with water added) in the microwave oven in the bowl in which you serve it. In three to five minutes your soup will be hot.

In this section, as in all sections of the book, directions are given for both conventional and microwave cooking.

SOUP'S ON

FOR
THE ONE OR
TWO OF YOU

MINESTRONE SUPPER BOWL

1 small onion	½ cup cooked or canned red beans
1 small potato, peeled	¼ cup elbow macaroni
2 green beans	1½ cups hot broth or water
1 stalk celery	Salt, pepper, oregano, parsley
1 small carrot	Grated Parmesan cheese
½ cup canned tomatoes, chopped	

*Cut onion and potato into small uniform dice;
cut beans, celery and carrot into thin slices.*

Range

Simmer ingredients except cheese in pan 20 to 25 minutes, covered, until vegetables are tender.

Microwave

Combine ingredients except cheese in large soup bowl or casserole. Cover with flat plate or wax paper. Cook about 12 minutes, until vegetables and pasta are tender.

Cooking Time Saved: 8 to 13 minutes

*Add more broth or water if necessary. Sprinkle with grated cheese.
Makes 1 large or two smaller servings.*

FRESH GREEN PEA SOUP

1 cup chicken broth
½ cup fresh green peas (or frozen peas, slightly thawed)
1 small onion, chopped

Salt, pepper, dash nutmeg
¼ cup light cream or yogurt
1 strip bacon, cooked and crumbled

Whirl broth, peas, onion and seasonings in blender, or force through a sieve or food mill.

Range

Bring mixture to boil in small pan. Reduce heat, simmer 5 minutes. Stir in cream or yogurt, heat without boiling. Pour into soup bowl.

Microwave

Pour mixture into soup bowl, cover with flat plate or wax paper. Heat 3 minutes. Add cream or yogurt, stir smooth.

Garnish with crumbled bacon. Makes 1 serving.

CHINESE CHICKEN SOUP

1 cup chicken bouillon
¼ cup slivers of raw chicken breast
1 mushroom, sliced
1 scallion, sliced
1 stalk watercress

Range

Bring bouillon to boil in small pan. Add chicken, return to simmer, cover, poach 5 minutes. Add mushroom and scallion, poach 5 minutes longer. Add watercress. Spoon into soup bowl.

Microwave

Combine bouillon and chicken in soup bowl, cover with flat plate or wax paper, cook 2 minutes. Add mushroom and scallion, cook, covered, about 1½ minutes. Add watercress.

Makes 1 serving.

EGG DROP SOUP

1 cup chicken broth
½ teaspoon soy sauce
½ egg (or 1 egg white or yolk), beaten with a fork

Range

Bring broth and soy to boil in small pan. Add egg, stir gently until egg sets. Pour into soup bowl.

Microwave

Heat broth and soy in soup bowl, 1½ minutes, until steaming. Stir in egg. Cook 1½ minutes, until egg sets.

Makes 1 serving.

ONION SOUP

2 tablespoons butter or margarine or oil
2 large sweet onions, cut into rings
2 cups hot broth
¼ pound Gruyère cheese, cubed
2 to 3 slices French bread, toasted

Range

Heat fat in soup pan. Add onions and cook slowly until wilted. Add broth, bring to boil. Place cheese in soup bowls, cover with hot broth and onions, top with bread.

Microwave

Divide fat into 2 soup bowls. Add onion rings and cook 4 minutes. Add broth, cook 4 minutes. Add cubed cheese, top with bread.

Makes 2 servings.

FOR
THE FAMILY

VICHYSSOISE (LEEK AND POTATO SOUP)

2 tablespoons butter
2 leeks or 4 scallions,
white part only, sliced
1 medium onion, finely chopped
2 small potatoes, peeled and diced
2 cups boiling water or broth

Salt, white pepper
1 cup milk
1 cup heavy or light cream
Garnishes: butter or margarine,
chopped chives

Range

In soup pot, melt butter or margarine, add leeks or scallions and onions, cook until soft but not browned. Add potatoes, water, salt and pepper to taste. Bring to a boil, simmer 30 minutes. Press soup through a sieve, or whirl in a blender to make a smooth puree. Add milk and cream, heat. Refrigerate.

Microwave

Cook butter or margarine, leeks or scallions, onion and potatoes in 2-quart casserole or soup bowl, 7 minutes, covered. Add water, salt and pepper to taste. Cook, covered, 5 minutes. Press soup through a sieve or whirl in blender to make a smooth puree. Add milk and cream, heat 2 minutes, covered. Refrigerate.

Cooking Time Saved: 18 minutes

Serve chilled; sprinkle with chopped chives. Makes 4 to 6 servings.

FRESH TOMATO SOUP

5 or 6 medium tomatoes, chopped
1 tablespoon butter or margarine or oil
1 clove garlic, minced
½ medium onion, chopped
1 cup hot water or chicken broth

3 sprigs parsley
½ teaspoon basil
½ teaspoon salt
1 tablespoon cornstarch

Range

Cook tomatoes in butter or margarine with garlic and onion until soft, about 10 minutes. Add water, herbs and salt. Simmer 15 minutes over low heat. Force soup through a sieve or food mill. Stir cornstarch with a little water, add to soup, cook, stirring, until thickened.

Microwave

Combine tomatoes with butter or margarine, garlic and onion in 2-quart casserole. Cook until tomatoes are soft, about 10 minutes, stirring once. Add water and herbs, cook 3 minutes longer. Force soup through a sieve or food mill. Stir cornstarch with a little water, add to soup, cook 3 minutes.

Cooking Time Saved: About 10 minutes

Adjust seasoning. Serve hot or chilled. Makes 3 to 4 servings.

VEGETABLE SOUP

2 tablespoons oil
1 carrot, diced
1 stalk celery, sliced
1 onion, diced
2 large potatoes, diced
2 tomatoes, peeled and diced

3 cups very hot vegetable or beef broth
1 tablespoon parsley, chopped
1 tablespoon chopped chives
½ teaspoon marjoram
Salt, pepper

Range

Heat oil, add carrot, celery, onion and potatoes. Cook 10 minutes, stirring often, until golden. Add tomatoes, broth and seasonings. Simmer about 30 minutes.

Microwave

Pour oil over carrot, celery, onion and potatoes in 2-quart serving bowl. Cook about 5 minutes, stirring once. Add tomatoes, broth and seasonings, cook about 10 minutes longer.

Cooking Time Saved: 25 minutes

Makes 4 to 6 servings.

SPINACH SOUP

1 package (10 ounces)
frozen chopped spinach
2 tablespoons butter or margarine
2 tablespoons grated onion

1½ tablespoons flour
3 cups milk
3 chicken bouillon cubes

Range

Cook frozen spinach in ¼ cup water in a tightly covered skillet until tender. Do not drain. Force through a sieve or food mill, or puree in blender. Melt butter or margarine in soup pot, add onion, cook until golden. Stir in flour, cook until combined. Add milk gradually, stir until smooth and thickened. Add bouillon cubes, stir until dissolved. Add pureed spinach, heat to serving temperature.

Microwave

Cook frozen spinach in covered bowl about 7 minutes, until tender. Do not drain. Force through a sieve or food mill, or puree it in blender with milk. Cook butter or margarine and onion in covered serving bowl 1 minute. Add flour, stir. Add spinach, milk and bouillon cubes, stir well. Cook 5 minutes, stirring at 2-minute intervals, until soup is hot, thickened and smooth.

Season to taste. Makes 5 to 6 servings.

FRESH MUSHROOM SOUP

1½ cups fresh mushrooms
3 cups hot chicken broth
2 tablespoons butter, softened
2 tablespoons flour
1 cup milk, room temperature

Wipe mushrooms clean, trim ends of stems. Chop very finely, or puree in an electric blender with a little of the broth.

Range

Melt butter in saucepan, stir in flour, gradually add broth. Bring to a boil, stirring constantly. Simmer over low heat, stirring, until soup is thickened and smooth. Add raw mushrooms and milk, heat, stirring. Do not boil. Pour into soup bowls.

Microwave

Blend butter and flour to make a paste, add to broth in 2-quart glass casserole. Cook 1 minute, stir. Add mushrooms and milk, cook 3 minutes. Stir halfway through the cooking time.

Makes 6 servings.

SPLIT PEA SOUP

1 cup split green peas
5 cups boiling water
Ham bone with meat clinging to it
1 onion, stuck with 2 cloves

2 carrots, sliced
¼ teaspoon pepper
1 teaspoon salt

Range

Combine all ingredients in a large soup pot. Bring to a boil, cover, simmer 2½ hours, until peas are tender, adding more water as needed.

Microwave

Combine split peas with 3 cups boiling water and remaining ingredients in a 4-quart serving bowl. Cook, covered, 20 minutes, stirring every 10 minutes. Add remaining water as needed, cover, cook 25 minutes longer.

Cooking Time Saved: 1 hour, 45 minutes

Cut meat from ham bone, add to soup; discard bone and onion. Adjust seasoning. Makes 4 servings. Sieve soup before adding ham, if desired.

CHICKEN SOUP WITH BREAD DUMPLINGS

1½ pounds chicken pieces, (wings, giblets, etc.)
1 quart boiling water
Salt
½ teaspoon peppercorns
1 small onion, studded with 2 cloves

2 carrots, diced fine
Herb bouquet of celery tops, parsley, dill and bay leaf, tied in cheesecloth
Bread Dumplings, (page 75)

Range

Cover chicken with water, bring to boil, simmer 30 minutes. Skim. Add remaining ingredients. Cover, simmer about 1½ hours, until chicken and vegetables are tender.

Microwave

Combine all ingredients in a 3-quart bowl or casserole. Cover, cook 30 minutes, stirring every 10 minutes. Skim.

Cooking Time Saved: 1 hour, 30 minutes

Strain the soup, discard vegetables and herb bouquet. Remove chicken from the bones, reserve for other uses. If desired, skim excess fat, reserve for other uses. Prepare Bread Dumplings, cook as directed. (See page 75.) Makes 4 servings.

BREAD DUMPLINGS

2 slices day-old white bread,   1 egg, beaten
crusts trimmed   Salt, pepper to taste
1 teaspoon minced parsley

*Whirl bread in blender container to make fine crumbs, or crumble finely.
Add parsley, egg, salt and pepper. Chill.*

Range	Microwave
Drop from a teaspoon into boiling soup in soup pot. Cover, simmer about 5 minutes.	Drop from a teaspoon into serving bowl of boiling soup. Cover, cook about 3 minutes.

Makes 8 small dumplings.

Tip: *These dumplings may also be cooked on top of stews or in boiling water.*

BLACK BEAN SOUP

1 cup cooked or canned   1 clove garlic, minced
black beans, drained   1 tablespoon oil
1 cup boiling chicken broth   ¼ teaspoon dry mustard
1 carrot, diced   1 teaspoon Worcestershire sauce
1 stalk celery, diced   Salt, pepper
1 small onion, diced   2 thin slices ham, slivered

*Force beans through a sieve or food mill or whirl in blender with
a little chicken broth to puree.*

Range	Microwave
Cook carrot, celery, onion and garlic in oil in a small saucepan, 12 minutes or until tender. Stir in pureed beans, mustard, Worcestershire sauce, salt and pepper, remaining broth and slivered ham. Simmer 15 minutes.	Cook carrot, celery, onion, garlic and oil in covered 1-quart serving bowl 3 minutes. Stir in pureed beans, mustard, Worcestershire sauce, salt and pepper, remaining broth and slivered ham. Cook, covered, 3 minutes, stir, cook uncovered 3 minutes longer.
	Cooking Time Saved: about 18 minutes

Makes 2 hearty servings.

SPRING GREEN SOUP

1 package (10 ounces) frozen chopped spinach
1 cup boiling water
1 can (10½ ounces) condensed cream of mushroom soup

1 cup sour cream
Pinch dried basil
Salt, pepper

Range

Cook spinach in boiling water 3 minutes. Force through a sieve or food mill, or whirl in blender to make a puree. Add soup, bring to a boil, stirring, about 6 minutes. Reduce heat, and simmer for 5 minutes stirring occasionally.

Microwave

In large serving dish, cook spinach 2 minutes. Add boiling water and force through a sieve or food mill, or whirl in blender to make a puree. Blend with soup in serving bowl, cook 5 minutes, until steaming hot. Stir halfway through the cooking time.

Stir in sour cream and basil, adjust seasoning to taste. Makes 4 servings.

SCOTCH BROTH

Bones and scraps of meat left from roast leg of lamb
2 quarts boiling water
1 onion, stuck with 4 cloves
¼ teaspoon peppercorns
1 tablespoon salt

1 bay leaf
3 carrots, sliced
2 celery stalks, diced
2 small turnips, sliced
⅓ cup pearl barley
½ teaspoon marjoram

Range

In soup pot cover lamb bones with boiling water, add onion, peppercorns, salt and bay leaf. Cover, simmer 1½ hours. Remove bones, dice meat. Strain broth, skim if necessary. Add meat pieces, vegetables, barley and marjoram. Cover, simmer 45 minutes, until barley is tender.

Microwave

Cover lamb bones in a 4-quart bowl with boiling water, add onion, pepper, salt and bay leaf. Cover, cook 10 minutes. Remove bones, dice meat. Strain broth, skim if necessary. Add meat pieces, vegetables, barley and marjoram. Cover, cook 15 minutes, until barley is tender.

Cooking Time Saved: 1 hour, 50 minutes.

Makes 6 or more servings.

76

NEW ENGLAND CLAM CHOWDER

1 strip bacon, diced
1 medium onion, chopped
2 medium potatoes, finely diced
1 can (8 ounces) minced clams

½ cup water
2 cups milk
Salt, pepper, hot pepper sauce

Range

Cook bacon and onion in saucepan until golden. Add potatoes. Drain liquid from clams, add liquid and water to pan. Cover, bring to a boil, cook until potatoes are very tender, about 15 minutes. Add milk and seasonings, heat just to boiling, stir in clams, cook 2 minutes longer.

Microwave

Cook bacon, onion and potatoes in covered 2-quart bowl 5 minutes. Stir halfway through cooking time. Drain liquid from clams, add liquid and water to bowl. Add milk and seasonings. Cover, cook 5 minutes. Stir in clams, let stand 2 minutes, covered, before serving.

Makes 3 to 4 servings.

MANHATTAN CLAM CHOWDER

2 tablespoons butter or margarine
1 stalk celery, diced
1 onion, finely diced
1 carrot, finely diced
1 large potato, finely diced
½ cup hot water

1 can (1 pound) tomatoes, chopped
Bit of bay leaf
⅓ teaspoon thyme
1 teaspoon salt
Dash pepper
1 can (8 ounces) minced clams

Range

Heat butter or margarine. Cook celery and onion until golden. Add carrot and potato, water and tomatoes. Add herbs, salt and pepper to taste. Simmer ½ hour. Add clams with liquid, heat.

Microwave

Cook butter or margarine, celery, onion, carrot, potato in 2-quart soup bowl or casserole about 5 minutes. Add water, tomatoes, herbs and seasonings, stir. Cook 12 minutes, covered. Add clams with liquid, cook 1 minute, until steaming hot.

Cooking Time Saved: 15 minutes

Makes 6 servings.

FISH STEW

2 tablespoons oil	Salt to taste
1 onion, diced	⅛ teaspoon each pepper, thyme,
1 clove garlic, minced	paprika, saffron
2 cups boiling water	1 tablespoon chopped parsley
½ cup white wine	2 pounds assorted raw fish fillets
1 can (1 pound) stewed tomatoes	(cut in chunks) and seafood
	Sliced French bread

Range

Heat oil in large pan, cook onion and garlic 3 minutes or until translucent. Add boiling water, wine and tomatoes, cook 10 minutes. Add seasonings, fish and seafood. Cover, cook 15 minutes, or until fish flakes easily with a fork.

Microwave

Cook oil, onion and garlic in a 3-quart serving bowl 2 minutes. Add boiling water, wine, tomatoes, seasonings, fish and seafood. Cover, cook 10 minutes, stirring occasionally. Test fish by flaking with a fork.

Cooking Time Saved: 10 minutes

*Place thick slices of toasted French bread in soup plates, serve stew over bread.
Makes 6 to 8 servings.*

CRAB BISQUE

1 cup crabmeat (8 ounces)	Salt, cayenne
4 tablespoons butter or margarine	Pinch nutmeg
2 tablespoons flour	Sherry (optional)
2½ cups milk or half and half	

*Use fresh-cooked, canned or frozen crabmeat; shred finely and discard
any shells or membranes.*

Range

Melt butter or margarine in saucepan, stir in flour. Gradually add milk; cook, stirring, until soup is smooth and thickened. Add crab meat and seasonings, heat to serving temperature.

Microwave

Work softened butter or margarine into a paste in a 2-quart soup bowl or casserole. Add milk, cover, cook 3 minutes. Stir. Add crabmeat and seasonings, cook 1½ minutes longer.

*For variety, finely chopped shrimp and lobster may be used instead of crabmeat.
Serve with a dash of sherry in each plate, if desired. Makes 4 servings.*

SALAD SOUP

1½ cups leftover tossed green salad
with about 2 tablespoons salad dressing
½ cup raw or cooked
vegetables or peeled tomatoes
1 cup hot chicken broth
Salt, pepper

Combine all ingredients, whirl in blender or force through food mill to puree.

Range	Microwave
Pour into saucepan, bring to a boil over medium heat. Adjust seasoning. Ladle into soup bowls.	Divide into 3 soup bowls. Heat about 5 minutes. Rearrange bowls half way through the cooking time. Adjust seasoning.

Sprinkle with croutons. Makes 3 servings.

CHEESE SOUP

1 small onion, sliced thin
¼ cup butter or margarine
2 tablespoons flour
¼ teaspoon dry mustard

1 cup boiling chicken broth
2 cups hot milk
1 cup grated Cheddar cheese
(4 ounces)

Range	Microwave
Cook onion in butter or margarine until translucent, sprinkle with flour and mustard, stir until smooth. Gradually add broth, cook over low heat, stirring, until mixture is smooth and thickened. Cover, simmer 15 minutes, stir often. Add milk, heat to boiling point. Add cheese, stir until cheese melts.	Combine onion with butter or margarine in 2-quart serving bowl. Cover, cook 4 minutes, until onion is tender. Stir in flour and mustard. Add boiling broth and hot milk, cook until milk bubbles, about 4 minutes, stirring once. Add cheese, stir until cheese melts.

Cooking Time Saved: 15 minutes |

Makes 4 servings.

CREAM OF AVOCADO SOUP

1 avocado, peeled and pitted
1 cup half-and-half
2 cups water

½ garlic clove
2 chicken bouillon cubes
2 tablespoons lemon juice

*Force avocado through a sieve and combine with half-and-half,
or whirl it in the blender with half-and-half*

Range

Bring water to a boil in a saucepan with garlic clove and bouillon cubes. Stir. Discard garlic, add avocado and half-and-half, heat without boiling. Refrigerate.

Microwave

Put water in 2-quart casserole with garlic clove and bouillon cubes. Cook until water boils. Stir, discard garlic, add avocado combined with half-and-half, heat 3 minutes. Refrigerate.

Cold lemon juice, serve chilled. Makes 4 servings.

MIDNIGHT ONION SOUP

2 tablespoons butter or margarine
4 onions, sliced thin
4 cups hot beef broth
1 tablespoon Worcestershire sauce

Salt, pepper
6 slices toasted French bread
6 tablespoons grated Parmesan cheese

Range

Melt butter or margarine in saucepan, cook onions slowly, over low heat, until golden and translucent, about 20 minutes. Divide into 5 or 6 individual casseroles, top each serving with toast, sprinkle with Parmesan cheese.

Microwave

Cook butter or margarine and onions in 3-quart casserole, covered until onions are colored, about 15 minutes. Add broth and seasonings to taste, cover, cook 10 minutes. Divide into 5 or 6 individual bowls, top each serving with toast, sprinkle with Parmesan cheese.

Makes 5 to 6 servings.

APRICOT SOUP

1 package (11 ounces)
dried apricots
4 cups water
⅓ cup sugar

2 tablespoons
quick cooking tapioca
1 to 2 tablespoons lemon juice
Sour cream

*Soak apricots in water in a 2-quart bowl
1 hour. Add sugar.*

Range

Simmer fruit in saucepan until very tender, about 45 minutes. Force fruit and liquid through a foodmill or sieve to make a puree; or whirl in an electric blender. Add tapioca, return to saucepan, cook, stirring, until thick.

Microwave

Add tapioca, cover, cook about 5 minutes. Stir, cover, cook 5 minutes. Force fruit and liquid through a foodmill or sieve to make a puree; or whirl in an electric blender.

Cooking Time Saved: about 35 minutes

*Add lemon juice to taste. Serve hot or cold.
Top with sour cream, if desired. Makes 6 servings.*

BORSCHT

1 pound beets (3 medium) peeled and sliced thin
2 cups boiling water or broth
2 tablespoons sugar

3 tablespoons lemon juice
Salt to taste
1 egg, beaten
Sour cream or boiled potato garnish

Range

Combine beets and water in a saucepan, cover, bring to a boil. Reduce heat, simmer until beets are tender, about 35 minutes.

Microwave

Combine beets and water in a serving bowl, cover, cook about 17 minutes, until tender.

Cooking Time Saved: 18 minutes

*Add sugar, lemon juice, and salt to taste. Add a little hot soup to egg, stir
and combine with remaining soup. Serve chilled, garnished with sour cream,
or hot, with a boiled potato in each plate. Makes 3 to 4 servings.*

AVGOLEMONO (Greek Lemon Soup)

2 cups chicken broth
¼ cup cooked rice
1 egg
Juice of ½ lemon

Range

Bring chicken broth to a boil with rice in a small saucepan. Beat egg, add lemon juice and a little of the hot broth, return to pan.

Microwave

In 1-quart serving bowl, heat broth to a boil with rice, about 4 minutes. Beat egg, add lemon juice and a little of the hot broth, return to bowl.

Serve at once. Makes 2 to 3 servings.

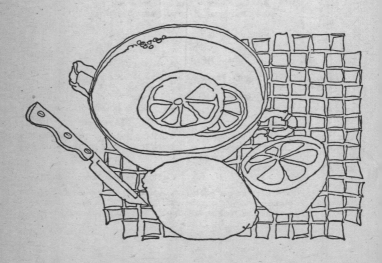

THE MAIN EVENT

(ALSO KNOWN AS THE ENTRÉE,
THE MAIN DISH
AND THE ANSWER TO
"WHAT'S FOR DINNER?")

In this section we have included meat, fish and poultry recipes that can be prepared either with conventional cookery or the microwave oven. Because you already know about conventional cookery, there are a few things we want to add about microwave cooking.

Meats: Choose a tender, well fat-marbled cut of meat that is uniform in size. A roast about five inches in diameter is ideal. Do not salt the roast before cooking it in the microwave oven because salt absorbs the moisture in the meat and toughens the outer layer. You may, however, use herbs, soy sauce, paprika, Worcestershire sauce. If the roast is not uniform in size, cover the smaller or thinner portion with a piece of aluminum foil for the first half of the cooking period and then remove it when the roast is turned. Cooking times vary, of course, depending on whether you prefer meat rare, medium or well-done. Consult the cooking chart in this section for times. This is the recommended way to roast meat in the microwave oven:

1. Place the meat fat side down on an inverted saucer that will withstand heat of meat and drippings in a glass baking dish.

2. Cover the meat with wax paper or a paper towel so the oven will not be spattered.

3. After half the cooking time has elapsed, open the oven door and turn the roast fat side up.

4. After roasting is completed remove the roast from the oven, cover with aluminum foil, and let stand for a half hour. This is done to permit heat equalization. If you are using a meat thermometer, remove the meat from the oven when internal temperature is about 20° lower than temperatures suggested for desired doneness. Temperature will increase during recommended standing time. Use only special microwave-proof thermometer.

Poultry: If you are cooking a large turkey, tie the legs and wings of the bird closely to the body. The wings, ends of the legs and tail should be covered with aluminum foil for the first half of the cooking period to prevent overcooking of these parts.

1. Brush the bird with melted shortening and place breast side up on inverted saucers in a glass baking dish.

2. To hold a large bird in place, custard cups may be wedged in the baking dish against the bird.

3. After one-quarter the cooking time has elapsed, open the oven door and turn the bird on its side. Repeat turning at intervals as directed in recipe (Page 119).Each time you do this, baste the bird with drippings in dish. Remove excess drippings from dish, if necessary.
4. After roasting, remove the bird from the oven, cover with aluminum foil, and let stand for a half hour to permit heat equalization.

   Fish: The most important thing in cooking fish or shellfish is to avoid overcooking. You can test doneness by checking to see if the fish flakes with a fork and shell fish is opaque. You'll help both flavor and appearance if you brush fish fillets with melted butter or margarine and sprinkle them with paprika.

In this section, as in all sections of the book, directions are given for both conventional and microwave cooking.

THE MAIN EVENT

FOR THE ONE OF YOU

SCAMPI WITH RICE PILAF

2 teaspoons oil
1 tablespoon chopped onion
1 clove garlic, minced
⅓ cup rice
·¾ cup boiling water
1 chicken bouillon cube

¼ cup white wine
Salt, pepper
¼ pound shrimp, cleaned and deveined
1 teaspoon butter or margarine

Range

Heat oil in a saucepan, add onion and garlic, cook until onions are wilted. Stir in rice, water, bouillon cube, wine, salt and pepper. Transfer to a baking dish, cover, bake 15 minutes at 425°F. Meanwhile, arrange shrimp in a separate casserole, dot with butter or margarine. Bake at 425°F, 10 minutes; serve scampi on rice with pan juices spooned over them.

Microwave

Combine oil, onion, garlic in a 1-quart casserole, cook 2 minutes. Stir in rice, boiling water, bouillon cube, wine, salt and pepper. Cover with wax paper, cook 12 minutes or until water is absorbed, stirring twice. Arrange shrimp on rice, dot with butter or margarine. Cover and cook 1 minute or until shrimp is opaque and pink.

Cooking Time Saved: 15 minutes

Makes 1 serving.

SPAGHETTI CARBONARA

2 ounces thin spaghetti
2 cups boiling water
½ teaspoon salt
1 slice bacon, chopped
1 tablespoon finely chopped onion

3 tablespoons grated Parmesan cheese
3 tablespoons minced
boiled ham (or prosciutto)
Pepper to taste
Fresh parsley, minced

Range

Cook spaghetti in salted boiling water, about 12 minutes or until tender. Meanwhile cook bacon and onion in small saucepan, until bacon is crisp, stirring often. Drain spaghetti, turn into a warmed bowl, stir in bacon-onion mixture, cheese, ham and pepper.

Microwave

Combine spaghetti, boiling water and salt in a 2-quart casserole, cover, cook 7 minutes. Remove casserole from microwave, let stand, covered. Meanwhile, combine bacon and onion in serving dish, cook 3 minutes, until onion wilts. Drain spaghetti, add to bacon-onion mixture, stir in cheese, ham and pepper.

Garnish with parsley. Makes 1 serving.

CHINESE BEEF STEW

¾ pound round steak, thinly sliced
4 teaspoons flour
¼ teaspoon ground ginger
Salt, pepper
1 tablespoon oil

1 clove garlic, crushed
1 can (8 ounces) stewed tomatoes
1 tablespoon soy sauce
½ teaspoon crushed red pepper (optional)

Coat beef with flour seasoned with ginger, salt and pepper.

Range

Heat oil and garlic in small skillet. Add steak, cook over low heat, stirring, until browned on all sides. Add stewed tomatoes, soy sauce, crushed red pepper, simmer 5 minutes until steak is tender.

Microwave

Combine steak, oil and garlic in 2-quart casserole. Cook, covered, 1 minute. Add stewed tomatoes, soy sauce, crushed red pepper. Cook, covered, 4 minutes.

Serve with noodles or boiled rice. Makes 2 servings.
Freeze remaining stew in a small oven casserole. Warm in 325°F oven
25 minutes, or in microwave 6 to 9 minutes depending on the amount, turning once.

Cooking time saved in rewarming: about 19 minutes

SEAFOOD NEWBURG

1 tablespoon butter or margarine
1 tablespoon flour
½ cup milk
Salt, pepper

Dash paprika
3 ounces cooked or canned lobster, shrimp or crabmeat
2 teaspoons white wine
1 slice toast (cut into 4 triangles)

Range

In a heavy saucepan melt butter or margarine. Add flour, cook, stirring, until blended. Add milk and seasonings. Simmer until thick and smooth, about 10 minutes, stirring often. Stir in seafood, cook until heated through. Remove from heat, stir in wine.

Microwave

Soften butter or margarine, blend with flour in serving bowl. Stir in milk, seasonings. Cook, covered, 2½ minutes, stir. Add seafood, cook, covered, 1 minute. Stir in wine.

Cooking Time Saved: about 12 minutes

Serve on toast points.
Makes 1 serving.

SAVORY POTATO MEDLY

1 medium potato
¼ pound chicken livers, halved
1 tablespoon chopped onion
2 pieces bacon, chopped
1 tablespoon sour cream

Range

Cook potato in boiling salted water about 30 minutes, or until tender. Meanwhile, cook livers, onion and bacon over low heat, stirring, until bacon is crisp and liver is no longer pink.

Microwave

Cook potato on paper towel, 2 minutes. Turn potato over and allow to stand 2 minutes in microwave. Combine liver, onion and bacon on dish, cover with paper towel and cook for 2 minutes. Stir and cook 2 minutes longer or until potato and liver test done.

Cooking Time Saved: 24 minutes

Peel potato and split in half. Arrange halves on serving dish,
cover with liver mixture. Top with sour cream, if desired. Makes 1 serving.

LEMON AND HERB CHICKEN WITH BROCCOLI

½ chicken breast (boned)
1 tablespoon lemon juice
½ teaspoon tarragon
Salt, pepper

2 tablespoons butter or margarine
2 thin lemon slices
Pinch paprika
1 large broccoli spear

Range

Place chicken in an ovenproof casserole; sprinkle with lemon juice, tarragon, salt and pepper; dot with butter or margarine; top with lemon slices, sprinkle with paprika. Bake at 325°F for 35 minutes, basting frequently. Meanwhile, bring 2 cups salted water to a boil on top of stove, add broccoli and cook, covered, 10 to 12 minutes, until just tender. Arrange chicken on broccoli in serving dish. Serve pan juices as a sauce.

Microwave

Place broccoli on serving dish. Dot with butter or margarine. Cook 3 minutes, turn over. Cover with chicken breast. Sprinkle lemon juice, tarragon, salt, pepper. Top with lemon slices, sprinkle with paprika. Cook 4 minutes. Spoon pan juices over chicken and broccoli. Note: If additional browning is desired, cook chicken 6 inches from broiler heat for about 4 minutes. In this case, transfer chicken to a dish that will withstand the direct heat of the broiler.

Cooking Time Saved: 28 minutes

Makes 1 serving.

LAMB SHANK WITH RICE

2 tablespoons finely
chopped green pepper
2 tablespoons finely chopped onion
1 garlic clove, finely minced
1 tablespoon lemon juice
¼ cup tomato juice
3 tablespoons barbecue sauce

Dash salt
Dash black pepper
1 lamb shank (frozen or thawed)
⅔ cup water
1 teaspoon butter or margarine
Dash salt
¼ cup rice

*Combine pepper, onion, garlic, lemon and tomato juice, barbecue sauce,
salt and pepper in a 1-quart casserole. Add lamb shank,
turn in mixture, coating all sides.*

Range

Roast shank at 325°F for 45
minutes (1 hour if frozen), turning
and basting frequently. Twenty-five
minutes before lamb is finished
cooking, bring water, butter or
margarine and salt to boil top stove
in small pan. Add rice, cover,
simmer 20 minutes until water is
absorbed. Serve with lamb.

Microwave

Combine water, butter or margarine,
salt and rice in serving bowl, cover
with wax paper. Cover lamb casserole
with wax paper. Cook together about
9 minutes, or until shank is tender,
turning shank twice. (If lamb is frozen
cook it about 14 minutes.)

Cooking Time Saved: 45 minutes

Makes 1 serving.

FOR
THE TWO
OF YOU

BLANQUETTE OF VEAL

½ pound boneless veal (shoulder or breast) cut in 1" cubes
Water to cover
¾ cup water
½ cup pearl onions, peeled
1 carrot, peeled and cut in ½-inch rounds

1 bouquet garni (½ celery stalk, 1 bay leaf, 1 clove garlic, pinch thyme, tied in cheesecloth)
1 teaspoon butter or margarine, softened
2 teaspoons flour
¼ cup cream
Salt
White pepper

Parboil veal in water to cover for 5 minutes, drain.

Range

In saucepan, combine veal, ¾ cup water, onions, carrots and bouquet garni. Bring to a boil; reduce heat and simmer, covered, for 1 hour or until meat is tender. Remove meat and vegetables to a serving dish. Blend softened butter or margarine and flour to make a paste, add to hot liquid, cook until sauce is thickened.

Microwave

In a glass bowl, combine veal, ¾ cup water, onions, carrots and bouquet garni. Cook, covered, 15 minutes. Discard bouquet garni, cook 8 minutes. Remove meat and vegetables to a serving dish. Blend softened butter or margarine with flour to make a paste, add to liquid and cook, uncovered, until sauce is thickened, 4 minutes.

Cooking Time Saved: 35 minutes.

Add cream, adjust seasonings and pour sauce over meat and vegetables.
Makes 2 servings.

LAMB TENDERLOIN

1 lamb loin roast (1½ pounds),
boned and trimmed
¼ cup red wine vinegar
¼ cup oil
2 cloves minced garlic
1 teaspoon salt

¼ teaspoon thyme
¼ teaspoon paprika
¼ teaspoon freshly ground pepper
1 teaspoon butter or margarine
2 teaspoons flour

*Combine vinegar, oil, garlic and seasonings to make a marinade, cover meat,
let stand 1 hour, turning frequently. Remove meat from marinade.*

Range

Arrange meat on rack·in roasting
pan. Roast at 325°F, 20 minutes for
medium rare. Meanwhile, heat
marinade in a saucepan. Blend
butter or margarine and flour, and
add to marinade. Cook until
thickened, adjust seasonings, spoon
over cooked lamb tenderloin on
serving platter.

Microwave

Set a 6-inch saucer upside down in a
10-inch pie plate. Put tenderloin on
saucer and pour marinade over meat.
Cook, uncovered, 3 minutes. Remove
meat to serving plate. Blend butter or
margarine and flour, add to marinade,
cook 3 minutes. Adjust seasonings,
spoon over cooked tenderloin.

Cooking Time Saved: 14 minutes

CHINESE PEPPER STEAK

¼ cup oil
¾ pound steak (round or chuck),
sliced into thin strips
1 medium onion, sliced thin
1 green pepper, seeded and sliced thin
1 tomato, peeled and cut in 8 slices

2 cloves garlic, minced
1 tablespoon cornstarch
½ cup cold water
2 tablespoons soy sauce
1 teaspoon sugar

Range

Heat oil in skillet or wok and brown
meat quickly. Remove to serving
dish. Add vegetables to pan and
cook, stirring, until just tender. Add
cornstarch dissolved in water, soy
sauce and sugar. Cook, stirring,
until sauce is thickened and clear.
Add meat, heat through, serve
immediately.

Microwave

Heat oil in a 10-inch glass pie plate.
Add vegetables and cook, covered, for
8 minutes. Add cornstarch dissolved
in water, soy sauce, sugar and strips
of meat. Stir well and cook, covered,
for 2 minutes. Stir, remove cover,
cook 2 minutes.

Makes 2 servings.

BEEF STROGANOFF

2 tablespoons oil
½ pound round steak, sliced in thin strips
½ cup sliced mushrooms
¼ cup minced onions
2 garlic cloves, minced
½ cup warm water
1 beef bouillon cube

1 tablespoon steak sauce
½ teaspoon prepared mustard
1 teaspoon butter or margarine, softened
2 teaspoons flour
2 tablespoons sour cream
1½ cups boiled noodles

Range

Heat oil in a heavy skillet and quickly brown strips of beef. Push meat to side of pan. Sauté mushrooms, onions and garlic in the skillet until wilted. Add water, bouillon cube, steak sauce and mustard. Stir, cover, cook 45 minutes. Blend softened butter or margarine and flour to a paste, stir into sauce. Stir until smooth and thickened, about 3 minutes. Add sour cream.

Microwave

Heat oil in a 10-inch glass pie plate for 2 minutes. Add mushrooms, onions and garlic, cover with wax paper, cook 3 minutes. Add remaining ingredients except sour cream and noodles, cook, uncovered, 8 minutes. After 4 minutes, rotate the dish ½ turn and stir. Stir in sour cream.

Cooking Time Saved: 39 minutes

Serve on buttered noodles. Makes 2 servings.

POT AU FEU
(Boiled Dinner)

½ pound stewing beef, cut in 1-inch cubes
½ chicken breast
2 beef bouillon cubes
1 bouquet garni (bay leaf, pinch thyme, 2 cloves, celery stalk, tied in cheesecloth)

6 pearl onions
½ cup sliced celery
1 carrot, peeled and quartered
1 potato, peeled and quartered
2 small leeks, halved
Salt, pepper

Range

Put meat and chicken into a heavy saucepan, add water to cover, bring to a boil. Skim. Add bouillon, bouquet garni, onion and celery. Simmer, covered, about 2 to 2½ hours, or until the meat is tender. Add carrots, potato and leeks during final ½ hour of cooking. Discard bouquet garni.

Microwave

Place meat, chicken, water to cover bouillon cubes, bouquet garni, onions and celery in a 3-quart glass casserole. Cover and cook 20 minutes. Discard bouquet garni, add carrot, potato and leeks, cook 10 minutes, uncovered. Rotate casserole ½ turn, stir, cook 10 minutes until vegetables are tender.

Cooking Time Saved: About 1¾ hours

*Adjust seasoning with salt and pepper. Serve broth separately.
Arrange meat and vegetables on serving platter and moisten with broth.
Makes 2 servings.*

BEEF LOAF

¾ pound lean ground beef
¼ cup tomato sauce
1 teaspoon Worcestershire sauce
2 tablespoons chopped green peppers
1 small onion, chopped

⅓ cup bread crumbs
½ teaspoon salt
⅛ teaspoon pepper
1 egg
2 tablespoons ketchup

Combine all ingredients, except ketchup, blend well. Shape into a loaf and place in a 10-inch glass casserole.

Range

Bake beef loaf, uncovered at 350°F, for 35 minutes. Top with ketchup and bake 15 minutes longer.

Microwave

Top loaf with 2 tablespoons ketchup. Cook in microwave 5 minutes, rotate ½ turn, baste with pan juices, cook 8 minutes. Let stand 10 minutes.

Cooking Time Saved: 37 minutes

SHRIMP CREOLE

4 tablespoons oil
1 onion, minced
3 cloves garlic, minced
1 green pepper, chopped
2 tablespoons minced parsley,
1 chicken bouillon cube
1 teaspoon salt

4 dashes hot pepper sauce
¼ cup water
1 can (8 ounces) tomato sauce
1 cup okra
9 ounces shrimp, cleaned
and deveined
1½ cups cooked rice

Range

Heat oil, cook onion, garlic and green pepper until onion is translucent. Add remaining ingredients except shrimp and rice. Bring to a boil, simmer 20 minutes, covered. Add shrimp, cook until pink, about 5 minutes.

Microwave

Combine oil, onions, garlic, peppers and tomato in a 1-quart casserole. Cover and cook 4 minutes. Rotate dish ½ turn, stir, cook 2 minutes. Add remaining ingredients except shrimp and rice, cook, uncovered, 6 minutes. Stir in shrimp and cook 1½ to 3 minutes or until shrimp are pink.

Cooking Time Saved: 15 minutes

Serve on rice. Makes 2 servings.

STUFFED LOBSTER TAILS

2 frozen rock lobster tails
1 teaspoon butter or margarine
2 teaspoons flour
½ cup cream or milk
Salt

1 teaspoon lemon juice
2 dashes hot pepper sauce
Pinch nutmeg
1 tablespoon diced pimiento
½ teaspoon paprika

Range

Plunge frozen lobster tails into boiling water and simmer 3 minutes. Split membranes on underside, remove meat without breaking shell, and cut into ½-inch slices. Melt butter or margarine in a saucepan, add flour, cook 3 minutes, stirring. Combine cream, salt, lemon juice, hot pepper sauce, nutmeg and add, slowly, to butter and flour. Cook until smooth and thickened. Add chunks of lobster meat and pimiento, cook 3 minutes. Adjust seasoning, spoon mixture into shells, sprinkle with paprika.

Microwave

Place frozen lobster tails on a plate and cook 45 seconds to defrost. Split underside, remove meat, cut into ½-inch slices. Cook cream in an 8-inch glass pie plate 3 minutes. Combine softened butter or margarine and flour to make a paste. Stir into cream. Cook, uncovered, 3 minutes. Add lemon juice, spices, pimiento and lobster meat, stir well, cook about 2 minutes, or until lobster meat tests done. Adjust seasoning and spoon into lobster shells. Sprinkle with paprika.

Cooking Time Saved: 14 minutes

Makes 2 servings.

FILLET OF SOLE AMANDINE

12 ounces fillets of sole
(or other fish fillets)
¼ cup butter or margarine
1 tablespoon lemon juice
1 tablespoon dry white wine

Salt, paprika
Hot pepper sauce
¼ cup slivered almonds,
browned in butter

Range

Arrange fish in baking dish. Top
with 3 tablespoons butter or
margarine, lemon juice, wine, salt,
paprika and hot pepper sauce to
taste. Cover with wax paper and
bake at 325°F for 12 minutes, until
fish flakes readily. Remove fish to
serving platter, sprinkle with
browned almonds, and cover with
lemon butter sauce.

Microwave

Arrange fish in a 10-inch glass pie
plate. Dot with butter or margarine,
sprinkle with browned almonds,
lemon juice, dry white wine, salt,
paprika and hot pepper sauce. Cover
with wax paper and cook about 4
minutes or until fish flakes readily.

Makes 2 servings.

LEMONY GLAZED CHICKEN

1 broiler-fryer chicken
(2 pounds), split
½ teaspoon salt
1 teaspoon paprika

2 tablespoons honey
2 tablespoons lemon juice
2 tablespoons butter
or margarine

*Rub chicken with salt and paprika. Coat with lemon juice
mixed with honey. Dot with butter or margarine.*

Range

Place seasoned chicken in a small
roasting pan. Bake at 350°F about
40 minutes, or until cooked
through, basting occasionally with
pan juices.

Or: Broil skin side down for 25
minutes; turn, baste, broil 15
minutes longer.

Microwave

Place chicken halves in a 10-inch glass
pie plate, skin side down. Cook
uncovered, 4 minutes. Turn chicken
pieces skin side up, baste with pan
juices and cook about 8 minutes
longer.

Cooking Time Saved: 28 minutes

*To test for doneness, insert a fork between thigh and body.
The juices should run clean, without a trace of pink. Makes 2 servings.*

SUPREMES OF CHICKEN WITH CLAM SAUCE

1 whole chicken breast, boned and split
2 teaspoons butter
1 teaspoon lemon juice
1 can (8 ounces)
.minced clams

1 teaspoon butter or margarine
2 teaspoons flour
¼ cup cream
Hot pepper sauce
Salt, pepper

Range

Put chicken in a saucepan. Add butter or margarine, lemon juice, salt, pepper and ¼ cup liquid drained from clams. Cover, simmer 25 minutes, until chicken is cooked.

Microwave

Arrange chicken on a 10-inch glass pie plate. Cover with butter or margarine, lemon juice, salt, pepper and ¼ cup liquid drained from clams. Cover, cook about 4 minutes or until chicken tests done.

Remove chicken to a serving platter, keep warm. Blend softened butter or margarine and flour to make a paste, add to sauce. Add cream and hot pepper to sauce to taste.

Cook, stirring, until sauce is smooth and thickened. Add clams, adjust seasoning, heat.

Add clams, cook 1 minute; stir. Adjust seasoning.

Cooking Time Saved: about 20 minutes

Spoon sauce over chicken. Makes 2 servings.

ROCK CORNISH GAME HENS AUX CERISES

2 Rock Cornish hens
2 tablespoons butter or margarine
Salt, pepper
1 can (8 ounces) pitted bing cherries

¼ cup dry red wine
1 teaspoon lemon juice
1 tablespoon cornstarch

Rub Rock Cornish hens with butter or margarine. Season with salt and pepper.

Range

Roast hens on a rack in a roasting pan, at 400°F for about 1 hour. Test by inserting a fork between thigh and body; the juices should run clear. Transfer birds to a serving platter. In saucepan mix liquid from cherries, wine, lemon juice and cornstarch. Simmer, stirring, until sauce is thickened and clear, add cherries, heat.

Microwave

Arrange birds breast-side down on saucers in a 10-inch glass pie plate. Cover with wax paper, cook 10 minutes. Brush hens with drippings, turn breast-side up, cover, cook about 10 minutes longer or until they test done. Let stand 5 minutes. In small bowl combine liquid from cherries, wine, lemon juice and cornstarch. Cook until sauce is thickened and clear, 4 minutes. Add cherries, heat.

Cooking Time Saved: 30 minutes

Pour sauce over Rock Cornish hens on platter. Makes 2 servings.

EGGPLANT PARMESAN

1 eggplant (¾ pound)
¼ cup oil
1 small onion, minced
½ green pepper, seeded and minced
3 cloves garlic, minced

¼ cup mushrooms, sliced
1 cup spaghetti sauce
3 tablespoons grated Parmesan cheese
6 thin slices mozzarella cheese

Wash eggplant, slice ½-inch thick.

Range

Quickly brown eggplant slices in hot oil on both sides, remove and drain on absorbent paper. Sauté onion, pepper, garlic and mushrooms in same pan. Add spaghetti sauce and Parmesan cheese, simmer 20 minutes.

Microwave

Arrange eggplant slices in a single layer in a 13-by9-by2-inch glass baking dish. Brush with oil, cover with wax paper, cook 4 minutes. Turn eggplant slices over, cover, cook 4 minutes longer. Remove and drain on absorbent paper. In the same dish, cook onions, peppers, garlic and mushrooms, covered, 8 minutes. Add spaghetti sauce and Parmesan cheese and cook, uncovered, for 10 minutes.

In a 1-quart casserole arrange layers as follows:
spaghetti sauce, topped with eggplant, another layer of sauce, and
mozzarella cheese. Repeat until all ingredients are used.

Range

Bake in 350°F oven, 40 minutes, until bubbling and well browned.

Microwave

Cook, uncovered, 10 minutes.

Cooking Time Saved: 40 minutes

Makes 2 servings.

FOR SMALL FAMILIES

PORK CHOPS WITH APPLESAUCE

6 pork chops, 1 inch thick
2 medium baking potatoes, peeled, sliced thin
1 medium onion, sliced thin
Salt, pepper

¼ teaspoon thyme
¼ teaspoon marjoram
1 can (1 pound, 4 ounces) applesauce
Cloves, cinnamon

Range

Brown chops quickly on both sides in a heavy skillet, remove from pan. In skillet, layer potato slices, onion slices, and chops. Sprinkle with salt and pepper, thyme and marjoram. Season applesauce with cloves and cinnamon to taste, pour over chops. Cover skillet. Simmer slowly over low heat 30 minutes, until chops are thoroughly cooked and vegetables are tender. Add a little water during cooking, if necessary.

Microwave

In a 12-inch pie plate, layer potato slices, onion slices, and pork chops. Season with salt and pepper, thyme and marjoram. Season applesauce with cloves and cinnamon to taste, pour over chops. Cover and cook 14 minutes, basting occasionally with applesauce.

Cooking Time Saved: about 20 minutes.

Makes 6 servings.

SAVORY POT ROAST

4 pounds chuck roast
1 large onion, sliced
½ cup lemon juice
¼ cup sugar
Water

½ teaspoon gravy browner
(microwave only)
4 tablespoons flour (microwave only)
Salt, pepper

Range

Brown meat, fat side down, in Dutch oven, add onion, brown lightly. Add lemon juice, sugar, 1½ cups water and salt and pepper to taste. Cover, simmer until meat is tender, about 3 hours.

Microwave

Combine onion, lemon juice, sugar and gravy browner in 6-quart casserole fitted with a lid. Add chuck roast, fat side up, cook 15 minutes. Turn meat over. Combine a little water with flour to make a paste, stir into casserole, add water barely to cover, and cook 15 minutes, covered. Turn meat over. Cook 1 hour, turning meat every 15 minutes. Let stand 20 minutes before slicing. Season with salt and pepper.

Cooking Time Saved: 1½ hours

Makes 6 to 8 servings.

STUFFED MEAT LOAF ROLL

2 pounds ground meat loaf mixture
(veal, pork and beef)
1 slice stale bread, cut into small cubes
½ cup milk
2 eggs
2 teaspoons salt
1 teaspoon freshly ground
black pepper

¼ cup chopped green pepper
¼ cup chopped onion
2 tablespoons chopped parsley
1 cup grated mild Cheddar
or Swiss cheese.
½ cup tomato sauce or ketchup

*Soak bread cubes in milk. Combine with remaining ingredients, except cheese
and tomato sauce. On a sheet of wax paper spread mixture to form a
10- by 12-inch rectangle. Sprinkle with grated cheese and roll up like a jelly roll.
Place seam side down in a lightly greased 1½-quart ovenproof glass loaf dish.*

Range
Bake meat loaf, uncovered, at 325°F
for 45 minutes. Cover with tomato
sauce and cook ½ hour longer.

Microwave
Cover meat loaf with tomato sauce
and bake, uncovered, 6 minutes.
Rotate dish ½ turn, cook 6 minutes
longer. Let stand 10 minutes before
serving.

Cooking Time Saved: 40 minutes

Makes 6 servings.

NEW ENGLAND BOILED DINNER

1 corned beef brisket, about 3 pounds
2 quarts cold water
1 onion, quartered and studded with 6 cloves
2 carrots, peeled and quartered
1 turnip, peeled and quartered

½ teaspoon peppercorns
Herb bouquet (2 bay leaves, 2 celery tops, 6 sprigs parsley)
1 small head cabbage, quartered
8 small potatoes

Range

Cover beef with cold water in a large soup pot or Dutch oven, bring to a boil and skim surface. Add onion, carrots, turnip and seasonings. Reduce heat, cover, simmer 3 hours. Add cabbage and potatoes, cover, simmer 30 minutes, or until meat is tender.

Microwave

Cover beef with water in a 4-quart bowl or 4½-quart casserole. Add onion, carrots, turnip and seasonings. Weight meat with a plate to keep it submerged, cover with wax paper. Cook 25 minutes. Turn meat over, let stand 10 minutes. Cook 25 minutes, turn meat again, let stand 10 minutes. Add cabbage and potatoes, cook 25 minutes. Let stand 10 minutes before serving.

Cooking Time Saved: 1 hour, 45 minutes

Slice beef across the grain, surround with vegetables and moisten with broth. Makes 8 servings.

OLD-FASHIONED BEEF STEW

2 pounds beef chuck, in 1-inch cubes
½ cup flour seasoned with
salt and pepper
2 tablespoons oil
2 large onions, sliced thin
Water

2 beef bouillon cubes
¼ teaspoon pickling spices
4 carrots, peeled and quartered
4 small potatoes, peeled and
quartered
Dumplings, below

Dust beef cubes with seasoned flour.

Range

Brown beef in hot oil in large, heavy pan. Add onions, water to cover, bouillon cubes and spices. Bring to a boil, stir. Simmer, covered, 1 hour. Add more water if necessary. Add carrots and potatoes, simmer 30 minutes, or until meat and vegetables are tender. Adjust seasoning. Drop dumplings on to stew, simmer covered, 15 minutes.

Microwave

Sprinkle oil over beef and onions in a 3-quart casserole, cook covered 5 minutes. (Or, brown meat and onions in oil on range.) Add water top of cover, bouillon cubes and spices. Cover, cook 45 minutes, rotating casserole ¼ turn and stirring well every 15 minutes. Add carrots and potatoes, cook, covered, 15 minutes. Drop dumplings on top of stew, simmer, covered, 5 minutes longer.

Cooking Time Saved: 35 minutes

Makes 8 servings.

DUMPLINGS

1 egg
¾ cup milk
1 tablespoon oil

1½ cups flour
1½ teaspooons baking powder
½ to ¾ teaspoon salt

*Beat egg with milk and oil. Toss flour, baking powder and salt to mix,
add to egg mixture, stir to combine.
Drop mixture from a tablespoon onto simmering stew.*

Range

Cook, covered, about 15 minutes.

Microwave

Cook, covered, about 5 minutes.

Cooking Time Saved: 10 minutes

Makes 8 dumplings.

SMOKED TONGUE WITH RAISIN SAUCE

3½-to 4-pound smoked tongue
1 onion
1 carrot, peeled
2 bay leaves
Water to cover

Range

Place tongue, onion, carrot and bay leaves in a Dutch oven, add water to cover, simmer in covered pot for 3 to 3½ hours or until tongue is tender.

Microwave

Place tongue, onion, carrot and bay leaves in a 4-to 5-quart casserole, add water to cover. Cover casserole, cook 25 minutes. Let stand 10 minutes, turn tongue. Cover, cook 25 minutes, let stand 10 minutes.

Cooking Time Saved: about 2 hours

Reserve broth. Plunge tongue into cold water to cool. Split skin near the base with point of knife and pull off. Cut away fatty part. Slice thinly. Serve with Raisin Sauce, below.

Makes 8 servings.

RAISIN SAUCE

1 cup strained tongue broth
1 tablespoon corn starch
¼ cup wine vinegar
¼ cup brown sugar
¼ cup seedless raisins

Range

Combine cornstarch with a little of the tongue liquid. Combine with remaining ingredients in saucepan. Bring to a boil, simmer, stirring, until sauce is slightly thickened and smooth.

Microwave

Combine ½ cup strained tongue broth with cornstarch in small serving bowl. Cook, covered, 1 minute. Stir in remaining ingredients. Cook, covered, 5 minutes.

Makes about 1½ cups.

SALMON LOAF

1 can (1 pound) salmon
¾ teaspoon salt
¼ teaspoon pepper
1 teaspoon lemon juice
1 teaspoon Worcestershire sauce

1 tablespoon grated onion
2 eggs
1 cup milk
2 tablespoons melted
butter or margarine
½ cup soft bread crumbs

*Drain salmon, discard skin and bones, and mash. Add seasonings,
onion and eggs, blend well. Combine milk, melted butter or margarine
and bread crumbs, let stand 5 minutes, blend with salmon.
Pour mixture into a well-greased 1- or 1½-quart ovenproof glass loaf dish.*

Range

Bake salmon loaf at 350°F for 45 minutes or until firm.

Microwave

Cook salmon loaf, covered, 12 minutes or until firm. Let stand 5 minutes.

Cooking Time Saved: 28 minutes

Unmold to serve. Makes 4 servings.

109

BAKED STUFFED FISH

1 whole fish, about 2 pounds (carp, bluefish, mackerel)	2 cups soft bread cubes
1 slice bacon, minced	½ teaspoon salt
1 onion, minced	¼ teaspoon pepper
2 tablespoons minced green pepper	¼ teaspoon thyme
	1 tablespoon butter or margarine

Have fish cleaned, leave head and tail intact, if desired, for dramatic effect.

Range
Cook bacon in skillet over medium heat until translucent, add onion and green pepper, cook until onion is transparent and bacon crisp.

Microwave
Place bacon on shallow dish, cover with a paper towel, cook 1 minute. Add onion and green pepper, cook 2 minutes.

Toss with bread cubes and seasonings. Fill fish cavity and insert toothpicks or skewers on each side, about 2 inches apart, down the length of the split. Lace closed, as you would a shoe, with strong white thread.

Range
Arrange fish on rack in shallow baking pan, brush with butter or margarine. Bake at 375°F, 30 to 40 minutes, until fish flakes easily with a fork.

Microwave
Cook on shallow dish 6 to 8 minutes, turning dish once, until fish flakes easily with a fork. Let stand 2 minutes.

Cooking Time Saved: 20 to 30 minutes

Makes 4 servings.

ROASTED STUFFED CHICKEN

4-pound roasting chicken
Salt, pepper
1 small onion, minced
1 stalk celery with top, minced
1 chicken liver, diced

3 tablespoons butter or margarine
6 slices bread, trimmed and cubed
Poultry seasoning
1 egg, beaten
Oil

Season chicken with salt and pepper inside and out.

Range

Prepare stuffing: cook onion, celery and chicken liver in butter or margarine until onion is translucent. Add bread cubes and seasonings to taste. Add egg. Fill body cavity of chicken with stuffing, truss, tying legs close to the body. Rub with oil. Roast chicken, breast side down first, about 25 minutes per pound; at the half way point, brush with pan juices, turn. Let stand 10 to 15 minutes before carving.

Microwave

Prepare stuffing: combine onion, celery and chicken liver in shallow 10-inch square casserole. Cook 2 minutes, stir, cook 1 minute longer. Stir in bread cubes and seasonings to taste; add egg. Stuff body cavity of chicken, truss, tying legs close to the body. Rub with oil. Place chicken, breast side down, in same casserole. Cover with wax paper, cook 7 minutes. Turn onto one side, cook 7 minutes; turn breast side up, rotate dish, cook 7 minutes. Let stand covered with foil, 10 to 15 minutes before carving.

Cooking Time Saved: about 1 hour 5 minutes

Makes 6 servings.

BARBECUED CHICKEN

1 chicken (about 3 pounds)
cut into 8 serving pieces ·
Flour (range only)
Salt, pepper (range only)
1 small onion, minced
2 tablespoons oil

3 tablespoons vinegar
1 tablespoon sugar
1 teaspoon Worcestershire sauce
½ teaspoon salt
2 cloves garlic, minced

Range

Shake chicken pieces with flour, salt and pepper in a paper bag. Arrange on greased baking sheet, skin side up, and bake at 375°F for 30 minutes. Meanwhile, combine remaining ingredients in a small saucepan, bring to a boil, simmer about 5 minutes. Spoon over chicken pieces, bake 30 minutes longer, basting often with sauce.

Microwave

Arrange chicken pieces, skin side up, in a 13- by 9-inch baking dish. Combine remaining ingredients, pour over chicken. Cover with wax paper, cook 7 minutes. Rotate pan ½ turn and baste with sauce. Cook 7 minutes longer.

Cooking Time Saved: 50 minutes.

Makes 4 servings.

STUFFED CABBAGE

12 large cabbage leaves
1 pound ground beef
1 egg
1 cup cooked rice
2 tablespoons grated onion

2 tablespoons chopped parsley
1 teaspoon salt
½ teaspoon pepper
1 can (8 ounces) tomato sauce
½ cup water (range only)

*Cover cabbage leaves with boiling water, let stand a few minutes.
Combine beef, egg, rice, onion, parsley, salt and pepper.
Drain cabbage leaves. Divide meat mixture onto softened cabbage leaves,
roll up, folding in ends to make a secure package.*

Range

Arrange stuffed cabbage leaves in a Dutch oven. Add tomato sauce and water. Simmer, covered, 1 hour or until meat is well cooked.

Microwave

Arrange stuffed cabbage leaves in an 8-inch square baking dish. Cover with tomato sauce. Cook, covered, about 14 minutes or until meat is well cooked. Remove, let stand 4 minutes before serving.

Cooking Time Saved: 42 minutes

Makes 4 to 6 servings.

CHICKEN IN WHITE WINE

1 chicken (about 3 pounds)
cut into 8 serving pieces
Salt, pepper
¾ cup dry white wine
4 tablespoons butter or margarine

½ teaspoon tarragon
½ cup cream or milk
1 can (8 ounces) mushroom caps,
cut in half

Arrange chicken pieces in a shallow casserole. Sprinkle with salt and pepper, add white wine. Allow to marinate for 1 hour at room temperature. Remove chicken. Reserve marinade.

Range

Arrange chicken, skin side down, in a baking dish. Dot with butter or margarine and sprinkle with tarragon. Bake at 350°F, 30 minutes. Turn chicken pieces, add marinade, cream and mushrooms, cook 20 minutes longer, or until chicken is tender.

Microwave

Arrange chicken in a 13- by 9-inch baking dish. Dot with butter or margarine, sprinkle with tarragon. Cook, covered, 5 minutes. Rotate dish and baste chicken. Cook 5 minutes longer. Add marinade, cream and mushrooms, and cook uncovered 5 minutes or until chicken is tender.

Cooking Time Saved: 35 minutes

Makes 4 servings.

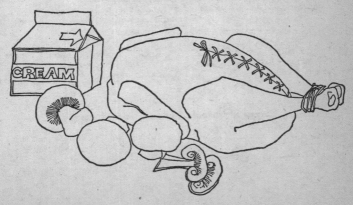

113

SPINACH LASAGNE

1 onion, chopped
3 cloves garlic, minced
2 tablespoons oil
¾ pound ground beef
1 can (8 ounces) tomato sauce
1 can (6 ounces) tomato paste
1 teaspoon Italian seasoning
Salt
2 eggs

1 package frozen chopped spinach,
thawed and drained
2 cups ricotta or cottage cheese
⅓ cup grated Parmesan cheese
1 package (12 ounces) lasagne
noodles, cooked just tender
½ pound mozzarella cheese, grated
(2 cups)
Salt and pepper

Range

In saucepan, cook onion and garlic
in oil until onion is translucent.
Add beef, cook, stirring, until it
loses its red color. Add tomato
sauce, tomato paste and seasonings
to taste. Cover, simmer 45 minutes.

Microwave

Cook onion, garlic and oil in a
covered 3-quart casserole, 4 minutes.
Stir in beef, cook 4 minutes longer.
Stir in tomato sauce, tomato paste
and seasonings to taste. Cook,
covered, 5 minutes, rotate casserole ½
turn, stir, cook 5 minutes longer.

Combine eggs, spinach, ricotta, Parmesan cheese, salt and pepper to taste.
To assemble: pour half the tomato sauce into the bottom of a 9- by 13-inch baking dish.
Cover with a layer of one-third the cooked noodles,
then a layer of half the spinach and cheese mixture.
Add a second layer of noodles, remaining spinach
and cheese, and a third layer of noodles. Top with the remaining tomato sauce.
Sprinkle with mozzarella cheese.

Range

Cover pan with foil, bake at 375°F
for 30 minutes. Remove foil, bake
10 minutes longer.

Microwave

Cook, uncovered, 15 minutes. Rotate
casserole ¼ turn every 5 minutes
during cooking.

Cooking Time Saved: about 1 hour

Let stand 10 minutes before serving. Makes 12 servings.

FOR FAMILIES
WHO EAT
IN TWO SHIFTS

PIZZA

1 envelope active dry yeast
1⅓ cups warm water
2 tablespoons oil
4 cups flour
1½ teaspoons salt

Sprinkle yeast on warm water, stir to dissolve. Add oil, flour and salt, knead dough to make a smooth, satiny ball. Turn to coat in greased bowl. Cover, let rise in a warm place 2 hours.* Punch down, divide dough in half.

Range

Oil one 12-inch pizza pan and one 10-by 15-inch jelly roll pan. Roll and stretch dough to fit pans, press firmly into pans, making crust slightly thicker at the edges. Spread with choice of toppings, below. Bake at 450°F about 30 minutes, until crust is browned and crisp.

Microwave

Cut one 12-inch circle and one 12-inch square from brown paper. Grease well, dust with flour. Roll and stretch dough to fit paper, making crust slightly thicker at the edges. Place on prepared paper. Spread with choice of toppings. Cook 3 minutes, rotate pizza ½ turn, cook 2 minutes. Slide onto cookie sheet, bake in range at 500°F. 6 minutes.

Rising Time Saved: about 1 hour

Cooking Time Saved: 20 minutes

*To reduce rising period, heat dough in microwave 25 seconds, turn over in bowl, let stand 2 minutes. Heat 25 seconds, turn dough, let stand 15 minutes, heat 25 seconds. Let rise in a warm place 45 minutes, or until doubled.

PIZZA SUPPER FOR KIDS

1 cup bottled pizza sauce or spaghetti sauce
¼ pound sliced salami or peperoni
¼ pound mozzarella cheese, shredded
½ teaspoon mixed Italian herbs

Spread sauce on round pizza, keeping edges free. Sprinkle with salami, cheese and herbs. Cook as directed. Makes about 6 servings.

PIZZA APPETIZER FOR ADULTS

1 cup bottled pizza sauce or spaghetti sauce
12 anchovy fillets

1 can (4 ounces) mushroom caps
¼ pound mozzarella cheese, shredded
½ teaspoon mixed Italian herbs

Spread sauce on rectangular or square pizza, keeping edges free. Sprinkle with anchovy fillets, mushroom caps, cheese and herbs. Cook as directed. Cut hot pizza into squares.
Makes about 16 appetizer servings.

MEATBALLS

2 pounds ground beef
2 slices bread, crumbled
¼ cup milk
1 egg
¼ cup chopped onion

2 tablespoons chopped parsley
2 teaspoons salt
¼ teaspoon pepper
Melted butter, margarine or bacon fat for frying

Mix beef with remaining ingredients, shape into 1½-inch balls.

Range

Heat butter or margarine or bacon fat in a large skillet. Brown meatballs.

Microwave

Roll meatballs in butter or margarine or bacon fat, spread ½ the meatballs on oven tray or in shallow dish. Cook 3 minutes, turn, cook 2 minutes. Repeat with remaining meatballs.

Drain meatballs on paper towels.
Use half the meatballs for Spaghetti and Meatballs for the youngsters, use the rest for Meatballs Stroganoff to serve adults.
Makes about 30 meatballs.

SPAGHETTI AND MEATBALLS

½ recipe meatballs (page 116)
1 can (14 ounces) spaghetti sauce
½ pound spaghetti, cooked

Range
Cover meatballs with sauce, simmer 15 minutes.

Microwave
Cover meatballs with sauce in 1-quart casserole. Cover, cook 7 minutes.

Cooking Time Saved: 8 minutes

Serve over cooked spaghetti. Makes 4 to 6 servings for children.

MEATBALLS STROGANOFF

½ recipe meatballs, above
1 can (10½ ounces) condensed cream of mushroom soup
½ cup milk or water
½ cup sour cream
½ pound egg noodles, cooked

Range
In a saucepan cover meatballs with soup mixed with milk. Bring to a boil, simmer 15 minutes. Stir in sour cream, heat without boiling.

Microwave
Combine meatballs, soup and milk in 2-quart serving bowl. Cook 7 minutes. Stir in sour cream.

Cooking Time Saved: 8 minutes

Serve over cooked egg noodles. Makes 3 to 4 servings for adults.

BAKED CHICKEN MEAL IN TWO STAGES

1 broiler-fryer (about 3 pounds), cut
into 8 serving pieces
½ cup melted butter or margarine
Flour, salt, pepper, paprika
4 small onions, cooked or canned

1 small garlic clove, minced
1 can (4 ounces) mushrooms
⅓ cup red wine
⅓ cup chicken bouillon
1 tablespoon tomato paste
Pinch basil

Brush chicken with butter or margarine, dust with flour seasoned with salt, pepper and paprika.

Range

Arrange chicken, skin side up, on
greased baking sheet. Bake at 425°F
for 10 minutes, reduce temperature
to 325°F. Bake 30 minutes or until
chicken is done.

Microwave

Arrange chicken pieces side by side
on serving dish, cover with wax
paper, cook about 7 minutes. Turn,
cook about 7 minutes longer. Let
stand 10 minutes before serving.

Cooking Time Saved: about 25
minutes

Test by piercing thigh meat with a fork; juices should run clear. Serve favorite pieces to the children, prepare rest of chicken for adults.

Range

Heat remaining butter or margarine
in skillet, add onions and garlic,
brown lightly. Add remaining
ingredients, bring to a boil, simmer
10 minutes.

Microwave

Put onions and garlic in serving dish,
sprinkle with remaining butter or
margarine, cook 1 minute. Add
remaining ingredients, cook 5
minutes.

Add chicken, baste with sauce, heat. Serves 2 to 3 children and 2 adults.

ROAST TURKEY–TURKEY A L'ORANGE

1 Turkey, about 10 pounds
Salt, pepper, poultry seasoning
Oil
Sauce a l'Orange (page 120)

Rub turkey inside and out with salt, pepper and poultry seasoning.

Range

Arrange turkey on a rack in a roasting pan, breast side down. Roast at 325°F about 20 minutes per pound, 1 hour, 20 minutes for a 10-pound bird. Turn breast side up after first hour of cooking. Let stand 15 minutes before serving.

Microwave

Arrange turkey breast side down on two saucers in a shallow baking dish. Cook about 10 minutes per pound, 1 hour, 40 minutes for a 10-pound bird as follows: Divide cooking time into quarters; turn bird on one side after first quarter, then on the other side, and finish breast up. When the turkey begins to brown, cover tail, wing tips and leg ends with small pieces of aluminum foil. The foil should not touch the walls of the oven. Let stand, covered, 20 to 30 minutes before serving.

Cooking Time Saved: about 2 hours

Makes 6 servings.

For children, cut off drum sticks and wings.
For adults, slice breast meat, arrange on a large serving platter.
Pour Sauce à l'Orange over turkey slices.

SAUCE A L'ORANGE

2 cups water (Range only)
Rind of 1 orange, thinly slivered
1 tablespoon sugar
2 tablespoons vinegar

1 cup turkey or chicken broth
2 tablespoons cornstarch
½ cup orange juice
Salt, pepper

Range

Bring 2 cups of water to a boil in a saucepan, add orange rind, simmer 5 minutes. Drain, rinse in cold water. In a heavy saucepan, cook sugar and vinegar until caramelized. Add turkey broth, orange rind, cornstarch dissolved in orange juice, salt and pepper to taste. Simmer 15 minutes.

Microwave

Cook sugar and vinegar in a 1-quart covered casserole until caramelized about 5 minutes. Add turkey broth and orange rind, cook uncovered 5 minutes. Add cornstarch dissolved in orange juice, salt and pepper to taste. Stir well, simmer 5 minutes, or until thickened.

Cooking Time Saved: 10 minutes

Makes 4 cups.

CHUCK FILLET ROAST

Beef chuck fillet, about 3 pounds
Garlic powder
Salt, pepper

Paprika
Gravy browner
Oil

Sprinkle meat with garlic powder, pepper and paprika.
Rub with gravy browner and oil.

Range

Roast meat on a rack in a baking pan at 325°F for about 20 minutes per pound for rare to medium. Baste often with pan juices during roasting.

Microwave

Set meat on two inverted saucers, fat side down, in a 13- by 9-inch baking dish. Cover with wax paper, cook 5½ minutes per pound for rare, 6 minutes for medium rare. At half way point, rotate dish ½ turn and turn meat fat side up. Baste meat with pan juices.

Cooking Time Saved: 42 minutes

Let roast stand 20 minutes, covered with foil, before carving.
Makes 8 servings.

FIVE BOY LAMB STEW/CURRY

For Children

2 tablespoons oil	4 tablespoons flour
2 cloves garlic, minced	1 teaspoon ginger
1 small onion, chopped	1½ teaspoons salt
2 pounds boneless lamb cubes	½ cup water
	2 carrots, peeled and diced

Range

Heat oil in heavy pot, add garlic and onion, cook until golden. Toss lamb with flour, ginger and salt. Brown in oil, stirring. Add water and carrots simmer 45 minutes until lamb is tender.

Microwave

Cook oil, garlic, onion and carrot 1 minute in 3-quart casserole. Toss lamb with flour, ginger and salt, add to vegetables. Cook 4 minutes. Stir in water. Cook, covered, about 5 minutes or until meat is almost tender. Let stand, covered, 5 minutes to finish cooking.

Cooking Time Saved: about 45 minutes

For children, serve stew with choice of condiments, below.

For Adults

2 tablespoons oil	1 tart apple, peeled, cored and chopped
1 tablespoon curry powder	Salt, pepper
2 tablespoons chopped onion	Cooked rice
1 clove garlic, minced	Condiments: grated coconut, chutney, raisins, cucumber and chopped peanuts
¼ cup minced green pepper	

Range

Heat oil, add curry powder, onion and garlic, cook stirring, until onion is golden. Add green pepper and apple, cook until apple is soft. Stir mixture into cooked lamb stew, reheat.

Microwave

Combine ingredients in small bowl, cook, covered, 5 minutes until apple is soft. Add to prepared lamb stew, stirring to combine, reheat.

Adjust seasoning to taste. Serve with rice and bowls of condiments.
Serves 2 to 3 children and 2 adults.

CHILI CON CARNE

1 pound ground beef
1 onion, chopped
1 garlic clove, minced
2 teaspoons chili powder
1 can (1 pound) tomatoes

1 teaspoon salt
1 can (1 pound) red
kidney beans, drained
For adult recipe: Monterey Jack
cheese, crushed red pepper, minced
onion

Range

In a skillet, cook beef, onion and
garlic until meat loses its color. Add
chili powder, tomatoes and
seasonings; simmer 10 minutes. Add
beans, simmer 1 hour until thick.

Microwave

Cook meat, onions and garlic in a
2-quart casserole, 4 minutes. Stir after
2 minutes. Add tomatoes and
seasonings; cook 3 minutes. Stir, add
beans, cook 2 minutes.

Cooking Time Saved: 30 minutes

For children, serve with corn chips.

*For adults, adjust seasoning with more chili powder,
crushed red pepper and minced onion to taste.
Divide into two ovenproof bowls, top with strips of cheese.*

Range

Bake at 325°F or until cheese is
melted and bubbly, about 20
minutes.

Microwave

Cook until cheese is melted and
bubbly, 2 minutes.

Cooking Time Saved: 18 minutes

Serves 2 to 3 children and 2 adults.

ROLLED RIB ROAST

1 rolled boneless rib roast

Range

Arrange meat on rack in roasting pan, roast at 325°F for about 20 minutes per pound, until thermometer inserted in center, away from fat, reads 140°F.

Microwave

Arrange meat on inverted saucers in baking dish, fat side down. Cover with a paper towel, cook 5 minutes per pound for rare. Give dish a ¼ turn every 10 minutes, turn fat side up at the halfway point. At the end of cooking time, remove meat, insert thermometer. It should read 120°F. Let stand wrapped in foil 20 to 30 minutes before carving; the temperature will increase to 140°F during standing time.

CUMBERLAND SAUCE

1 cup currant jelly
1 teaspoon prepared mustard
1 tablespoon grated orange rind
1 tablespoon lemon juice
½ cup pan juices from Rolled Rib Roast

Range

Warm currant jelly in small pan until it just melts.

Microwave

Melt jelly in small serving bowl, 2 minutes.

Add remaining ingredients, stir well to blend. Serve with slices of beef. Makes 1½ cups.

FISH FILLETS
(Plain and Véronique)

1½ pounds fish fillets,
fresh or frozen
Seasoned dry bread crumbs
Butter or margarine

1 tablespoon lemon juice
Seasoned flour
1 cup seedless grapes
½ cup dry white wine

Range
Thaw fish sufficiently to separate fillets, if frozen.

Microwave
Thaw fish sufficiently to separate fillets, if frozen, about 3 minutes in package in microwave.

Sprinkle with lemon juice. Serve with cole slaw and French fried potatoes.

Range
Véronique:

Adults: Dust fish fillets with seasoned flour. In skillet, brown lightly on both sides in butter or margarine. Transfer to heated serving dish. Add grapes and wine to pan, simmer 5 minutes, pour over fish.

Plain
Children: Coat children's portions with seasoned crumbs. Brown lightly on both sides in a skillet in butter or margarine.

Microwave
Véronique:

Adults: Arrange fish fillets on baking dish, dot with 2 tablespoons butter or margarine. Add wine, if desired. Cover, cook 2 minutes, rotate dish ½ turn, cook 2 minutes longer. Add grapes, cover, cook 2 minutes longer.

Plain
Children: Melt 2 tablespoons butter or margarine on plate, coat fish with butter, then with seasoned crumbs. Arrange on individual plates, cook 4 minutes.

Serves 2 to 3 children and 2 adults.

124

FOR CHILDREN TO MAKE BY THEMSELVES

DO-YOUR-OWN-THING FISH STICKS

1 package fish sticks (10 pieces)
Toppings:
Cheese slices, tomato slices, pickles,
Mayonnaise, tartar sauce

Range

Arrange fish sticks on baking pan,
top to taste. Bake at 350°F for about
20 minutes (or according to
directions on fish package) until
piping hot.

Microwave

Arrange fish sticks on an 8-inch
square glass baking dish. Top to taste,
cook 4 minutes.

Cooking Time Saved: 16 minutes

Makes 5 servings.

TUNABURGERS

1 can (7 ounces) tuna
3 tablespoons mayonnaise
Salt, pepper
2 or 3 hamburger rolls, split
Sliced stuffed olives or diced almonds

Break tuna into small pieces, combine lightly with mayonnaise and salt and pepper to taste. Spread on both halves of hamburger rolls. Sprinkle with sliced olives or diced almonds.

Range
Brown under the broiler. Be careful not to burn almonds, if used.

Microwave
Heat on paper plates 2 minutes, until bread and filling are hot.

Makes 2 or 3 servings.

SLOPPY JOES

1 pound ground beef
1 tablespoon instant minced onion
½ teaspoon salt
Pepper

1 can (10¼ ounces) condensed tomato soup
¼ cup ketchup
6 hamburger buns, split

Range
Cook beef, onion and seasonings in skillet, stirring with a fork, until meat browns. Add soup and ketchup, bring to a boil, reduce heat, simmer 5 minutes. Adjust seasoning with salt and pepper. Serve on toasted hamburger buns to make open-faced sandwiches.

Microwave
Combine ingredients in glass dish. Cover. Cook, rotating dish occasionally, about 8 minutes. Serve on buns heated in microwave 20 seconds.

Makes 6 servings.

MUFFIN PIZZAS

English muffins
Spaghetti or pizza sauce
Mozzarella, Swiss or Cheddar cheese, shredded·
Italian herbs

*Split English muffins with a fork, toast if desired, spread with
prepared spaghetti or pizza sauce from a jar.
Top with shredded cheese, sprinkle with mixed Italian herbs.*

Range	Microwave
Bake at 450°F on cookie sheet until the cheese melts and muffins are piping hot, about 10 minutes.	Heat on serving plate until cheese melts, 45 seconds for 2 halves, 1½ minutes for 4 halves.
	Cooking Time Saved: about 8 minutes

MACARONI AND BACON

1 package (9 to 10 ounces) frozen macaroni and cheese
4 strips bacon

Range	Microwave
Heat macaroni according to directions about 40 minutes. During last 10 minutes, place bacon on rack over a shallow baking pan, bake at 400°F until crisp and brown. Drain on paper towels.	Remove frozen macaroni from metal package, place in serving dish. Cover, cook 9 minutes, turning once. Wrap bacon in paper towels, place beside macaroni during last 5 minutes of cooking.
	Cooking Time Saved: about 30 minutes

Crumble bacon over macaroni. Makes 2 servings.

FROZEN DINNERS
.(THAT CHILDREN CAN MAKE FOR THEMSELVES, TOO)

❧

ITALIAN DINNER PLATE
SPAGHETTI AND MEATBALLS
BROCCOLI PARMESAN

¼ pound ground beef
½ slice bread, crumbled
2 tablespoons grated Parmesan cheese
½ teaspoon garlic salt
Pinch Italian seasoning

½ cup spaghetti sauce
2 ounces spaghetti, cooked and drained
1 package (10 ounces) frozen broccoli
Grated Parmesan cheese, garlic salt

Combine beef with bread, Parmesan cheese, garlic salt, Italian seasoning. Shape into 4 or 5 balls.

Range

Brown meatballs on all sides on a lightly greased skillet. Drain off excess fat, add spaghetti sauce, cover, simmer 5 minutes. Arrange cooked, drained spaghetti on foil tray or pie plate, top with meatballs and sauce. Thaw broccoli just long enough to separate pieces. Place ⅓ broccoli on plate with spaghetti, return remainder to freezer for other use. Sprinkle with Parmesan cheese and garlic salt. Wrap tray in aluminum foil, store in freezer. When ready to serve, slit foil with knife to allow steam to escape and bake at 350°F for 25 minutes.

Microwave

Arrange meatballs on plate, cook 3 minutes, drain off excess fat. Add spaghetti sauce, cook ½ minute. Arrange cooked, drained spaghetti on plastic-coated paper plate, top with meatballs and sauce. Thaw broccoli in package in microwave just long enough to separate pieces, about 1½ minutes. Place ⅓ broccoli on plate with spaghetti, return remainder to freezer for other use. Sprinkle with Parmesan cheese and garlic salt. Wrap plate in plastic or freezer paper. Store in freezer. When ready to serve, slit paper with knife to allow steam to escape. Cook 6 minutes.

Cooking Time Saved: 19 minutes

Makes 1 serving.

HAM DINNER PLATE

HAM WITH JELLY SAUCE
CANDIED SWEET POTATOES
SPINACH IN CREAM

Fully cooked ham steak
(about 4 ounces)
2 tablespoons currant jelly
1 tablespoon butter or margarine,
melted
1 tablespoon brown sugar

Pinch ground cloves
1 or 2 cooked or
canned sweet potatoes
½ cup cooked, chopped spinach
1 teaspoon cornstarch
1 tablespoon cream

Arrange dinner on a foil tray for conventional cooking, or on a heavy plastic-coated paper plate for microwave cooking. Coat both sides of ham steak with jelly, place on plate. Combine melted butter or margarine, brown sugar and cloves. Coat sweet potatoes with mixture, add to plate.
Combine spinach, cornstarch and cream, stir until smooth. Add to plate.

Range

Wrap tray in aluminum foil, store in freezer. When ready to serve, slit foil with knife to allow steam to escape, bake at 350°F for 25 minutes.

Microwave

Wrap plate in plastic or freezer paper, store in freezer. When ready to serve, slit paper with knife to allow steam to escape. Cook about 5 minutes, turning plate once.

Cooking Time Saved: 20 minutes

Makes 1 serving.

CHICKEN DINNER PLATE

BAKED OR ROAST CHICKEN
SCALLOPED POTATOES
BUTTERED GREEN BEANS

Baked or roast chicken quarter (page 118)
½ cup scalloped potatoes (page 190)
1 tablespoon butter or margarine
½ cup individually frozen green beans
Salt, pepper

Range

Arrange chicken piece and potatoes in a foil tray or pie plate. Melt butter or margarine, toss with green beans, salt and pepper to taste, add to foil tray. Wrap tray in aluminum foil, store in freezer. When ready to serve, slit foil with knife to allow steam to escape, bake at 350°F for 30 minutes.

Microwave

Arrange chicken piece and potatoes on a plastic-coated paper plate. Melt butter or margarine (20 seconds), toss with green beans, salt and pepper to taste, add to plate. Wrap plate in plastic or freezer paper. Store in freezer. When ready to serve, slit paper with knife to allow steam to escape. Cook 7 minutes.

Cooking Time Saved: 23 minutes

Makes 1 serving.

FISH DINNER PLATE

FISH FILLETS CREOLE
CHEESY POTATOES
PEAS O'BRIEN

1 pound frozen fish fillets
¼ teaspoon salt
⅛ teaspoon pepper
¼ teaspoon crushed basil
2 cups fluffy mashed potatoes

½ cup shredded American cheese
1 package (10 ounces) frozen peas
1 tablespoon chopped red pepper
1 tablespoon oil
1 can (8 ounces) stewed tomatoes

Arrange each dinner on a foil tray for conventional cooking, or plastic-coated paper plate for microwave cooking. Thaw fish just enough to separate fillets, (about 2 minutes in microwave). Season with salt, pepper and basil. Divide onto four plates. Combine potatoes with cheese, mound on plates with fish. Thaw peas just enough to separate (about 1 minute in microwave), combine with pepper and oil. Add to plates with fish and potatoes.

Range

Wrap plate in aluminum foil, store in freezer. When ready to serve, slit foil with knife to allow steam to escape. Bake at 400°F for 25 minutes. Meanwhile, heat tomatoes in small saucepan.

Microwave

Wrap plate in plastic or freezer paper, store in freezer. When ready to serve, slit paper with knife to allow steam to escape. Cook 1 dinner 4 minutes. Place stewed tomatoes in a small serving bowl beside dinner, cook 3 minutes.

Cooking Time Saved: **21 minutes.**

Pour tomatoes over fish. Makes 4 servings.

MEAT AND POULTRY TIMETABLE

	Internal Temp. (In microwave ovens allow recommended standing time)	Microwave Time min./pound	Range (325°F) min./pound
Beef Rolled rib or rump	140°F (Rare) 160°F (Medium)	5-6 6-7	20-25 25-30
Pork Fresh roast, boneless Ham, precooked	170°F 130°F	8-9 6-8	35-40 20-25
Lamb Leg with bone Rolled	160°F (Medium) 170°F (Well done) 160°F (Medium) 170°F (Well done)	5-6 6-7 7-8 8-9	25-30 30-35 35-40 40-45
Veal Roast	180°F	9	30-40
Poultry Chicken Turkey	180°F 180°F	6-8 10	25 20-25

ENTERTAINING

One of the best features of microwave cooking for children is the fact that no one gets burned with hot plates or utensils. Most cooking utensils stay cool and comfortable to the touch. And no one ever forgets to turn off a microwave—it goes off automatically when the timer shuts off.

ENTERTAINING

FOR INTIMATE LITTLE SIT-DOWN DINNERS
(for 8 or fewer)

SMALL BASHES (up to 20 people)

FOR
INTIMATE LITTLE
SIT-DOWN
DINNERS
(FOR 8 OR FEWER)

EGGPLANT CAVIAR

2 small eggplants
2 large ripe tomatoes, peeled
1 medium onion, peeled and quartered

½ cup olive oil
3 tablespoons lemon juice
Salt, freshly ground black pepper

Trim stem ends from eggplant.

Range
Bake eggplant on a lightly greased baking sheet at 400°F for 40 minutes, until very soft.

Microwave
Place eggplant on microwave tray, cover with wax paper, cook 6 minutes. Turn, cook 10 minutes, until very soft.

Cooking Time Saved: 24 minutes

Let cool, peel and discard skin. Chop eggplant pulp, tomatoes and onions. Mix with olive oil, lemon juice and seasonings. Chill. Serve as an appetizer salad, on lettuce, or as a dip with crackers or chips.

CASTILIAN SHRIMP

1½ pounds shrimp
1 medium onion, minced
4 cloves garlic, minced
¼ cup oil
1 can (1 pound) Italian style
tomatoes, drained and chopped

1 tablespoon lemon juice
2 teaspoons chili powder
Sugar, oregano, salt, pepper to taste
10 pimiento-stuffed olives
·2 tablespoons chopped parsley
Cooked rice

Shell and devein fresh shrimp, or defrost and drain cleaned frozen shrimp.

Range

In saucepan, cook onion and garlic
in oil until translucent. Add
tomatoes, lemon juice and
seasonings, simmer 20 minutes. Add
shrimp, olives, chopped parsley,
simmer 5 minutes or until shrimp
are pink.

Microwave

Cook onion and garlic in oil in a
covered 3-quart casserole for 4
minutes. Add tomatoes, lemon juice
and seasonings, cover, and cook 10
minutes. Add shrimp, olives and
parsley. Cook 3 minutes or until
shrimp are pink.

Cooking Time Saved: about 14
minutes

Serve over cooked rice. Makes 4 servings.

CHAWAN MUSHI

8 raw shrimp, peeled, deveined,
split in half
½ pound raw white chicken meat,
slivered
2 tablespoons cornstarch

4 eggs
3 cups chicken broth
Salt, white pepper
Soy sauce, ½ teaspoon or to taste

*Toss shrimp and chicken slivers with cornstarch; divide into 4 individual casseroles.
Beat eggs well, combine with chicken broth and seasonings, pour into casseroles.*

Range

Cover casseroles with lids, set in pan
of hot water, bake at 350°F for
about 50 minutes, until custard is
set.

Microwave

Pour 2 inches boiling water into a 12-
by 18-inch glass baking dish. Arrange
casseroles in water two at a time,
cover with wax paper. Cook about 17
minutes. Rotate the dishes halfway
through cooking time.

*Slivered scallions, sliced water chestnuts, bamboo shoots or watercress sprigs
are optional additions to the custard. Makes 4 servings.*

BARBECUED TURKEY BREAST

1 turkey breast, about 3 pounds ·   2 tablespoons Worcestershire sauce
2 tablespoons butter or margarine   ¼ cup ketchup
1 clove garlic, crushed   1 tablespoon sugar
¼ cup vinegar   Salt, pepper to taste

Turkey leg quarters may be cooked by this method.
Allow slightly longer time than for the breasts.

Range

Melt butter or margarine, add garlic, cook 2 minutes. Discard garlic. Add remaining ingredients, heat to the boiling point. Brush turkey with sauce, arrange on rack, skin side down, roast at 325°F for about 30 minutes, basting often with sauce. Turn, roast about 30 minutes longer until turkey is tender and cooked through. Baste often.

Microwave

Put butter or margarine and garlic in glass baking dish large enough to hold turkey. Cover, cook 1 minute, discard garlic. Add remaining ingredients, heat to boiling point, about 3 minutes. Brush turkey breast with sauce, arrange in baking dish, skin side down. Cover with wax paper, cook 15 minutes. Rotate dish ½ turn, cook uncovered, skin side up, 10 to 12 minutes. Baste, cover with foil, let stand 10 minutes before carving.

Cooking Time Saved: about 35 minutes

Makes 8 servings.

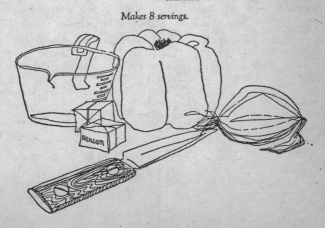

CHICKEN FLORENTINE

1 small onion, minced	4 tablespoons cream
4 cloves garlic, minced	4 chicken breasts, split and boned
¼ cup butter or margarine	¾ cup cream
2 packages (10 ounces each)	¼ cup dry white wine or sherry
frozen spinach	1 cup sliced mushrooms
½ teaspoon nutmeg	1 tablespoon beurre manié
Salt, pepper	(page 4)

Thaw spinach (2 minutes in microwave). Chop, squeeze dry.

Range

Sauté onion and garlic in butter or margarine until wilted. Add spinach, seasonings and 4 tablespoons cream, cook 10 minutes, until most of the liquid has evaporated. Divide spinach into 8 equal mounds in a 13-by 9-inch baking dish. Top with chicken breasts. Add ¾ cup cream, wine and mushrooms. Cover and bake at 350°F for 35 minutes, until chicken is done. Remove chicken to a serving platter. Add beurre manié to cooking liquid, simmer 10 minutes, stirring often, until sauce is thickened.

Microwave

Cook butter or margarine, onions, garlic and spinach in a 2-quart covered casserole 6 minutes. Stir well, add seasonings and 4 tablespoons cream. Cook, uncovered 4 minutes. Divide spinach into 8 equal mounds in a 13-by 9-inch baking dish. Top with chicken breasts. Add ¾ cup cream, wine and mushrooms. Cook, covered 10 minutes. Remove chicken to serving platter, cover, and let stand. Add beurre manié to pan juices, stir, cook 3 minutes.

Cooking Time Saved: 35 minutes

Season sauce to taste and pour over chicken breasts.
Makes 8 servings.

CHICKEN KIEV

2 whole chicken breasts
(about 10 ounces each)
½ stick (¼ cup) butter or margarine
2 tablespoons parsley
⅓ cup fine bread crumbs

Salt, pepper
1 egg
1 tablespoon water
Fat for deep frying (range only)

Remove bones and skins from chicken breasts, pound with a mallet or heavy plate to flatten. Cut in half. Slice butter into pieces 2-inches long, ¼-inch thick. Put a piece of butter or margarine on narrow end of chicken piece. Sprinkle with parsley. Roll up, beginning at the narrow end, in jelly roll fashion, folding in the edges to cover the butter. Secure rolls with wooden toothpicks, chill at least ½ hour (or overnight, if desired). Dip rolls into crumbs seasoned with salt and pepper, then into egg beaten with water, and again into crumbs. Chill 1 hour.

Range

Heat deep fat to 375°F. Fry rolls until richly browned, about 8 minutes. Drain on paper towels.

Microwave

Arrange rolls on glass bake-and-serve platter. Cover with wax paper, cook 2 minutes, turn rolls, remove cover, cook 3 minutes longer. Let stand 2 minutes before serving.

Cooking Time Saved: No pan of oil to preheat and no clean-up after deep fat frying.

Makes 4 servings.

CHICKEN MOLÉ

3 pounds chicken parts
(breasts, thighs and legs)
¼ cup lard or shortening
1 green pepper, seeded
1 medium onion, peeled
1 tablespoon sesame seeds
3 cloves garlic

⅓ cup blanched almonds
1 cup solid-pack tomatoes, drained
1 square (1 ounce) unsweetened
chocolate
1 tablespoon chili powder
Dash each ground cloves, cinnamon,
coriander and anise seed
1 cup chicken bouillon

Range

Brown chicken parts in lard or
shortening in a heavy skillet over
medium heat, about 30 minutes.
Remove to a flameproof casserole,
or Dutch oven fitted with a lid.

Microwave

Melt lard or shortening in a 13- by
9-inch baking dish, about 2 minutes.
Add chicken, cover, cook skin side
down for 6 minutes. Rotate dish ½
turn, cook 6 minutes longer.

*Puree remaining ingredients in a blender, or grind twice with finest
blade of food chopper to make molé sauce. Pour over chicken pieces.*

Range

Cover dish, simmer 30 minutes,
stirring and basting occasionally.

Microwave

Cook, covered, 8 minutes. Baste
chicken and rotate dish ½ turn, cook
7 minutes longer.

Cooking Time Saved: about 30
minutes.

Makes 8 servings.

CHICKEN CORDON BLEU

2 whole chicken breasts
(about 10 ounces each)
¼ pound Swiss cheese, thinly sliced
¼ pound ham, thinly sliced
4 tablespoons flour
1 egg, beaten

½ cup fine dry bread crumbs
Oil for frying (range)
2 tablespoons butter or
margarine (microwave)
Salt, pepper

*Remove bones and skins from chicken breasts, pound with a mallet or
heavy plate to flatten. Cut in half. Arrange a slice of Swiss cheese
and a slice of ham on each chicken piece. Fold short sides over
filling and roll up from the wide side. Secure rolls with toothpick;
dust with flour, dip in beaten egg, coat with bread crumbs.*

Range

Heat 1-inch oil to 350°F in a heavy
skillet. Brown chicken rolls on all
sides. Arrange in baking dish, brown
in oven at 375°F. for 8 to 10
minutes, until chicken is firm and
juices run clear.

Microwave

Arrange chicken rolls on microwave
tray, dot with butter or margarine.
Cover with wax paper, cook 4
minutes. Remove wax paper, cook 2
minutes more, until chicken is firm
and juices run clear.

Season to taste with salt and pepper. Makes 4 servings.

LANCASHIRE HOT POT

3 medium potatoes, peeled and
cut in ½-inch slices
1 large onion, thinly sliced
6 lamb shoulder chops, 1-inch thick

½ teaspoon salt
½ teaspoon pepper
1 cup warm beef broth
4 tablespoons butter or margarine

*Spread potato slices in 12-inch square baking dish, top with onion
slices and chops. Season vegetable layers with salt and pepper.
Pour beef broth down the side of the dish, dot with butter or margarine.*

Range

Cover dish, bake at 350°F for 2¼
hours until meat and potatoes are
very tender. Uncover, bake 10
minutes longer.

Microwave

Cover dish, cook 15 minutes, or until
meat and potatoes are tender. Rotate
dish ½ turn after first 7 minutes of
cooking.

Cooking Time Saved: about 2 hours

Makes 6 servings.

BEEF BOURGUIGNONNE

½ pound bacon, diced
2 pounds boneless chuck,
cut in ¾-inch cubes
4 medium carrots, peeled, cut
in ½-inch rounds
1 cup minced onions
4 cloves garlic, minced
1 teaspoon sugar

¼ teaspoon thyme
1 cup dry red wine
2 cups beef broth
Salt, freshly ground pepper
2 tablespoons flour
1 tablespoon butter or margarine,
softened
1 can (8 ounces) mushroom caps

Range

In a heavy 3-quart saucepan, sauté bacon until crisp, remove, drain. Brown meat cubes quickly in bacon drippings, remove. Add carrots, onion and garlic, sauté until onions are translucent. Add remaining ingredients except flour, butter or margarine and mushrooms. Simmer, covered, 1½ to 2 hours until meat is fork tender. Thicken sauce with flour blended with softened butter. Add mushrooms. Simmer 10 minutes, until sauce is thickened to the desired consistency.

Microwave

Cook bacon in a covered 3-quart casserole for 8 minutes until fat is rendered. Add meat, onions, carrots and garlic. Cook, covered, 5 minutes, until meat loses its red color. Add remaining ingredients except flour, butter and mushrooms. Cover, cook 20 minutes. Stir in flour mixed with softened butter or margarine. Add mushrooms. Cook, covered, 20 minutes until meat is fork tender. Rotate casserole ½ turn and stir well every five minutes during final 20 minutes of cooking.

Cooking Time Saved: 1 hour

Makes 8 servings.

STANDING RIB ROAST

6 to 8-pound standing rib roast
1 clove garlic
Rub meat with garlic.

Range

Place seasoned standing rib roast fat side up on a rack in an open roasting pan. Roast at 325°F for 18 to 20 minutes per pound for medium rare. Remove roast from oven. Let stand 20 minutes before carving.

Microwave

Place standing rib roast fat side down on two inverted saucers in a 13-x 9-inch baking dish. Cover top loosely with paper towelling. Allow about 5 minutes per pound for rare. After 25 minutes, let stand 5 minutes. Turn meat fat side up, cover loosely with paper and cook 15 minutes longer. Wrap meat in aluminum foil, let stand 20 minutes.

Cooking Time Saved: over 2 hours

Makes about 8 servings.

Note: *A standard meat thermometer or one specially designed for microwave is helpful in verifying internal temperature.*

RISOTTO WITH MUSHROOMS

4 tablespoons butter or margarine
1 small onion, chopped
1 clove garlic, minced

½ cup sliced mushrooms
1½ cups long grain rice
3 cups hot chicken broth

Range

Heat butter or margarine in skillet, cook onion, garlic and mushrooms until wilted. Add rice, stir until golden. Add hot broth, bring to a boil. Transfer to a casserole, cover. Bake at 325°F for about 20 minutes, until rice is tender and liquid absorbed.

Microwave

In a 2-quart serving casserole, combine butter or margarine, onion, garlic, mushrooms and rice. Stir, cover, cook 5 minutes. Stir in hot broth, cover, cook 10 minutes longer. Rotate casserole ½ turn, stir, cook 4 minutes longer, until rice is tender and liquid absorbed. Let stand, covered, 4 minutes before serving.

Makes 8 servings.

STUFFED LAMB SHOULDER

1 shoulder of lamb (about 3 pounds)	¼ pound chicken livers, minced
4 strips bacon, diced	1 cup soft bread crumbs
1 small red pepper, chopped	Salt, pepper, paprika
¼ pound mushrooms, sliced	

Have the meat man bone the shoulder, shaping a pocket for stuffing.

Range

Brown bacon in skillet, add vegetables, and cook until onions are translucent. Add chicken livers and cook 10 minutes or until livers lose their pinkness. Fill lamb pocket with stuffing, sew closed. Sprinkle meat with seasonings, roast at 325°F for about 2 hours (40 minutes to the pound). Remove and let stand 15 minutes before serving.

Microwave

Cook bacon, covered, in an 8- by 10-inch, glass baking dish 4 minutes, or until crisp. Add vegetables, stir, cook 3 minutes. Add crumbs and seasonings and mix well. Fill lamb pocket and sew closed. Place meat on 2 inverted saucers in a 9- by 13-inch baking dish. Cook uncovered 20 minutes. Turn meat over, cook 15 minutes longer, or 12 minutes per pound in all. Remove, cover tightly with aluminum foil, and let stand 15 minutes before slicing.

Cooking Time Saved: 1½ hours

Makes 8 servings.

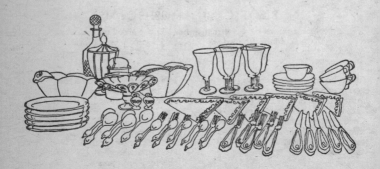

INDIAN LAMB CURRY

2 pounds boneless lamb, cut in
1-inch cubes
4 tablespoons oil
2 tablespoons curry powder
1 large onion, peeled and minced
3 medium carrots, peeled and minced
1 tart green cooking apple,
peeled, cored and minced

2 cloves garlic, minced
2 tablespoons tomato puree
2 tablespoons lemon juice
¼ cup coconut milk or light cream
2 teaspoons salt
1 cup yogurt
½ cup warm water

Range

Sauté lamb in oil over high heat with curry. Remove meat and add the onions, carrots, apples and garlic to pan. Cook over low heat, stirring, until vegetables are wilted and apple reduced to a pulp. Add remaining ingredients and lamb to the saucepan, simmer 1½ hours, or until lamb is very tender.

Microwave

In 3-quart casserole, mix oil with curry, add onion, carrots, apple and garlic. Cook, covered, 10 minutes. Stir in cubes of lamb, cover, cook 8 minutes. Stir in remaining ingredients, cook, covered, 30 minutes. Rotate casserole ½ turn and stir well every 10 minutes. Let stand, covered, 10 minutes before serving.

Cooking Time Saved: 50 minutes

Serve with small bowls of chutney, grated coconut, shredded cucumber and yogurt, salted peanuts, minced green onions, raisins.
Makes 8 servings.

APPLE CHUTNEY

5 cups peeled, cored and chopped apples or pears
1 lemon, seeded and chopped
1 cup white sugar
1 cup light brown sugar, packed

1½ cups seedless raisins
2 tablespoons chopped candied ginger
1½ teaspoons salt
¼ teaspoon crushed dried red pepper
1½ cups cider vinegar

Range

Combine ingredients in large saucepan. Simmer 45 minutes to 1 hour, uncovered, until mixture is thick and syrupy.

Microwave

Combine ingredients in 4-quart casserole. Cook, covered, 10 minutes. Uncover, cook 25 minutes or until thick and syrupy. Let stand 5 minutes.

Store in refrigerator. Makes 5 cups.

SWEET AND SOUR PORK

2 pounds boneless pork, cut in
¾-inch cubes
4 medium carrots, peeled and sliced
4 tablespoons oil
1 medium onion, sliced
2 green peppers, seeded and sliced
1 teaspoon black pepper
1 tablespoon Worcestershire sauce

¼ teaspoon hot pepper sauce
½ cup soy sauce
½ cup brown sugar
¼ cup vinegar
1 cup pineapple chunks
(reserve syrup)
4 tablespoons cornstarch, stirred into
½ cup pineapple syrup

Range

Brown pork and carrots slowly in
hot oil, in a wok or heavy saucepan.
Add onion and peppers, cook until
just tender. Stir in remaining
ingredients, cook 10 minutes, until
sauce is clear and thick and pork is
cooked through. Adjust seasoning.

Microwave

Cook carrots and oil in a 3-quart
covered casserole 4 minutes. Stir in
onion, peppers and pork cubes, cover,
cook 5 minutes. Add remaining
ingredients, cook 10 minutes, until
sauce is clear and thick and pork is
cooked through. Rotate dish ½ turn
and stir well after 5 minutes.

Cooking Time Saved: 10 minutes

Makes 8 servings.

BARBECUED PORK TENDERLOIN

1 boneless pork tenderloin,
about 1½ pounds
1 can (8 ounces) tomato sauce
¼ cup cider vinegar
½ cup water
2 teaspoons salt
Dash cayenne pepper

1 teaspoon dry mustard
¼ teaspoon garlic powder
½ teaspoon onion powder
2 tablespoons brown sugar
¼ cup lemon juice
2 tablespoons oil

Range

Combine tomato sauce and
remaining ingredients in saucepan,
bring to a boil, simmer 5 minutes.
Cool. Marinate tenderloin in sauce
30 minutes at room temperature.
Remove meat from marinade,
arrange on rack in roasting pan.
Roast at 325°F about 1½ hours,
basting often with marinade.

Microwave

Combine tomato sauce and
remaining ingredients in shallow
8-inch square casserole, cook 4
minutes. Cool. Marinate tenderloin
in sauce 30 minutes at room
temperature. Put casserole into
microwave, cover meat with wax
paper, cook 10 minutes. Baste with
marinade in dish, let stand 5 minutes.
Cover, cook 10 minutes, basting
often. Let stand 5 minutes.

Cooking Time Saved: about 1 hour

Makes 4 servings.

RABBIT WITH SOUR CREAM

2 rabbits, about 1½ pounds each,
cut into serving pieces
¼ pound bacon, diced
3 tablespoons flour
1½ cups sour cream

1 cup milk
¼ cup lemon juice
Salt, pepper
2 tablespoons chopped parsley
for garnish

Range
Arrange rabbit pieces in baking dish,
sprinkle with bacon dice. Bake at
475°F for 25 minutes. Reduce
temperature to 350°F, bake 25
minutes.

Microwave
Arrange rabbit pieces in baking dish,
dot with bacon, cover with paper
towel, cook 20 minutes.

*Stir flour into sour cream, mix with milk, lemon juice and seasonings,
pour over rabbit.*

Range
Bake 20 minutes, until rabbit is
tender, basting occasionally.

Microwave
Cover with wax paper, cook 10
minutes until tender.

Cooking Time Saved: 40 minutes

Sprinkle with chopped parsley before serving. Makes 8 servings.

SPINACH SALAD WITH HOT BACON DRESSING

2 pounds spinach
4 strips bacon, in large dice
1 onion, chopped
½ cup oil
½ cup vinegar

1 tablespoon sugar
1 teaspoon salt,
freshly ground black pepper
2 teaspoons cornstarch
½ cup water

Wash and trim spinach. Arrange in salad bowl.

Range

Sauté onion and bacon in oil in a skillet until onions are wilted and bacon is crisp. Drain and reserve drippings. Combine vinegar, sugar, salt and pepper and bring to a boil. Blend cornstarch with water and reserved drippings. Stir into hot liquid. Simmer 8 minutes until slightly thickened. Add onions and bacon.

Microwave

Place bacon in a 1-quart casserole. Cover, cook 2 minutes. Stir, cook 2 minutes longer. Add onion and oil, cover, cook 4 minutes longer, until bacon is brown. Mix remaining ingredients, add to casserole, stir. Cook dressing, covered, 3 minutes, until slightly thickened.

Cooking Time Saved: 12 minutes

Pour over spinach in salad bowl. Makes 8 servings.

CAFFE BORGIA

¼ cup instant coffee or instant espresso
¼ cup instant chocolate drink mix
3 cups hot water
½ cup whipped cream
Grated orange rind

Range

Combine coffee or espresso powder and instant chocolate mix in a small saucepan. Gradually stir in hot water. Bring almost to boiling point over moderate heat.

Microwave

Combine coffee or espresso powder and instant chocolate mix in a 1-quart measuring cup. Gradually stir in hot water. Cook until just steaming, about 4 minutes.

Pour into demi-tasse cups. Top with whipped cream and grated orange rind. Makes about 8 servings.

SMALL BASHES

QUICK QUICHE LORRAINE

1 package refrigerated
crescent dinner rolls
6 slices bacon, cooked and drained
2 cups grated Swiss cheese
2 cups half-and-half

4 eggs, beaten
⅛ teaspoon nutmeg
¼ teaspoon salt
⅛ teaspoon white pepper
¼ teaspoon paprika

Grease 9- by 13-inch glass baking dish. Cover baking dish with rectangles of crescent dough, pressing perforations to close seams and make a solid crust. Cover dough with bacon and sprinkle with grated Swiss cheese. Blend half-and-half with beaten eggs, add nutmeg, salt and pepper, pour into crust. Sprinkle with paprika.

Range

Bake quiche at 375°F for 40 minutes, until crust is browned and a knife inserted near the center comes out clean.

Microwave

Place baking dish near front of oven. Cook 3 minutes. Push to back of oven, cook 3 minutes. Give dish ½ turn, return it to front of oven, cook 2 minutes. Push to back of oven, cook 2 minutes.

Cooking Time Saved: 30 minutes

Let stand 10 minutes before serving. Makes 20 appetizer servings.

SCAMPI MAISON

2 pounds large shrimp, shelled
and deveined
½ cup olive oil
½ cup butter or margarine
3 cloves garlic, minced
2 teaspoons salt

Freshly ground black pepper
¼ cup vermouth or dry white wine
1 tablespoon brandy
1 tablespoon parsley, minced
2 tablespoons lemon juice

Split shrimps without separating the halves, flatten to shape butterflies.

Range

Heat oil and butter or margarine in
a large skillet, add garlic cloves and
cook until golden. Add remaining
ingredients, except lemon juice, heat.
Add shrimp, cook until just pink,
turning and stirring to cook evenly.
Add lemon juice.

Microwave

Arrange prepared shrimps in single
layer on 10-inch round serving
platter, add remaining ingredients.
Cover with wax paper and cook 1½
minutes. Rotate plate ½ turn, cook
1½ minutes longer.

Serve with picks. Makes 20 to 30 cocktail servings.

SEAFOOD DIM SUM

¼ pound crabmeat or fillet of
white fleshed fish
4 mushrooms
⅛ teaspoon sugar

Salt, pepper
1 tablespoon oil
1 teaspoon finely chopped ginger root
1 package refrigerated
Parkerhouse rolls

*Shred crabmeat, discarding shells and membranes, or shred fish. Trim mushrooms, wipe
clean, chop finely. Combine with crab or fish, add sugar, salt and pepper.*

Range

Heat oil in small skillet, add ginger
root and mushroom-crab mixture.
Cook over high heat for 2 to 3
minutes, stirring constantly.

Microwave

Heat oil and ginger root in a small
shallow dish for 3 minutes. Add
mushroom-crab mixture, cook 2
minutes. Stir.

*Flatten refrigerated rolls to make rounds. Put a spoonful of
filling in the center of each round, bring edges
of dough to center, pinch to make a tight package, roll gently into a ball.*

Range

Steam 5 or 6 at a time in a Chinese
basket steamer, or on a rack over
boiling water in a covered pot,
about 5 minutes, until dumplings
are firm and puffed.

Microwave

Cover microwave tray with wax
paper, arrange dumplings in a ring,
cover with wax paper, cook 2
minutes.

Makes 10 dim sum.

CHICKEN CACCIATORE

4 broiler-fryers (2½ pounds each)
1 cup oil
3 cups sliced onions
3 cups seeded and sliced green peppers
2 cups washed and sliced mushrooms
1 can (1 pound) tomato sauce
1 cup dry red wine
8 cloves garlic, minced

2 beef bouillon cubes
3 cans (1 pound each) tomatoes, drained and chopped
1 teaspoon oregano
2 teaspoons basil
Salt
Pepper

Cut each chicken into 8 pieces. Reserve wing tips and backs for other uses.

Range

Heat oil in a heavy 4-quart saucepan. Add onions, green peppers and mushrooms. Cook until wilted. Drain vegetables and divide into two 3-quart ovenproof casseroles. Brown chicken pieces, a few at a time, in oil remaining in the saucepan, drain, divide into casseroles. Add the rest of the ingredients to the saucepan and bring to a boil. Add to casseroles and bake, uncovered, at 375°F for about 1 hour, until chicken is tender and juices run clear.

Microwave

Heat oil in 4-quart glass casserole, 5 minutes. Add onions, peppers and mushrooms. Stir, cover, cook 15 minutes. Give the casserole a ¼ turn and stir the vegetables every 5 minutes. Transfer half the vegetables to a second 4-quart casserole, add 16 chicken pieces to each. In saucepan, bring remaining ingredients to a boil over direct heat on top of range, pour over chicken. Cook one casserole at a time, covered, until chicken is tender and cooked through, about 25 minutes, turning once. Let stand, covered, 10 minutes before serving.

Makes 20 servings.

ROAST TURKEY

Stuff turkey with Fruit Stuffing (page 156) or choose your own favorite.
Close opening and truss with twine and wooden skewers. Sprinkle with black pepper,
poultry seasoning, paprika or a little ginger, or rub with garlic to taste.

Range

Sprinkle bird with salt, brush with
butter. Roast on rack in pan, breast
up, uncovered, at 375°F. Allow
about 20 minutes per pound. Baste
often. Turkey is done when meat
thermometer, inserted between
thigh and body, reads 185°F. Or
insert a fork between body and
thigh. The juices will run clear. Let
stand 20 minutes before carving.

Microwave

Coat bird with oil. Do not use salt.
Place 2 saucers upside down in a
baking dish large enough to hold the
turkey. Rest bird on the saucers,
breast down. Cover with waxed
paper. Allow about 10 minutes per
pound total cooking time for turkeys
up to 12 pounds, 7 to 9½ minutes per
pound for larger birds. Divide
cooking time in fourths. Turn one
side up, then other side up. Finish
cooking breast side up. During the
last half of cooking time when turkey
begins to brown, cover wing tips and
ends of drumsticks with small pieces
of aluminum foil. Foil should not
touch walls of the oven. After 80
minutes cooking time, test for
doneness by inserting a fork between
thigh and body. If juices run clear, the
bird should be served at once. If the
juices have a pink tinge, cover the
bird with foil and let stand 15 to 20
minutes to finish cooking outside the
oven.

Cooking Time Saved: 2½ hours for a
12-pound turkey

Note: *Cooking times are approximate, since they vary according to the shape and*
conformation of the bird.

FRUIT STUFFING FOR TURKEY

½ pound prunes
2 large apples, peeled, cored and sliced
½ cup butter or margarine
½ loaf day-old bread (½ pound) cubed

½ teaspoon poultry seasoning
½ teaspoon salt
2 teaspoons lemon juice
2 eggs (lightly beaten)

Range

Simmer prunes in water to cover until tender. Drain and pit. Cook apples in melted butter or margarine until just tender.

Microwave

Cover prunes with hot water, cook 8 minutes. Drain and pit. Cook apples in butter or margarine in a shallow baking dish about 10 minutes.

Soak bread cubes in water, squeeze dry. Combine with fruit, poultry seasoning, salt, lemon juice and eggs. Mix well. Use to stuff a 10-to 14-pound turkey.

GLAZED HAM MELBA

10-pound pre-cooked, bone-in ham
1 package (10 ounces) frozen raspberries, thawed and drained
2 tablespoons prepared mustard
¼ cup brown sugar
2 tablespoons lemon juice

Arrange ham on baking dish, score fat in diamonds, ½-inch deep. Force raspberries through a strainer, or puree in the blender. Combine with remaining ingredients. Spread thickly on ham.

Range

Bake ham at 375°F for about 1 hour, 20 minutes, basting often.

Microwave

Cook ham 20 minutes, rotating dish a ½ turn every 5 minutes. If fat does not brown to desired degree, set ham under broiler at the end of cooking time for a few minutes. In this case, transfer ham to a dish able to withstand the direct heat of the broiler.

Cooking Time Saved: 1 hour

Makes 20 servings.

CANDIED SWEET POTATOES

6 pounds cooked
or canned sweet potatoes
1 cup brown sugar
¼ cup corn syrup

¼ cup butter or margarine
¼ cup lemon juice
Salt, pepper to taste

Spread sweet potatoes in a 9-by-13-inch baking dish.
Top with brown sugar and corn syrup. Dot with butter or margarine, sprinkle
with lemon juice and season to taste with salt and pepper.

Range	Microwave
Bake, uncovered, at 375°F for 10 minutes, basting often. Turn potatoes, bake 30 minutes longer, basting often.	Cover with wax paper. Cook 6 minutes. Rotate dish ½ turn, baste with pan sauce. Cook, uncovered, 7 minutes. Turn potatoes, baste, cook 7 minutes longer.

Cooking Time Saved: 20 minutes

Makes 20 servings.

CARROT AND RAISIN SALAD

1 cup raisins
2 cups water
3 teaspoons sugar
½ teaspoon salt
1½ teaspoons lemon juice
4 pounds carrots, peeled and grated

¾ cup mayonnaise
¾ cup French salad dressing
Salt
Pepper
Lemon juice

Range	Microwave
Combine raisins with water, sugar, salt and lemon juice in a saucepan. Bring to a boil, remove from heat, let stand until raisins are plump. Drain, cool.	Combine raisins, water, sugar, salt and lemon juice in a 1-quart casserole. Cook 8 minutes. Let stand until raisins are plump. Drain, cool.

Combine raisins with grated carrots, mayonnaise and salad dressing.
Add seasoning to taste. Makes 20 servings.

CAPER AND CROUTON SALAD

2 large heads chicory
2 large heads romaine
¼ cup mayonnaise
¾ cup olive oil
¼ cup lemon juice or vinegar
Freshly ground black pepper

1 teaspoon capers
Salt to taste
4 slices bread
½ cup butter or margarine
Garlic salt

Wash and clean chicory and romaine and drain well.
Break chicory and romaine into bite-sized pieces. Place in refrigerator
to crisp. Combine mayonnaise, oil, lemon juice, pepper, capers and
salt, stir to combine. Cut bread slices into cubes.

Range

Melt butter in a small skillet. Add bread cubes, sprinkle with garlic salt. Stir over moderate heat about 10 minutes, until cubes are golden.

Microwave

Melt butter in a shallow dish, about 1 minute. Add bread cubes and garlic salt, stir to coat. Cook 3 minutes, stir, cook about 3 minutes longer, until cubes are golden and crisp.

Arrange chicory and romaine in bowl. Add croutons.
Pour dressing over salad, toss to coat. Makes about 20 servings.

❧

MEXICAN TOSSED GREEN SALAD

3 large heads romaine lettuce
1 large head chicory
1 medium head escarole
1 ripe avocado, peeled and pitted
2 egg yolks

½ cup lemon juice
2 cups salad oil
Salt, pepper
2 cups corn chips

Wash and drain greens, dry, break into bite-size pieces and crisp in
refrigerator until serving time. In electric blender container,
combine avocado, egg yolks and lemon juice. Blend until smooth.
Gradually blend in oil, a drop at a time at first,
then in a steady stream. Adjust seasoning to taste with salt,
pepper and more lemon juice. Chill.

Range

Just before serving salad, spread corn chips on a baking sheet, bake at 350°F until hot and crisp, about 10 minutes.

Microwave

Just before serving salad, spread corn chips on tray, heat 3 minutes.

Cooking Time Saved: 7 minutes

Pour salad dressing over greens in bowl, sprinkle with hot corn chips.
Makes 20 servings.

CHILI CON CARNE

¾ cup oil
3 large onions, minced
4 green peppers, minced
8 cloves garlic, minced
5 pounds ground beef
2 cans (1 pound 13 ounces each)
tomatoes
3 cans (1 pound each)
red kidney beans, drained

2 teaspoons celery seed
1 tablespoon ground cumin
2 bay leaves
½ cup chili powder (or to taste)
2 tablespoons salt
1 tablespoon freshly ground
black pepper

Range

Heat oil in a 6-quart pot and cook onions, peppers and garlic until lightly colored. Add meat and cook, stirring, until meat is browned. Add remaining ingredients, stir, bring to a boil, reduce heat. Simmer 2 hours, stirring often and adding water as needed to prevent burning.

Microwave

Combine oil, onions, peppers and garlic in a glass baking dish. Cook, uncovered, 5 minutes, rotate dish ¼ turn, cook 5 minutes longer, stirring twice. Remove. Cook meat in a 4-quart glass baking dish 10 minutes, turning and stirring every 2 minutes. Blend onions and meat with remaining ingredients, divide mixture into two 4-quart baking dishes. Cook one dish at a time, 20 minutes, turning and stirring every 5 minutes.

Cooking Time Saved: 1 hour

Makes 20 servings.

JAMBALAYA

10 hot Italian sausages, cut in half
1 cup oil
2 large onions, chopped
8 cloves garlic, minced
3 green peppers, seeded and chopped
3 cups cooked, diced chicken
3 cups cooked, diced ham

3 cups rice
1 can (1 pound, 12 ounces) tomatoes
6 cups hot chicken broth
1 teaspoon cayenne
1 teaspoon salt
1 teaspoon freshly ground pepper

Range

Brown sausage in large skillet or saucepan. Remove, drain fat. Add oil to fat to make 1 cup. Heat oil and fat, add chopped onion, garlic and peppers, cook until soft. Add chicken, ham and sausage, cook 5 minutes. Add rice, stir until golden. Add tomatoes, hot broth and seasonings. Simmer, covered, 1 hour and 20 minutes.

Microwave

Cook sausage in large casserole 15 minutes. Remove, drain fat, add oil to fat to make 1 cup. Cook chopped onions, garlic and peppers in oil and fat in covered 3-quart casserole until wilted, about 5 minutes. Add rice, stir, cook 2 minutes. Divide into two 9-by 13-inch baking dishes or equivalent casseroles. Divide chicken, ham, sausage, tomatoes, hot broth and seasonings into dishes, stir. Cook one dish at a time, covered, 35 minutes.

Makes 20 servings.

CHOUCROUTE GARNI

3 pounds knockwurst or frankfurters
3 pounds kielbasa (Polish sausage)
8 pounds saukerkaut (bulk or canned)
6 cloves garlic
1 teaspoon freshly ground black pepper
1 tablespoon juniper berries
2 tablespoons caraway seeds

½ pound salt pork or bacon, in thin slices
1 quart dry white wine
2 large onions, quartered and studded with cloves
20 smoked loin pork chops
20 small boiled potatoes

Cut sausages into large chunks, set aside. Rinse sauerkraut well, drain thoroughly. Add garlic, pepper, juniper berries and caraway seeds.

Range

Line 6-quart casserole with salt pork or bacon. Add sauerkraut, wine and onions. Top with sausages and chops. Cover, bake at 325°F for 1 hour and 45 minutes.

Microwave

Line two 4-quart casseroles with salt pork or bacon, fill each with half the sauerkraut mixture, half the wine and onions. Cover with lid, cook 25 minutes. Add sausages and chops, cover, cook casseroles, one at a time 15 minutes until meat is hot.

Cooking Time Saved: 25 minutes

Serve with boiled potatoes coated with melted butter or margarine and caraway seeds. Makes 20 servings.

BIGGER BASHES— THE COCKTAIL PARTY

PÂTÉ MAISON

1 pound bacon
1½ pounds chicken livers
2 eggs
8 cloves garlic, peeled
1 medium onion, peeled and quartered
¾ cup Cognac
1 teaspoon thyme or sweet marjoram

1 tablespoon peppercorns
Pinch nutmeg
1 teaspoon whole allspice
2 pounds ground lean pork
1½ pounds fresh ground pork fat
¾ pound ground ham or tongue
½ cup dry vermouth

Line two 5-by-9-inch glass loaf dishes crosswise with bacon strips, covering bottom and sides and allowing a 1-inch overhang around the sides. Whirl in a blender 1 pound chicken livers, eggs, garlic cloves, onion, Cognac, herbs and spices. Mix purée with remaining ingredients. Fill each dish with ¼ the pâté mixture, top with a row of whole chicken livers. Add remaining pâté, cover with ends of bacon strips.

Range

Cover dishes tightly with aluminum foil and set in a larger pan, in 2 cups of hot water. Bake at 325°F for 2½ hours.

Microwave

Pour 2 cups hot water in microwave tray. Cover baking dishes with wax paper and a 13-by 9-inch baking dish and cook 30 minutes. Rotate dishes ½ turn, cover, cook 20 minutes.

Cooking Time Saved: 1 hour, 40 minutes

Press pâté with 2-pound weight placed on sheet of foil and cool thoroughly. Chill and unmold before serving. Makes about 40 hors d'oeuvres servings.

COCKTAIL FRANKS IN SWEET AND SOUR SAUCE

½ cup prepared chili sauce
½ cup orange marmalade
1 teaspoon prepared mustard
1 pound cocktail franks

Range
Combine chili sauce, marmalade and mustard in a small saucepan. Heat to simmering. Add cocktail franks, cook over low heat 5 minutes, or until heated through.

Microwave
Combine chili sauce, marmalade and mustard in a 1-quart serving bowl. Add cocktail franks, cover, cook 3 minutes, until heated through.

Serve in bowl with toothpicks. Makes about 2 dozen appetizer servings.

RUMAKI

2 cups pineapple juice
1 cup soy sauce
½ cup grated ginger root
(or 2 tablespoons ground ginger)
2 tablespoons minced garlic
2 tablespoons dry mustard

½ cup brown sugar
1 can (16 ounces) water chestnuts
1 pound chicken livers, cut in half
8 scallions, cut in quarters lengthwise
1 pound bacon strips, cut in half
30 toothpicks

Combine pineapple juice, soy sauce, ginger, garlic, dry mustard and brown sugar in shallow dish to make marinade.
Make about 30 rumaki: fold half a chicken liver around a water chestnut, add a piece of scallion and wrap all with half a strip of bacon, secure with toothpick. Turn rumaki in marinade to coat, let stand in marinade 1 hour at room temperature. Reserve marinade for use with other meats.

Range
Broil rumaki 6 inches from heat, basting occasionally with drippings, for 30 minutes, until bacon is crisp and livers are firm.

Microwave
Arrange 15 rumaki directly on microwave tray or in a large shallow dish. Cover with paper toweling, cook 8 minutes. Remove paper toweling, cook 4 minutes more. Serve on microwave tray, if desired.

Cooking Time Saved: 13 minutes

Makes 30 appetizer servings.

HAM AND CHEESE ROLLS

¼ cup prepared mustard
1 tablespoon horseradish
¼ pound thin sliced boiled ham
¼ pound thin sliced Muenster cheese

*Combine mustard and horseradish. Cut ham and cheese slices into 3-
by 4-inch rectangles. Spread ham with horseradish sauce, top with
cheese slices. Roll up, jelly-roll fashion. Secure with toothpicks*

Range	Microwave
Place rolls on greased baking sheet. Bake at 400°F for 10 minutes, until cheese melts.	Arrange rolls on serving platter. Cook 2 minutes, until cheese melts.
	Cooking Time Saved: about 8 minutes

Makes 12 to 16 appetizer servings.

SCOTCH EGGS

10 hard cooked eggs, shelled
3 pounds sausage meat
1 teaspoon freshly ground black pepper
2 teaspoons fennel seed (or anise seed)

*Combine sausage meat with pepper and fennel seed.
Divide into 10 equal portions, shape 6 by 8-inch rectangles.
Place a hard cooked egg in the center of each rectangle,
wrap egg in sausage, mold into egg shape, seal well.*

Range	Microwave
Place Scotch eggs on baking sheet and bake at 375°F for 50 minutes until sausage is cooked through and browned.	Arrange Scotch eggs on microwave tray, cover with wax paper, cook 10 minutes. Rearrange eggs, cook 10 minutes.
	Cooking Time Saved: 30 minutes

*Cool, cut in ½-inch slices and serve with Mustard Mayonnaise Sauce, below.
Makes 40 hors d'oeuvres servings.*

*Mustard Mayonnaise Sauce: 2 cups mayonnaise, 2 tablespoons dry mustard,
2 tablespoons capers and juice and 1 tablespoon lemon juice.*

CHEESE-STUFFED MUSHROOMS

24 large mushrooms
4 ounces blue cheese, crumbled
2 eggs, separated
1 tablespoon lemon juice
1 tablespoon chopped parsely

*Wipe mushrooms clean with a damp cloth. Remove stems, chop half the
stems finely, reserve rest for another use. Mash cheese, combine with
chopped stems. Beat egg yolks with lemon juice, blend with cheese.
Beat egg whites until stiff, fold in. Pile mixture into mushroom caps.*

Range	Microwave
Arrange mushrooms on baking sheet. Bake at 400°F for 10 minutes, until puffed. Remove to serving tray.	Arrange on serving tray or platter, cook 5 minutes. Cooking Time Saved: 5 minutes

Garnish with chopped parsley. Serve at once. Makes 24 appetizer servings.

DUXELLES STUFFED MUSHROOMS

Ingredients as listed for Duxelles
(page 166)
1 cup cooked ham, minced finely
1 teaspoon freshly ground black pepper
½ teaspoon marjoram

¾ cup heavy cream
1 tablespoon Madeira
40 mushroom caps, about 2 inches in diameter
½ cup bread crumbs

*To the ingredients for Duxelles add ham, pepper, marjoram,
heavy cream and.Madeira.*

Range	Microwave
Simmer in a heavy saucepan until thickened, about 15 minutes. Cool, fill mushroom caps. Sprinkle stuffed caps with bread crumbs. Bake mushrooms at 375°F for 20 minutes, until stuffing is golden brown and puffed.	Cook in a 1-quart covered casserole for 6 minutes, cool. Fill mushroom caps, sprinkle with bread crumbs. Cook, uncovered, on microwave tray 8 minutes, until puffy. Cooking Time Saved: 20 minutes

Makes 40 servings.

*Note: Stuffed caps may be prepared and frozen in advance and heated in
the microwave for about 12 minutes or in the oven at 375°F for 25 minutes.*

DUXELLES (MUSHROOM PASTE)

1 pound mushrooms
(or pieces and stems)
2 medium onions, peeled
4 shallots, peeled (optional)

4 tablespoons butter or margarine
1 teaspoon salt
⅛ teaspoon nutmeg

Finely mince mushrooms, onions and shallots.
Wrap in a kitchen towel and wring out moisture.

Range

Melt butter or margarine in a heavy 2-quart casserole. Add mushrooms, onions, shallots and seasonings. Reduce heat and simmer, stirring occasionally, for 40 minutes, until vegetables are wilted and moisture has been absorbed.

Microwave

Heat butter or margarine in a covered 2-quart casserole for 2 minutes. Add mushrooms, onions, shallots and seasonings. Cover with wax paper and cook 14 minutes. Stir every 4 minutes.

Cooking Time Saved: 26 minutes

Makes 1 cup. Use as stuffing for mushroom caps. Or use Duxelles to improve
meat and poultry sauces, to dress vegetables and rice.

COCKTAIL TOMATOES

12 cherry tomatoes
6 anchovy fillets, rinsed and cut into small pieces
¼ pound cheese cut into ¼-inch cubes

Slice tops from tomatoes and scoop out centers.
Fill with anchovies and cheese.

Range

Arrange tomatoes stuffed side up on greased baking dish. Bake at 400°F for 6 minutes, until cheese melts. Remove to serving platter.

Microwave

Arrange tomatoes, stuffed side up, on shallow serving platter. Cook 1 minute until cheese melts.

Cooking Time Saved: 5 minutes

BRUNCHES

BRUNCH SPECIAL

8 strips bacon, diced
1 green pepper, finely diced
10 slices white or
whole wheat bread, cubed
½ pound Swiss cheese, grated

6 eggs
2 cups milk
¾ teaspoon salt
¼ teaspoon pepper

Range

Place bacon in cold skillet. Cook over low heat, turning often. Remove, drain off all but 2 tablespoons bacon fat. Cook green pepper in bacon fat until wilted.

Microwave

Place bacon and green pepper in a bowl, cover, cook 8 minutes, until bacon is crisp. Stir several times during cooking. Drain off fat.

Spread half the bread cubes in a shallow 2-quart casserole. Sprinkle with half the bacon, green pepper and cheese. Repeat layers. Combine eggs, milk and seasonings. Pour over layers, let stand 5 minutes or longer, or store in the refrigerator overnight to cook in the morning.

Range

Bake at 375°F for 40 to 45 minutes or until puffed and set.

Microwave

Cook 6 minutes, rotate dish ½ turn, cook 6 to 8 minutes longer, until puffed and set.

Cooking Time Saved: about 25 minutes

Makes 6 to 8 servings.

TOMATO FONDUE

2 tablespoons butter or margarine
3 medium tomatoes, peeled,
seeded and chopped
¼ teaspoon salt

1½ cups milk
½ pound grated American cheese
3 tablespoons flour
1 loaf French bread, cut into cubes

Range

Melt butter or margarine in a heavy casserole or fondue pot. Add tomatoes, cook over low heat until soft, stirring often. Stir in salt and milk, heat just to boiling. Toss cheese with flour, add to simmering fondue a handful at a time, stirring until smooth.

Microwave

Soften butter or margarine in 1½-quart casserole 30 seconds. Blend in flour, add tomatoes and salt. Cover, cook 1 minute. Add milk, stir to blend, cook 6 minutes, until hot. Stir in cheese, cook 1 minute longer, to heat through.

Serve with cubes of bread and long handled forks for dipping.
Makes 4 to 6 servings.

HAM QUICHE

Baked 9-inch pie shell
4 thin slices cooked ham, slivered
1 tablespoon chopped chives
¼ pound Swiss cheese, shredded

3 eggs, lightly beaten
1½ cups half-and-half
¼ cup grated Parmesan
or Romano cheese
Salt, pepper, cayenne

Sprinkle baked pie shell with ham, chives and Swiss cheese.
Mix eggs, half-and-half, grated cheese and seasonings to taste.
Pour into pie shell.

Range

Bake pie at 375°F for 40 to 45 minutes, until filling sets.

Microwave

Cook 9 minutes, rotate plate ½ turn, cook about 5 minutes longer, or until filling is set.

Cooking Time Saved: about 25 minutes

Makes 10 to 12 appetizer servings; 6 main course servings.

EGGS BENEDICT ROYALE

2 English muffins, split and toasted
4 slices ham or Canadian bacon
4 slices Monterey Jack or Swiss cheese
4 poached eggs (page 12)
1 cup Hollandaise sauce (page 207)

Range
Top each muffin half with a slice of ham and a slice of cheese. Place under broiler for about 5 minutes, or until cheese melts.

Microwave
Arrange muffin halves on serving platter. Top each half with a slice of ham and a slice of cheese. Cook 2 minutes, or until cheese melts.

*Before serving top each half with a poached egg
and ¼ cup Hollandaise sauce.
Makes 4 servings.*

CREAMED CHIPPED BEEF

1 can (10¾ ounces) cream of mushroom, celery or asparagus soup
½ cup milk
1 cup shredded chipped beef, rinsed

Dash pepper
4 slices toast, or 4 biscuits, split
Chopped parsley
Boiled onions (optional)

Range
Combine soup and milk in a 2-quart saucepan, heat until warmed through, stirring. Add chipped beef and pepper, heat until simmering.

Microwave
Combine soup and milk in a 2-quart casserole. Cook 2 minutes, covered, until warmed through. Add chipped beef and pepper, heat until simmering, about 3 minutes.

*Spoon over warm toast or biscuits on 4 individual serving plates. Sprinkle with chopped parsley, serve with boiled onions, if desired.
Makes 4 servings.*

KIELBASA AND COMPANY

2 tablespoons butter or margarine
1 large onion, sliced
1 cup rice
2 cups boiling water

2 beef bouillon cubes
1 large orange, peeled and sectioned
1 pound kielbasa or frankfurters,
in 1-inch slices

Range

Heat butter or margarine in large skillet, add onion, cook over low heat, stirring often, until onions are translucent. Add rice, stir until golden. Add water and bouillon cubes, cook until rice is tender, about 15 minutes. Add orange sections and kielbasa, cook until sausage is hot.

Microwave

Combine butter or margarine and onion in a 3-quart casserole. Cover, cook 3 minutes. Add rice, water and bouillon cubes, cook, covered 6 minutes. Stir, add kielbasa, cover, cook 6 minutes. Add orange sections, cook, uncovered, until rice is tender and liquid absorbed.

Makes 4 servings.

TOAD IN THE YELLOW HOLE

1 pound brown and serve sausages
1 large tomato, sliced
1 box (8 ounces) corn muffin mix
1 egg, lightly beaten
½ cup milk

Range

Cook sausage in skillet until well browned on all sides. Drain.

Microwave

Wrap sausage in paper towels, cook 2 minutes.

Place sausage in a 10-inch pie plate. Cover with tomato slices.
Mix remaining ingredients just until meat is moistened.
Pour the batter around the edges of the dish, leaving the center uncovered.

Range

Bake at 350°F for 25 minutes.

Microwave

Cook, uncovered, 5 minutes, rotate dish ½ turn, cook 3 minutes longer.

Cooking Time Saved: about 20 minutes

Makes 6 servings.

BREAD BECOMES CAKE

1 loaf (1 pound) unsliced bread   1 tablespoon cinnamon
½ cup melted butter or margarine   ¼ cup raisins
Jelly or marmalade   ¼ cup chopped nuts
¼ cup sugar   Brown sugar

*Trim crusts from bread, slice lengthwise into 5
thin slices. Flatten slices with a rolling pin,
brush with some of the melted butter or margarine
and spread with a thin layer of jelly or marmalade. Combine sugar,
cinnamon, raisins and nuts,
sprinkle over jelly. Roll up like jelly rolls, from
the long side, cut into ¼-inch slices.*

Range

Generously grease small muffin cups
and sprinkle with brown sugar.
Place slices, cut side down in muffin
cups. Brush with melted butter or
margarine. Bake at 350°F. for 10
minutes.

Microwave

Generously grease 6 glass cups and
sprinkle with brown sugar. Place
slices, cut side down in cups. Brush
with melted butter or margarine.
Cook 3 to 4 minutes.

Cooking Time Saved: about 6
minutes

*Serve warm. May be frozen and rewarmed.
Reheat in 350°F oven for 15 minutes; warm
in microwave 4 minutes. Makes 18 to 20 pinwheels.*

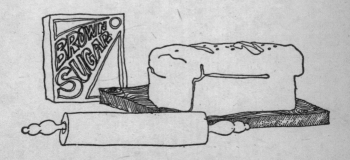

STREUSEL COFFEE CAKE

1½ cups flour
1½ teaspoons baking powder
½ teaspoon salt
½ cup butter
½ cup sugar
1 egg
½ teaspoon vanilla
½ cup milk

Topping:
¼ cup flour
¼ cup sugar
1 teaspoon cinnamon
¼ cup butter

*Toss together flour, baking powder and salt to mix.
Cream butter and sugar, beat in egg
and vanilla. Add milk and dry ingredients, beat
until smooth. Prepare topping: combine flour, sugar
and cinnamon. Cut in butter to make coarse crumbs. Set aside.*

Range

Grease and flour a 9-inch layer cake pan. Add batter, sprinkle with crumb topping. Bake at 350°F for 50 minutes, until cake tests done.

Microwave

Line a 9-inch glass layer cake dish with wax paper. Add batter, sprinkle with crumb topping. Cook 6 minutes, rotate dish ½ way after 3 minutes.

Baking Time Saved: 44 minutes

GREAT VEGETABLES
AND SAUCES
(Things You Never Thought of Making)

Because all of us are concerned about the nutritive value of the foods we eat, it is important to prepare vegetables well. Vegetables offer one of our best sources of vitamins and other nutrients. The vegetables included in this section are generally intended as side dishes, but some (ratatouille, for example) can be excellent main dishes, too.

Perhaps one of the greatest values of the microwave oven is its use in preparing vegetables, for both frozen and fresh vegetables benefit from preparation with microwave. Color and flavor are both improved.

Potatoes are easy to bake in the microwave oven. Be sure to place them in a circle and leave an inch between them, and remember to pierce the skin with a fork before baking. If you like potatoes moist, you will like the way they come out of your microwave oven. If you prefer potato skins crisp, heat them for a few minutes in your conventional oven after they have been baked with microwaves.

Now for a few tips:

Fresh Vegetables 1. Place in a glass dish with salt, butter or other seasonings on the bottom of the dish. Do not season the top because this tends to dehydrate the vegetables.

2. Cover the dish with a lid, plastic wrap, wax paper or a saucer. Stir at least once during the cooking time.

3. When cooking is completed, remove the dish from the oven and let vegetables stand, covered, 5 minutes before serving. This allows the heat to spread evenly.

Frozen Vegetables 1. Place in a glass dish with salt, butter or other seasonings on the bottom of the dish (see step 1 in fresh vegetables). If the vegetables are individually frozen, spread them evenly to the outside of the glass dish before cooking. If they are frozen solid, put them in the dish ice side up.

2. Cover with the casserole lid, plastic wrap, wax paper or a saucer; stir at least once during the cooking time.

3. When cooking is completed, remove from oven, and let stand, covered, for 5 minutes.

Sauces are the nemesis of most cooks, but microwaves make sauces easier to prepare. Microwave cooking keeps the sauces from becoming lumpy and reduces cooking time. The trick is to stir the sauce quickly every thirty seconds with a wooden spoon you can leave in the bowl.

In this section, as in all sections of the book, directions are given for both conventional and microwave cooking.

GREAT VEGETABLES
AND SAUCES

GREAT VEGETABLES
AND SAUCES

ARTICHOKES

4 artichokes
4 tablespoons oil
4 tablespoons vinegar
Salt, pepper
2 cloves garlic, minced (optional)

*Wash artichokes, cut off stem, trim sharp points of leaves with scissors.
Discard discolored or withered leaves.*

Range

Arrange artichokes in saucepan, side by side. Sprinkle with oil, vinegar and seasonings. Add boiling water to cover and garlic. Cover, boil 45 minutes or until bases are tender. Test with a fork.

Microwave

Arrange artichokes side by side in a deep dish with a lid. Sprinkle with oil, vinegar and seasonings. Add boiling water to cover and garlic. Cover with lid, cook 15 minutes, turning dish and basting every 5 minutes. Let stand 5 minutes, cook about 5 minutes longer or until bases are tender.

Cooking Time Saved: 20 minutes

*Serve hot with melted butter or margarine as a dip, or cold with French dressing.
Makes 4 servings.*

ASPARAGUS VINAIGRETTE

2 pounds asparagus
¾ cup oil
¼ cup vinegar
½ teaspoon salt
Pinch white pepper

½ teaspoon Worcestershire sauce
2 hard-cooked eggs, yolks only, mashed or sieved
3 pimiento-stuffed olives, chopped
1 tablespoon finely chopped parsley
1 teaspoon chopped chives

Snap and discard tough ends from asparagus. Wash stalks well.

Range

Stand asparagus upright in the bottom of a double boiler. Add boiling water to come half way up the spears, cover, cook quickly until tender, 12 to 15 minutes. Meanwhile, heat oil, vinegar, salt, pepper and Worcestershire sauce to the boiling point. Add egg yolks, olives and herbs, blend well.

Microwave

Stand asparagus upright in a 1-quart glass measuring cup; add boiling water to fill slightly less than half way. Cover the asparagus with a tent of wax paper. Cook about 5 minutes, until asparagus is fork-tender. Drain. Blend oil, vinegar, salt, pepper and Worcestershire sauce in a small bowl; cook until steaming hot, 3½ minutes. Add mashed egg yolks, olives and herbs, blend well.

Pour sauce over cooked asparagus on serving platter. Good hot or cold.
Makes 4 or more servings.

BOSTON BAKED BEANS

2 cans (16 ounces each) baked beans, drained
6 slices bacon, diced
1 small onion, minced
2 teaspoons dry mustard

½ teaspoon ground cloves
¼ cup molasses
¼ cup brown sugar
Salt, pepper to taste

Range

Combine ingredients in a 2-quart casserole. Bake, uncovered, at 375°F for 40 minutes. Stir often during cooking to prevent a crust from forming.

Microwave

Combine ingredients and cook, uncovered, 20 minutes, stirring beans every 5 minutes. Add a little water if necessary to moisten.

Cooking Time Saved: 20 minutes

Makes 6 to 8 servings.

GREEN BEANS AMANDINE

1 pound green beans
2 tablespoons butter or margarine
3 tablespoons slivered almonds

1 can (4 ounces) mushroom slices, drained
Salt, pepper
1 teaspoon lemon juice

Wash green beans, trim ends.

Range

Cook beans until tender in a small amount of salted water, about 12 minutes. Drain. Melt butter or margarine in a heavy skillet and sauté almonds and mushrooms until lightly browned. Toss with green beans, heat. Season to taste with salt, pepper and lemon juice.

Microwave

Pour ¼ cup salted water into a 1-quart casserole. Add green beans, cover. Combine butter or margarine, almonds and drained mushrooms in a small dish. Arrange dishes side by side in microwave. Cook 5 minutes. Stir contents of both dishes, cover beans, rotate both dishes ¼ turn, cook 5 minutes longer. Toss together, season to taste with salt, pepper and lemon juice.

Makes 4 servings.

DILLY GREEN BEANS

1 package (10 ounces) frozen green beans
or wax beans
Boiling water
¼ cup sour cream
½ teaspoon dill seed
Salt, pepper

Range

Cook beans as directed on package until barely tender in boiling salted water.

Microwave

Put ¼ cup boiling water into a serving dish, add a little salt. Add beans, cover, cook 4 minutes, stir, cook 2 minutes, until barely tender, let stand 2 minutes.

Drain beans, toss with sour cream, dill seed and salt and pepper to taste.
Makes 3 to 4 servings.

CAULIFLOWER POLONAISE

1 medium head cauliflower
⅓ cup butter or margarine
1 cup fine fresh bread crumbs
Salt, pepper

Trim leaves and stems from cauliflower.

Range

Cover cauliflower with boiling salted water, cook, covered, until just tender, about 25 minutes. Drain. Arrange in serving dish. Melt butter or margarine in a skillet, add bread crumbs, and salt and pepper to taste, stir over moderate heat until crumbs brown. Pour sauce over cauliflower.

Microwave

Arrange cauliflower in a glass baking dish in 2-inches hot water. Cover, cook 6 minutes. Turn with a pancake turner, cover, cook 6 minutes. Drain off cooking water. Add butter or margarine, cook until melted. Turn cauliflower, sprinkle with bread crumbs, spoon butter or margarine over crumbs. Cook, uncovered, about 4 minutes or until cauliflower is tender.

Cooking Time Saved: about 30 minutes

Makes 4 to 6 servings.

BROCCOLI PARMESAN

1 bunch broccoli
Salt, pepper
2 tablespoons oil
Grated Parmesan cheese

Trim stem ends of broccoli, wash thoroughly, discard any withered leaves. Cut slits in the bottom of large stalks for even cooking.

Range

Stand broccoli stalks upright in the bottom of a double boiler. Add 3 inches water, cover with inverted double boiler top, cook until stems are fork tender, about 10 minutes. Drain, arrange on flameproof serving dish. Season with salt and pepper, sprinkle with oil (or melted butter or margarine) and Parmesan cheese. Broil until cheese has melted.

Microwave

Lay broccoli stalks pinwheel fashion on a serving plate, flowers in the center. Cover with wax paper, cook 8 minutes. Drain, season with salt and pepper, sprinkle with oil (or melted butter or margarine) and Parmesan cheese. Cook 1 minute, to melt cheese.

Makes 4 to 6 servings.

BRUSSELS SPROUTS AU GRATIN

2 packages (10 ounces each) Brussels sprouts
3 tablespoons butter or margarine
1 cup white sauce (page 206)
½ cup grated Cheddar cheese

Range

Thaw sprouts at room temperature enough to separate, 15 to 20 minutes. Heat butter or margarine in a large skillet, add sprouts. Cover, simmer about 10 minutes. Sprouts. should be just tender, still brightly colored. Transfer to a 6-cup baking dish. Cover with white sauce, stir. Sprinkle with grated cheese. Bake at 350°F for about 15 minutes, until cheese melts and sauce is bubbly.

Microwave

Place frozen sprouts in a 6-cup baking dish. Add butter or margarine, cover, cook 10 minutes, until just tender and still brightly colored. Cover with white sauce, stir. Sprinkle with grated cheese. Cook 2 minutes, uncovered, until cheese melts and sauce is bubbly.

Cooking Time Saved: about 15 minutes

Makes 6 servings.

CHINESE-STYLE BRUSSELS SPROUTS

4 tablespoons butter or margarine
1 package (10 ounces) frozen Brussels sprouts
2 cloves garlic, minced
1 teaspoon grated ginger root
1 teaspoon lemon juice

Range

Melt butter or margarine in a heavy saucepan. Add remaining ingredients and sauté over low heat, covered, until vegetables are just tender, stirring often.

Microwave

Place all ingredients in a 1-quart casserole. Cover, cook 4 minutes. Rotate dish ½ turn, stir sprouts, cook 4 minutes.

Makes 4 servings.

CARAWAY CABBAGE

1 medium head cabbage
2 tablespoons butter or margarine
2 teaspoons caraway seed
Salt, pepper

Cut cabbage into narrow wedges.

Range

Cover cabbage with boiling salted water in a large saucepan, cook until tender, about 15 minutes. Drain. Add butter or margarine and caraway to cabbage, stir over low heat until piping hot.

Microwave

Place cabbage in a large serving dish. Add butter or margarine and caraway seeds. Cover, cook 8 minutes, until cabbage is tender.

Season to taste with salt and pepper. Makes 6 to 8 servings.

CARROTS AND APRICOTS

1 pound carrots, peeled and sliced
1 cup canned apricots, sliced
⅓ cup apricot syrup
1 tablespoon brown sugar
½ teaspoon cornstarch
¼ teaspoon ground cloves
Salt, pepper

Range

Cook carrots in boiling salted water to cover until fork-tender, about 10 to 15 minutes. Drain. Combine carrots and apricots in a 6-cup baking dish. Mix syrup, sugar, cornstarch and cloves, pour over carrots. Add salt and pepper to taste. Bake at 350°F for 30 minutes.

Microwave

Put sliced carrots in 6-cup glass casserole with 2 tablespoons water, salt and pepper to taste. Cover with wax paper, cook 7 to 10 minutes, until fork-tender. Drain. Blend syrup with remaining ingredients, except apricots, add to casserole, cover, cook 3 minutes, stir. Add apricots, cover, cook 1 minute, stir, cook 1 minute longer.

Cooking Time Saved: 30 minutes

Makes 6 servings.

CARROT CUSTARD

1 pound carrots, peeled and sliced
1 cup half-and-half or milk
2 teaspoons grated onion

3 eggs, beaten
1 teaspoon chopped parsley
Salt, pepper

Range

Cook carrots in boiling, salted water until tender, about 20 minutes. Drain. Mash carrots, mix with remaining ingredients, and season with salt and pepper to taste. Arrange in a greased 1-quart baking dish, set dish in a pan of hot water. Bake at 350°F for 45 minutes, until custard is set.

Microwave

In 1-quart dish, cook carrots in ¼ cup water 10 minutes. Drain, mash carrots, add remaining ingredients. Season to taste with salt and pepper. Set dish in ½-inch water in shallow baking dish. Cook 12 to 15 minutes, until custard is set.

Cooking Time Saved: 40 minutes

Makes 4 to 6 servings.

BRAISED CELERY

1 bunch celery
2 tablespoons oil
½ cup water
1 beef bouillon cube

Trim celery, wash thoroughly and scrape if necessary. Cut stalks into 3-inch lengths.

Range

In a saucepan, heat oil, cook celery until lightly golden. Add water and beef bouillon cube, bring to a boil, stir. Cover, simmer 15 minutes until celery is tender-crisp. Remove celery and cooking liquid to a serving bowl.

Microwave

Mix oil, water and bouillon cube in glass dish, cook until water boils. Stir to dissolve bouillon cube, add celery, cover, cook 5 minutes, until tender-crisp.

Cooking Time Saved: 10 minutes

Makes 4 to 6 servings.

BEETS

Wash 1 pound beets thoroughly, but be careful not to break the skin.
Trim the top, leave the root ends intact.

Range
Simmer in a saucepan in boiling
water to cover until tender, from 20
minutes to an hour or more,
depending on the age or toughness
of the beets. Or wrap beets
individually in foil, bake at 350°F
for 1 hour.

Microwave
Arrange on paper towel in tray, cook
8 to 10 minutes, until tender.

Cooking Time Saved: up to 50
minutes

Drop into cold water to cool slightly, peel, slice or dice. Serve with butter
or margarine, salt and pepper, or use to make Harvard Beets, below.

HARVARD BEETS

1 pound cooked beets, or
1 can (1 pound), sliced or diced
1½ teaspoons cornstarch
½ teaspoon salt

1½ tablespoons sugar
3 tablespoons wine vinegar
2 tablespoons butter or margarine

Drain beets and reserve liquid. Stir cornstarch with salt, sugar,
vinegar and ⅓ cup beet liquid.

Range
Melt butter or margarine in
saucepan. Add cornstarch mixture,
cook over low heat, stirring
constantly until sauce is thick and
smooth. Add beets, heat. Transfer
to serving dish.

Microwave
Cook butter or margarine in 1-quart
casserole 45 seconds. Stir in
cornstarch mixture, cover with wax
paper, cook 3 minutes. Stir, add
beets, cover, cook 3 minutes.

Makes 4 servings.

CORN ON THE COB

6 ears of corn
2 tablespoons butter or margarine, melted
Salt, pepper
2 tablespoons sugar (range only)

Range

Strip husks and silk from corn. Plunge corn into boiling salted water to cover. If desired, add 2 tablespoons sugar. Cook about 10 minutes, depending on size and age of ears. Serve hot with butter or margarine, salt and pepper to taste.

Microwave

Pull husks back, remove and discard silk. Rewrap ears in husks, tie with kitchen string. Arrange on glass dish. Cook 4 minutes, turn ears over, cook 4 minutes. Cool somewhat, remove husks, serve hot with butter or margarine, salt and pepper to taste.

CORN CASSEROLE

3 tablespoons butter or margarine
2 tablespoons chopped onion
⅓ cup chopped green pepper
3 tablespoons flour
1½ cups milk
2 eggs, lightly beaten

2 cups corn kernels,
fresh cut or drained canned
⅓ cup chopped pimiento (optional)
2 tablespoons chopped parsley
¾ cup grated cheese
Salt, pepper

Range

Melt butter or margarine in a 6-cup flameproof casserole, add onion and green pepper, cook until onion is translucent. Stir in flour, gradually add milk. Cook, stirring, until sauce is smooth and thick. Warm eggs with a little hot mixture, combine. Add corn and remaining ingredients, salt and pepper to taste. Bake at 350°F for 45 minutes, until custard is set.

Microwave

Cook butter or margarine, onion and green pepper in a 6-cup casserole, covered, about 4 minutes. Stir in flour. Heat milk in a measuring cup 4 minutes. Add to casserole gradually. Heat 1 minute. Warm eggs with a little hot mixture, combine. Add corn and remaining ingredients, salt and pepper to taste. Cover, cook 10 minutes.

Cooking Time Saved: 30 minutes

Makes 4 servings.

EASY EGGPLANT CASSEROLE

1 large eggplant, peeled and
cut into ½-inch cubes
2 eggs
½ cup milk or cream

Salt, pepper
1 cup stuffing mix
2 tablespoons butter

Range
Parboil eggplant in water to cover
for 10 minutes.

Microwave
Put eggplant in a 2-quart baking dish,
add boiling water to cover. Cover and
cook 10 minutes.

*Drain eggplant. Combine eggs, milk and salt and pepper to taste.
Stir in eggplant and ½ cup stuffing mix. Turn into a 2-quart baking dish,
sprinkle with remaining stuffing mix, dot with butter or margarine.*

Range
Bake, covered, at 350°F for 35 to 40
minutes, or until eggplant is tender.

Microwave
Cook, covered, 12 minutes, or until
eggplant is tender.

Cooking Time Saved: about 23
minutes

Makes 4 to 6 servings.

GHIVETCH

4 carrots
1 stalk celery
2 small onions
1 clove garlic

2 potatoes
2 tomatoes, peeled
1 cup boiling water or broth
Salt, pepper, marjoram

*Cut carrots, celery, onions, garlic and potatoes into very thin slices.
Cut tomatoes into wedges.*

Range
Fill a baking dish with vegetables
and liquid, add seasonings to taste.
Cover, bake at 400°F for 20
minutes. Remove cover, bake 15
minutes, until vegetables are tender.

Microwave
Fill 2-quart baking dish with
vegetables and liquid, add seasonings
to taste. Cover, cook 20 to 25
minutes, until vegetables are tender.

Cooking Time Saved: 10 to 15
minutes

Makes 6 or more servings. Good hot or cold.

LIMA BEAN CASSEROLE

2 packages (10 ounces each)
frozen lima beans
1 small onion, chopped
2 tablespoons butter or margarine

¼ cup dark corn syrup
1 cup sour cream
¼ cup tomato paste
Salt, pepper

Range

Cook lima beans until tender, as directed on package, fill baking dish. Brown onion lightly in a skillet, add remaining ingredients, blend well. Pour over lima beans, stir. Bake, uncovered, at 350°F for about 20 minutes.

Microwave

Cook lima beans in the packages, 10 to 12 minutes. Fill 6-cup glass dish. Stir in remaining ingredients, cook 5 minutes, until steaming hot.

Cooking Time Saved: about 15 minutes

Makes 6 servings.

HONEY LIMA BEANS

1½ cups dried baby lima beans
2 teaspoons salt
White pepper
3 tablespoons butter
½ cup honey

Range

In a large saucepan cover lima beans with boiling water, simmer 5 minutes, let stand 1 hour. Return to a boil, simmer, covered, until tender. Add salt and pepper, cover, simmer ½ hour longer, adding more water as necessary. Drain. Combine with butter or margarine and honey in a 2-quart casserole. Bake at 350°F for 1 hour, stirring often.

Microwave

In a 2-quart casserole, cover lima beans with boiling water, cook 5 minutes, let stand 1 hour. Add salt and pepper, cook 25 minutes, stirring every 5 minutes and adding more water as necessary. Drain, add butter or margarine and honey. Cook, uncovered, 5 minutes.

Cooking Time Saved: about 2 hours

Makes 6 servings.

BRAISED MUSHROOMS

1 pound fresh mushrooms   ½ teaspoon salt
¼ cup butter or margarine   1 teaspoon chopped parsley
1 teaspoon lemon juice   2 tablespoons sherry or white wine

Wipe mushrooms clean with a damp cloth, trim stem ends,
cut into quarters or lengthwise slices.

Range

Heat butter or margarine in a large skillet, add mushrooms and remaining ingredients, cook 10 to 12 minutes.

Microwave

Combine mushrooms with remaining ingredients in covered bowl. Cook 4 to 5 minutes. Stir half way through the cooking time.

Cooking Time Saved: 5 minutes

Makes 4 servings.

CREAMED MUSHROOMS

1 pound mushrooms
2 small onions, chopped
3 tablespoons butter or margarine (range only)
½ cup water (microwave only)
1½ cups white sauce (page 206)

Wash mushrooms, trim stem ends if necessary. Slice vertically.

Range

Cook mushrooms and onions in butter or margarine until wilted, about 3 minutes. Add white sauce and simmer, stirring occasionally, 8 minutes.

Microwave

Cook mushrooms and onions in ½ cup salted water until tender, about 4 minutes. Stir half way through cooking time. Use liquid to replace equal amount of milk in preparing white sauce. Combine sauce with vegetables and cook, covered, 2 minutes.

Cooking Time Saved: 5 minutes

Makes 6 servings.

NEW POTATOES

1 pound small new potatoes
4 tablespoons butter or margarine
1 tablespoon parsley, minced
Salt, pepper

Wash potatoes and peel a ½-inch band of skin from around the middle.

Range
Cook potatoes in boiling, salted water to cover until tender, about 20 minutes.

Microwave
Put potatoes in a 6-cup casserole with ¼ cup salted water. Cover, cook 10 minutes. Rotate dish ½ turn after 5 minutes.

Cooking Time Saved: 10 minutes

Drain potatoes and toss with butter or margarine and parsley. Sprinkle with salt and pepper to taste. Makes 4 servings.

POTATOES ANNA

4 medium potatoes
1 sweet onion
Salt, white pepper
⅓ cup butter or margarine, clarified (page 207)

Peel potatoes (ordinary boiling potatoes are best for this dish) and cut into thin slices. Drop into a bowl of ice water, drain just before using. Slice onion thinly. Line the bottom of a well-buttered baking dish with a layer of overlapping slices of potatoes. Top with a few onion rings, season with salt and pepper to taste. Repeat layers until all ingredients are used. Spoon clarified butter or margarine over potatoes. Cover the baking dish.

Range
Bake at 450°F for about 1 hour, until potatoes are tender.

Microwave
Cook 15 to 20 minutes, until potatoes are tender.

Cooking Time Saved: 40 minutes

Let stand 5 minutes. Invert on serving dish. Makes 4 to 6 servings.

CREAMED POTATOES WITH CHEESE

2 pounds potatoes
3 tablespoons butter or margarine
¼ cup flour
1½ cups hot milk

1 teaspoon salt
White pepper, paprika
6 ounces Cheddar or
Swiss cheese, grated

Peel potatoes and slice thinly.

Range

Melt butter or margarine in a saucepan, add flour, stir to blend. Gradually stir in hot milk, salt, seasonings to taste. Cook, stirring, until smooth and thickened. Fill a greased 2-quart baking dish with alternate layers of potatoes, sauce and cheese, ending with sauce and cheese. Bake at 350°F for 1 hour, until potatoes are tender.

Microwave

Soften butter or margarine in a 2-quart glass bowl, 15 seconds. Stir in flour and hot milk. Add cheese, stir, add seasonings to taste. Add potatoes, stir. Cook, covered, 25 minutes rotating the dish ½ turn and stirring every 5 minutes. Let stand 5 minutes before serving.

Cooking Time Saved: about 40 minutes

Makes 6 servings.

CREAMY SCALLOPED POTATOES

4 medium potatoes, peeled, thinly sliced
1 medium onion, thinly sliced
1 can (10½ ounces)
condensed cream of celery soup

½ cup milk
¼ cup bread crumbs
Salt, pepper
2 tablespoons butter or margarine

Layer potatoes and onions in a buttered 4-cup casserole. Combine soup and milk, add. Sprinkle with crumbs, salt and pepper to taste. Dot with butter or margarine.

Range

Bake, uncovered, at 350°F 40 minutes, until potatoes are tender and top is browned.

Microwave

Cook, uncovered, 12 minutes. Rotate dish ¼ turn every 4 minutes.

Cooking Time Saved: 30 minutes

Makes 6 servings.

MASHED POTATOES AND TURNIPS

3 medium baking potatoes
4 small turnips
Salt, pepper
2 tablespoons butter or margarine
¼ cup milk

Peel potatoes and turnips and cut into uniform ½-inch dice.

Range	Microwave
Cover turnips with boiling salted water. Cook 10 minutes. Add potatoes, cook until both vegetables are tender, about 25 minutes.	Put turnips and potatoes into a 13-by 9-inch glass baking dish with ½ cup boiling salted water. Cover, cook 10 minutes. Stir again, cook 5 minutes. Stir, cover, cook 5 minutes, until vegetables are tender.

Drain, mash, season to taste with salt, pepper and butter or margarine. Add milk to make a smooth, fluffy mixture.

Range	Microwave
Stir over low heat until warm.	Heat 3 minutes, until warm.
	Cooking Time Saved: 15 minutes

Makes 6 servings.

DOUBLE ONION CASSEROLE

1 can (10½ ounces) condensed cream of mushroom soup
2 cans (15½ ounces each) small white onions, drained
1 can (3½ ounces) French fried onion rings

Stir mushroom soup in a 6-cup casserole until smooth. Add onions, mix gently.

Range	Microwave
Top with French fried onion rings. Bake at 375°F for 30 minutes.	Cover, cook 4 minutes, stir. Top with French fried onion rings. Cook, uncovered, 1 minute longer.
	Cooking Time Saved: 25 minutes

Makes 6 servings.

GREEN PEAS FRANÇAISE

2 tablespoons butter or margarine
1 cup shredded lettuce
1 package (10 ounces) frozen green peas
Salt, pepper

Range

Melt butter or margarine in a
saucepan, add lettuce, cover, cook 5
minutes. Add peas and salt and
pepper, cook, covered, about 10
minutes, until peas are tender.

Microwave

Combine ingredients in a 1-quart
casserole. Cover, cook 2 minutes, stir,
cook 2 minutes longer.

Cooking Time Saved: 10 minutes

Makes 3 to 4 servings.

RATATOUILLE

1 onion, thinly sliced
1 clove garlic, mashed
1 green pepper, cut into thin strips
3 tablespoons olive oil
1 medium zucchini, thinly sliced
1 medium eggplant, peeled and cubed

2 tomatoes, cut into wedges
1 bay leaf
1 teaspoon basil
Salt, pepper
Chopped parsley

Range

In skillet, cook onion, garlic and
green pepper in hot oil 5 minutes,
add zucchini and eggplant, simmer
10 minutes. Add tomatoes, bay leaf,
basil, salt and pepper to taste.
Simmer 10 minutes longer, until
vegetables are barely tender.

Microwave

Cook onion, garlic and green pepper
in oil in 3-quart covered casserole, 3
minutes. Add zucchini and eggplant,
cook, covered, 5 minutes. Add
tomatoes, bay leaf, basil, salt and
pepper to taste. Cook, covered, 2
minutes, until vegetables are barely
tender.

Cooking Time Saved: 10 minutes

*Sprinkle with parsley. Serve hot or cold. Vegetables will be crisp,
but may be cooked longer as desired. Makes 6 servings.*

SPANISH RICE

¼ cup oil
1 onion, chopped
1 green pepper, chopped
1 cup rice

1 teaspoon salt
2 medium tomatoes, peeled
and chopped
2 cups boiling water

Range

Heat oil in a heavy 1-quart saucepan. Cook onion and pepper until golden. Add rice and salt, stir well to coat with oil. Add tomatoes and water, bring to boil, cover, simmer 15 minutes, until liquid is absorbed.

Microwave

Cook oil, onion and pepper in a 1-quart casserole, covered, 4 minutes. Stir, cook 2 minutes. Add rice and salt, stir. Add tomatoes and water, cover, cook 15 minutes, until rice is tender and liquid absorbed.

Makes 4 to 6 servings.

SWEET AND SOUR RED CABBAGE

1 medium head red cabbage
3 strips bacon, diced
1 large apple, peeled and diced
1 onion, diced

¼ cup lemon juice
¼ cup brown sugar
1 teaspoon salt
White pepper

Shred cabbage, cover with boiling water. Drain, repeat twice.

Range

Brown bacon in large pan, remove and reserve. In fat, cook apple and onion until soft. Add cabbage, stir for a moment. Add lemon juice, brown sugar, salt and pepper to taste. Add ½ cup water, cover the pan, and cook slowly for 45 minutes or longer, until cabbage is tender. Add more water, if necessary.

Microwave

Cook bacon in 3-quart casserole until crisp, about 3 minutes. Remove bacon and reserve. To fat add apple and onion, cook 3 minutes. Add cabbage, lemon juice, brown sugar, salt and pepper to taste. Stir, cook 5 minutes, stir, cook 5 minutes longer.

Cooking Time Saved: about 35 minutes

Adjust seasoning to taste with more salt and pepper, brown sugar and lemon juice. Serve sprinkled with crisp bacon. Makes 8 to 10 servings.

OKRA AND TOMATOES

1 pound okra, trimmed and sliced, or
1 package (10 ounces) frozen, sliced okra
1 small onion, chopped
¼ cup bacon fat

1 can (1 pound) tomatoes
½ teaspoon curry powder (optional)
1 tablespoon brown sugar
Salt, pepper, paprika

Range

Cook okra and onion in fat until onion is golden. Add tomatoes and seasonings, bring to a boil. Simmer, covered, until okra is tender, about 20 minutes.

Microwave

Combine okra and onion in fat in a 2-quart casserole. Cook 5 minutes, stir. Add tomatoes and seasonings, cover, cook 7 minutes, until okra is tender.

Cooking Time Saved: about 10 minutes

Makes 4 servings.

SCALLOPED TOMATOES

¼ cup butter or margarine
2 slices day-old bread, cut into cubes
1 can (1 pound) tomatoes, drained
2 cans (8 ounces each) tomato puree
¼ cup brown sugar
Salt, pepper

Range

Melt butter or margarine in skillet, add bread cubes, sauté until brown.

Microwave

Melt butter or margarine on a plate 30 seconds, add bread cubes, turn to coat.

In a 2-quart casserole combine tomatoes, tomato puree, brown sugar and salt and pepper to taste. Top with bread cubes.

Range

Bake at 350°F for 40 minutes, until bubbling hot.

Microwave

Cook 15 minutes, rotating dish ¼ turn every 5 minutes until bubbling hot.

Cooking Time Saved: 25 minutes

Makes 6 servings.

SUMMER SQUASH

2 pounds summer squash
¼ cup butter or margarine
1 clove garlic
Salt, pepper
1 tablespoon lemon juice

Wash squash, grate on a coarse grater. Squeeze in kitchen towel to remove excess moisture.

Range

Heat butter or margarine with garlic in a heavy skillet, add squash, salt and pepper to taste. Stir over moderately high heat 8 to 10 minutes, until squash is just tender. Add lemon juice. Transfer to serving dish.

Microwave

Combine butter or margarine, garlic, lemon juice, salt and pepper to taste in a 12- by 8-inch baking dish. Add squash, cover, cook 7 minutes, stirring every 2 minutes, until squash is tender.

Makes 6 or more servings.

BAKED WINTER SQUASH

2 pounds winter squash (hubbard or crookneck)
2 tablespoons butter or margarine
⅓ cup brown sugar
Salt, pepper
Ginger or cinnamon

Wash squash, split in half, remove seeds and pulp. Cut into slices, peel. Dot with butter or margarine, sprinkle with sugar and seasonings to taste.

Range

Cover, bake squash at 400°F for 30 minutes, remove cover, bake until tender. Transfer to serving dish.

Microwave

Pile squash in a 6-cup glass baking dish. Cover, cook 5 minutes. Stir, cover, cook 5 minutes longer.

Cooking Time Saved: about 20 minutes

Makes 6 servings.

BUTTERED TURNIPS

1 pound turnips, peeled
2 tablespoons butter or margarine
Salt, pepper

Cut turnips into 1-inch cubes.

Range

Cover with boiling salted water in pan and cook, covered, about 20 minutes, until fork-tender, drain. Melt butter or margarine in a skillet, cook turnips until lightly glazed, turning occasionally.

Microwave

Add turnips and ¼ cup boiling salted water to casserole, cover, cook 10 minutes until fork-tender, drain. Add butter or margarine, cook, uncovered, 1 minute, turn, cook 1 minute longer until glazed.

Cooking Time Saved: about 12 minutes

Sprinkle with salt and pepper. Makes 3 to 4 servings.

Tip: *Turnips cooked until tender as above may be mashed with butter or margarine, salt and pepper, like potatoes. Or, sprinkle the glazed turnips with 1 tablespoon pancake syrup, a little cinnamon or clove.*

SPINACH SMETANA

1 package frozen chopped spinach
1 teaspoon grated onion
Salt, pepper
¼ cup sour cream

Range

Cook spinach as directed on package; drain thoroughly. Add onion, salt and pepper to taste, and sour cream. Stir over low heat until hot. Remove to serving dish.

Microwave

Cook spinach in package 4 minutes. Drain well. Place in serving dish, add remaining ingredients, stir. Cook 2 minutes.

Makes 3 servings.

SPINACH WITH ROSEMARY

1 pound fresh spinach	½ teaspoon dried rosemary
2 tablespoons butter or margarine	Salt, pepper
2 tablespoons finely minced onion	1 hard-cooked egg, finely chopped

Wash spinach in several changes of water, discard tough and wilted portions of leaves.

Range	Microwave
Heat butter or margarine in a heavy skillet, add onion and rosemary, cook until onion is translucent. Add spinach, cook over moderate heat until spinach is wilted, about 10 minutes.	Cook butter or margarine, onion and rosemary in a 6-cup covered casserole 2 minutes. Add spinach, cover, cook 5 minutes.

Add salt and pepper to taste. Sprinkle with chopped hard-cooked egg.
Makes 4 servings.

SPINACH PUFF

3 cups mashed potatoes (instant if desired)	1 teaspoon salt
	Pepper, nutmeg
1 cup cooked spinach, chopped	4 eggs, separated
¼ cup butter or margarine, melted	

Mix vegetables with butter or margarine and seasonings to taste.
Add egg yolks, blend well. Beat egg whites until stiff, fold into spinach mixture.
Pile in a buttered 6-cup casserole.

Range	Microwave
Bake, uncovered, at 375°F for 40 minutes until puff is set and golden.	Cook, uncovered, 10 minutes, until puff is set.
	Cooking Time Saved: 30 minutes

Makes 6 servings.

ACORN SQUASH AND APPLES

2 acorn squash
2 tablespoons brown sugar
Salt, pepper

2 tablespoons butter or margarine
2 small apples, peeled,
cored and cut in half
Nutmeg or cinnamon

Split squash in half, scoop out seeds and pulp. Sprinkle hollows with half the sugar, add salt and pepper, dot with butter or margarine. Put half an apple into each squash half, sprinkle with remaining sugar and nutmeg or cinnamon.

Range

Arrange filled squash in a baking pan, add 1 cup water to pan. Bake at 400°F for 1 hour, until squash is tender.

Microwave

Cook, covered with wax paper, in a glass dish in ½ inch water, 8 minutes. Rotate dish ¼ turn, cook about 8 minutes longer, until tender.

Cooking Time Saved: 44 minutes

Makes 4 servings.

ZUCCHINI AND TOMATOES

2 tablespoons oil
1 clove garlic, slivered
3 medium zucchini,
scrubbed and sliced

1 can (1 pound) solid-pack
tomatoes, drained
Salt, pepper, sugar
1 teaspoon cornstarch (optional)

Range

Heat oil in skillet, brown garlic slivers lightly. Add zucchini slices, cook until translucent. Add tomatoes and seasonings to taste, simmer 30 minutes. If desired, thicken with cornstarch mixed with 1 tablespoon water. Bring to a boil, stir until sauce is clear. Transfer to serving dish.

Microwave

In 2-quart casserole heat oil and garlic 2 minutes. Add zucchini, tomatoes and seasonings, cook until zucchini is translucent, about 8 minutes. Stir occasionally. If desired, add cornstarch dissolved in 1 tablespoon water. Cook 2 minutes longer.

Cooking Time Saved: about 12 minutes.

Makes 6 servings.

VEGETABLE GOULASH

1 cup boiling water	1 medium eggplant, peeled and cubed
½ cup rice	3 tomatoes, cut into wedges
1 bouillon cube	1 teaspoon mixed Italian herbs
⅓ cup oil	Salt, pepper
3 large onions, thinly sliced	Pinch crushed red pepper
2 medium peppers, slivered	2 tablespoons chopped parsley

Range

Combine water, rice and bouillon cube in saucepan, bring to boil, reduce heat, cover, simmer about 15 minutes. Meanwhile, in skillet, heat oil, cook onions and peppers 5 minutes, add eggplant, stir in tomatoes, herbs and seasonings, cook 15 minutes. Transfer to serving casserole.

Microwave

Combine water, rice and bouillon cube in a 2-cup glass measuring cup or small bowl. Cover with wax paper, cook 5 minutes. Meanwhile, combine remaining ingredients in 4-quart casserole, cover and cook alongside rice, 15 minutes, until all the vegetables are tender.

Stir rice into casserole. Sprinkle with parsley. Makes 6 servings.

YAM AND MARSHMALLOW CASSEROLE

4 medium yams or sweet potatoes	¼ cup brown sugar
2 tablespoons butter or margarine	Salt, pepper, powdered cloves to taste
1 tablespoon lemon juice	1 cup miniature marshmallows

Range

Bake yams at 350°F for about 45 minutes or until very tender.

Microwave

Arrange yams on paper towel, cook 10 to 12 minutes, uncovered, until tender.

Cool slightly, peel and mash. Add remaining ingredients except marshmallows, beat well. Fill a 2-quart casserole. Sprinkle with marshmallows.

Range

Bake in 350°F oven 40 minutes.

Microwave

Cook, uncovered, 15 minutes.

Cooking Time Saved: about 1 hour

Makes 5 servings.

PARSNIPS AND ORANGES

1½ pounds parsnips
2 tablespoons butter or margarine
1 tablespoon honey

¼ cup orange juice
1 teaspoon grated orange peel
1 orange, peeled, cut into wedges.

Peel parsnips, using a floating knife peeler, if possible.
Cut into lengthwise slices, cut out core if it is woody.

Range

Cover with boiling salted water, cook 20 minutes or longer, until fork-tender, drain. In a saucepan, combine remaining ingredients, bring to a boil. Add parsnips, heat.

Microwave

Put ½ cup boiling salted water into a baking dish, add sliced parsnips, cover, cook 5 minutes, until fork tender, drain. In a serving bowl, heat remaining ingredients 3 minutes, add parsnips, stir, heat 2 minutes.

Cooking Time Saved: 10 minutes

Makes 4 servings.

VEGETABLES WITH STYLE

In addition to the recipes included in this section, here are some ideas for vegetables with style. With accents and seasonings, and by varying the liquids, you can change the nationality of even a plain white potato.

| STYLE | ACCENT | VEGETABLES | | | | SEASONING | LIQUID | TIME | |
		White	Yellow Orange Red	Green				Range	Microwave
All-American	2 tbs. butter or margarine	½ cup lima beans cooked	½ cup corn	1 cup peas frozen		salt, pepper sugar	½ cup milk or cream	12-14 min.	6-8 min.
German	2 tbs. bacon fat or 2 strips bacon, diced and cooked 1 small apple, chopped	1 small onion, sliced thin 1 small potato, sliced thin	2 carrots cut in ¼" lengthwise	¾ pound cabbage cut in thin slices or 1 cup drained saukerkraut		1 tbs. prepared mustard 1 tbs. caraway seed	½ cup beer	20-25 min.	10 min.
Swedish	2 tbs. chicken fat	1 leek, sliced thin 4 new potatoes, quartered	½ cup turnip, sliced thin	½ cup beans, cut in 1" lengths		chopped dill salt, pepper	¾ cup sweet cream or, milk	25-30 min.	12 min.

VEGETABLES WITH STYLE

STYLE	ACCENT	VEGETABLES			SEASONING	LIQUID	TIME	
		White	Yellow Orange Red	Green			Range	Microwave
California	2 tbs. corn oil ¼ cup peperoni, diced	1 medium onion, minced 1 cup white kidney beans or chick peas	1 large tomato, chopped	1 cup peas	2 tbs. chili powder	½ cup water or chicken broth	18-20 min.	10 min.
North Carolina	¼ cup salt pork, rinsed and diced 1 small onion, diced	3 small turnips, cut in ½" cubes	½ cup wax beans, cut in 1" lengths	½ cup spinach or mustard greens	salt, hot minced peppers or tabasco	½ cup water or vegetable broth	20-25 min.	10 min.
Louisiana	2 tbs. shortening	1 small onion, sliced thin	3 small yams, cut in 1" cubes	1 cup frozen or fresh okra	molasses brown sugar nutmeg	½ cup pineapple juice	35-40 min.	14 min.
French Jardinière	2 shallots or 1 small onion, minced 1 tbs. butter	2 medium potatoes, cut in ½" cubes 6 mushrooms sliced	2 carrots, cut in ¼" rounds	1 cup peas	salt, pepper chopped mint	¼ cup chicken beef, or vegetable broth	20-25 min.	10-12 min.

Italian	2 tbs. olive oil, 1 garlic clove, minced 1 small red onion, minced	3 celery stalks, cut in ½" slices	1 tomato, chopped	3 small zucchini, cut in ⅛" rounds	salt, pepper basil	¼ cup tomato sauce or juice	12-14 min.	8 min.
Indian	1 small cooking apple, chopped 1 tbs. butter	1 medium potato, cut in ½" dice 1 small onion, chopped	1 medium eggplant, cut in ½" cubes	1 small pepper, chopped	2 tbs. curry powder salt, pepper	¼ cup chicken broth	18-20 min.	8 min.
Chinese	3 scallions, sliced in 1" diagonals 2 tbs. peanut oil	½ cup water chestnuts, sliced bean sprouts		2 cups snow peas or Chinese cabbage	2 tsp. grated ginger	½ cup chicken broth 1 tsp. cornstarch	6-8 min.	4 min.
Japanese	2 tbs. sesame oil 1 garlic clove, minced	1 small onion, sliced thin	2 small summer squash cut in ¼" rounds	1 pepper cut in thin strips or 1 cup spinach	2 tbs. soy sauce 1 tbs. sugar 1 tbs. sesame seeds	¼ cup beef broth	6-8 min.	4 min.

VEGETABLE COOKING CHART

1 pound fresh or 1 package (about 10 ounces) frozen vegetables
(unless otherwise specified).
For uniform cooking, cut vegetables into uniform pieces.

	FRESH		FROZEN VEGETABLES*
	Range Minutes	Microwave Minutes	Microwave Minutes
ARTICHOKES, whole (3-4) hearts	30 10 to 15	20 5	— 4 to 5
ASPARAGUS, whole	10 to 20	4 to 4½	8 to 10
BEANS, green or wax	12 to 16	12 to 14	7 to 8
BEANS, lima	25 to 30	6 to 8	7 to 8
BEETS, whole sliced	20 to 60 15 to 25	15 to 17 6 to 8	— —
BROCCOLI, spears	10 to 15	7 to 10	7 to 9
BRUSSELS SPROUTS (1 pint)	15 to 20	5	8 to 10
CABBAGE, quartered shredded	10 to 15 5 to 10	10 to 14 7 to 9	— —
CARROTS, sliced whole	10 to 20 15 to 20	7 to 10 10 to 14	7 to 8 —
CAULIFLOWER, whole flowerets	20 to 25 8 to 15	8 to 10 7 to 8	— 8 to 9
CELERY, sliced	15 to 18	10 to 13	—
CORN, ON THE COB (4 ears) kernels (1½ cups) EGGPLANT, sliced or diced	5 to 10 5 10	7 to 9 6 to 7 8	10 5 to 6 —
GREENS, (Turnips, Kale)	10 to 15	6 to 7	10 to 11
MUSHROOMS	10-12	4 to 5	—

(VEGETABLE COOKING CHART)

	FRESH		FROZEN VEGETABLES*
	Range Minutes	Microwave Minutes	Microwave Minutes
OKRA	10 to 15	7 to 10	7 to 9
PARSNIPS	20 to 40	5 to 7	—
PEAS	12 to 16	8 to 10	7 to 8
POTATOES, baked	45 to 60	10	—
boiled, cut-up	10 to 15	8 to 10	—
SPINACH, leaf	3 to 5	6 to 7	10 to 11
chopped	—	—	6 to 7
SQUASH, summer, sliced	8 to 15	5 to 7	6 to 8
acorn, baked	45	5 to 10	—
Hubbard, boiled	25	6 to 8	—
mashed	—	—	5 to 6
TURNIPS, sliced	20 to 30	10 to 12	—

*Follow package directions for conventional preparation of frozen vegetables.

NOTE: Since there is considerable variation in vegetable sizes, shapes and tenderness, use times indicated as a guide for your own preparations, rather than as an absolute.

WHITE SAUCE (and VARIATIONS)

2 tablespoons butter or margarine
2 tablespoons flour
1 cup milk or ½ cup milk and
½ cup liquid from cooking vegetables
Salt, pepper, nutmeg

Range	Microwave
Melt butter or margarine. Stir in flour, cook a minute, stirring. Stir in milk, cook over moderate heat, stirring constantly, until sauce is thick and smooth.	Soften butter or margarine in small cup about 5 seconds. Stir in flour to make a paste. Heat milk in 1-pint measuring cup or bowl 2 minutes. Stir in flour paste, cook 2 minutes longer. Stir.

Add salt, pepper and nutmeg to taste. Makes 1 cup medium white sauce.

Variations:

Cheese Sauce:	add ½ cup grated Swiss or Cheddar cheese, or ¼ cup grated Parmesan cheese.
Egg Sauce:	add 2 hard-cooked chopped eggs and lemon juice to taste.
Mushroom Sauce:	add 1 can (4 ounces) mushrooms, drained.
Caper Sauce:	add 2 tablespoons drained, chopped capers.
Curry Sauce:	add curry powder to taste, beginning with ½ teaspoon.
Dill Sauce:	add 2 tablespoons chopped, fresh dill, plus lemon juice to taste.
Onion Sauce:	add 1 small onion chopped and cooked in 2 tablespoons butter or margarine until tender.

HOLLANDAISE SAUCE

¼ pound (½ cup) butter or margarine   1 tablespoon lemon juice
3 egg yolks   Dash cayenne pepper

Range
Combine ingredients in a small, chilled saucepan. Cook over low heat, stirring constantly with a whisk, until the mixture is smooth and thick.

Microwave
Cut butter or margarine into 4 pieces, soften in shallow bowl, 5 seconds. Stir egg yolks, lemon juice and seasonings together, add to butter or margarine, blend well. Cover bowl with wax paper, cook 5 seconds. Stir, cover, cook 10 seconds, repeat until sauce is hot.

Serve at once, or cover and store in the refrigerator. Makes about ¾ cup.

Range
To reheat, whisk sauce in the top of a double boiler.

Microwave
Reheat in the microwave, about 1½ minutes.

If the sauce should curdle, whisk in 1 tablespoon boiling water, a little at a time, to restore smoothness. Or, stir in 1 ice cube, over low heat.

CLARIFIED BUTTER

Range
Melt butter over low heat in a heavy saucepan.

Microwave
Put butter in a glass measuring cup, cook 2 minutes, until melted.

Allow sediment to settle. Spoon any foam from top. Pour off clear liquid, straining, if desired. Use the clarified butter for frying, as dip, or sauce. Save the sediment and use on vegetables.

Tip: Margarine may be clarified in the same way.

MAÎTRE D'HÔTEL BUTTER

Range
Soften ½ cup butter or margarine at room temperature an hour or longer.

Microwave
Soften butter or margarine 45 seconds.

Cream with 1 tablespoon chopped parsley, the juice of ½ lemon, salt and hot pepper sauce. Use to top broiled meats, fish or poultry.

WILTED COLE SLAW

1 medium head cabbage, shredded
2 egg yolks
¾ cup milk
2 tablespoons flour
1 tablespoon sugar
¾ teaspoon salt

1 teaspoon dry mustard
Dash cayenne pepper
2 tablespoons butter
¼ cup lemon juice
1 teaspoon celery seed
1 tablespoon instant minced onion

Range

Put shredded cabbage into a large saucepan. In the top of a double boiler over hot water, combine egg yolks and 2 tablespoons milk. Whisk in flour, sugar, salt, mustard and cayenne pepper. Add remaining ingredients, whisk over hot water until sauce is thick and smooth. Pour sauce over cabbage in saucepan, bring to a boil, cook, stirring, over moderate heat, until cabbage is hot and slightly wilted.

Microwave

Place cabbage in a large serving bowl. In a 2-cup bowl, beat egg yolks with 2 tablespoons of the milk. Add flour, sugar, salt, mustard and cayenne pepper. Add remaining ingredients. Stir, cook 4 minutes, stirring after each minute, until sauce is thickened. Pour over cabbage in bowl, cook 4 minutes, until cabbage is hot and slightly wilted.

Good hot or cold. Makes 8 or more servings.

HOT GERMAN POTATO SALAD

3 pounds potatoes
¼ pound bacon, diced
½ cup onion, sliced or chopped
½ cup hot water
½ cup vinegar
¼ cup vegetable oil

1 tablespoon sugar
2 teaspoons dry mustard
1 teaspoon celery seed
1 teaspoon nutmeg
1 teaspoon salt
½ teaspoon white pepper

Range

Peel potatoes, cut into quarters. Cook in boiling salted water for 25 minutes, or until tender. Drain. Brown bacon in a skillet, drain on paper towels. In the bacon drippings sauté onion until translucent. Add water, vinegar, oil and seasonings, simmer 10 minutes. Slice potatoes ¼ inch thick, fill serving bowl. Pour hot dressing over potatoes, add bacon, stir gently.

Microwave

Wash potatoes, arrange on paper towel with an inch of space between them. Cook 15 minutes, turning potatoes once halfway through cooking. Peel while warm, slice ¼ inch thick, fill serving bowl. In a 1-quart casserole, cook bacon and onions for 10 minutes, stirring every 2 minutes. Add remaining ingredients, cook until steaming hot, about 3 minutes. Pour hot dressing over potatoes, stir gently.

Serve warm. Makes 8 or more servings.

CAESAR SALAD

2 cups day-old bread cubes
(3 slices bread)
½ cup oil
1 clove garlic, pureed
1 egg
3 tablespoons lemon juice

1 teaspoon salt
Pinch each black pepper, dry mustard
2 quarts assorted salad greens,
torn into bite-sized pieces
10 anchovy fillets, rinsed, diced
½ cup grated Parmesan cheese

Range

Spread bread cubes on baking sheet, sprinkle with ¼ cup oil mixed with garlic. Bake at 300°F for 15 minutes until crisp and golden, stirring occasionally. Cook whole egg in boiling water for 1 minute.

Microwave

Spread bread cubes on glass pie plate, sprinkle with ¼ cup oil mixed with garlic, cook 6 minutes, stirring every 2 minutes. Break egg into buttered custard cup, cook 40 seconds, until white is just opaque.

Cooking Time Saved: about 10 minutes

Reserve bread cubes. Combine remaining oil with lemon juice in large salad bowl, add salt, pepper and dry mustard. Pile greens into bowl. Sprinkle greens with anchovy fillets, toss to coat leaves with dressing. Add egg, toss well. Add cheese and bread cubes, toss again, Serve at once. Makes 6 to 8 servings.

DESSERTS
(FRUITS, SAUCES, CAKES, PIES, PUDDINGS AND CUSTARDS)

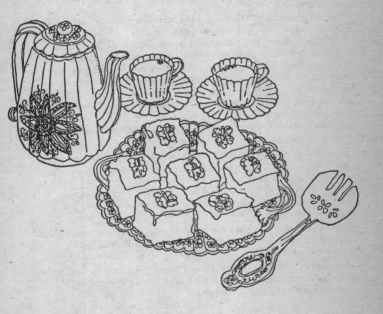

Just as good stories have happy endings, so good dinners have sweet endings. There are so many fine desserts to make in the microwave that it is difficult to decide which ones to include.

You will find that the microwave can make excellent coffee cakes and is particularly good for custards and puddings, fruits and sauces.

When you make a pudding or custard with milk in your microwave, be sure to stir frequently to prevent boiling over. All custards should be undercooked slightly, since they continue to cook after they are removed from the oven.

It is a popularly-held notion that the microwave oven cannot bake. But it can. It can bake from scratch or from a mix.

The basic directions for cake mixes are simple. Line the bottoms of two 8-inch round cake dishes with brown paper or wax paper. Prepare the cake mix as directed on the package. Fill the pans only half full, and if any batter remains, use it to make cupcakes. Run a knife through the batter a few times to release large air bubbles. Cover with a paper towel. Cook, one layer at a time, 5 to 6 minutes, turning the dish occasionally. Remove the paper towel, let the cake cool in the pan about 5 minutes, then invert on wire racks to finish cooling. Peel the paper from the bottom. Cupcakes take about 30 seconds each . . . or 3 minutes for 6 cupcakes.

- Bake cupcakes in ungreased custard cups or coffee cups, or line cups with paper liners.

- Be careful not to overbake cakes, or they may become tough and dry. Start with minimum recommended time, then watch carefully as you cook longer. Remember that the cake will continue to cook after it is removed from the microwave.

- Ring-shaped cakes bake more evenly and they are easy to prepare if a glass, about 3 inches in diameter, is placed in the center of the baking dish before the batter is added. The ring-shaped cake that results is attractive.

- To reheat individual servings of cakes or breads, place them on a napkin or paper plate in the microwave. Heat a single serving about 10 to 15 seconds, 2 servings about 20 seconds.

To make layer cake mixes richer, add any or all of the following:

2 tablespoons oil or butter

an extra egg

extra flavoring (1 teaspoon vanilla, ½ teaspoon almond extract, or ¼ teaspoon peppermint extract)

2 tablespoons grated orange rind

½ cup chopped nuts, candied fruit or chocolate chips

¼ cup poppy seeds

2 tablespoons instant coffee powder

In this section, as in all the sections of the book, directions are given for both conventional and microwave cooking.

DESSERTS

SAUCES FOR DESSERTS

CAKES FOR DESSERT

FROSTINGS FOR CAKES

DESSERTS

BABA AU RHUM

1 envelope yeast	4 cups flour
½ cup very warm water	½ cup butter or margarine, softened
¼ cup sugar	¾ cup water
1 teaspoon salt	¾ cup sugar
4 eggs, lightly beaten	½ cup dark rum

Dissolve yeast in warm water. Beat in sugar, salt and eggs. Gradually add flour and beat well. Add butter or margarine (softened 15 seconds in microwave, ½ to 1 hour at room temperature) and beat until satiny. Cover and let rise until doubled in bulk, about 1 hour. Punch down. Form into 8 balls, place in greased muffin cups. Cover and let rise until doubled in bulk (Reduce rising time by first heating in microwave 30 seconds.)

Range

Bake at 375°F for 20 to 25 minutes. Turn out onto cake racks to cool. Combine ½ cup water and the sugar in a heavy saucepan and cook over medium heat until light brown, about 18 to 20 minutes.

Microwave

Cook 8 minutes. Turn out onto cake racks to cool. Combine ½ cup water and the sugar in a 16-ounce measuring cup and cook 8 minutes until light brown.

Cooking Time Saved: about 30 minutes

Cool syrup slightly, stir in remaining ¼ cup water and rum. Prick Babas with a fork and baste liberally with sugar syrup. Makes 8 Babas.

APPLESAUCE

2 pounds apples
½ cup water
½ cup sugar,
or to taste (optional)

Wash and quarter apples. Discard stems and blossom ends.

Range

Combine apples and water in heavy saucepan. Cover, bring to a boil and simmer over low heat, stirring often, 15 to 20 minutes, until tender.

Microwave

Combine apples and water in 3-quart bowl. Cover, cook 8 to 10 minutes, stirring halfway through cooking period.

Cooking Time Saved: 10 minutes

Force fruit through a sieve or food mill. Add sugar to taste while hot. Cooking time depends on variety of apple used. Makes 6 servings.

BAKED APPLES

4 baking apples
3 tablespoons butter or margarine
⅓ cup brown sugar

3 tablespoons raisins
3 tablespoons chopped walnuts
¼ cup dry Sauterne or water

Core apples. Combine butter or margarine and sugar, add raisins and nuts, stuff into cavity of apples.

Range

Arrange in shallow dish, pour 1 tablespoon wine or water over each apple. Bake at 350°F for about 40 minutes, until tender. Transfer to serving dish, spoon sauce over fruit.

Microwave

Place apples in individual serving dishes, pour 1 tablespoon wine or water over each apple. Cover with wax paper. Cook 8 minutes, until tender.

Note: 2 apples cook in 4 minutes

Cooking Time Saved: 30 minutes

Exact cooking time will depend on variety and size of apples. Makes 4 servings.

POACHED APPLE RINGS

3 large cooking apples
3 tablespoons butter or margarine
Confectioners' sugar
2 tablespoons water or lemon juice

Wash, core and cut apples into ½-inch thick rings.

Range

Heat butter or margarine in a large skillet, add apples in a single layer. Sprinkle with sugar to taste, add water or lemon juice to pan, cover, poach gently until tender, about 12 minutes.

Microwave

Melt butter or margarine in large shallow dish, about 30 seconds. Add apples in a single layer. Sprinkle with sugar to taste. Add water or lemon juice to dish. Cover with wax paper, cook 5 minutes, until tender, rotating dish ¼ turn halfway through cooking.

Cooking Time Saved: 7 minutes

Exact cooking time will depend on variety and size of apples.
Makes 6 servings.

FRUIT COMPOTE

2 firm ripe pears
or apples
12 ounces dried
mixed fruit or prunes

1 orange
½ cup honey
½ cup white wine
Hot water to cover

Peel and core pears or apples, cut into bite-sized pieces. Arrange with dried fruit in a large shallow baking dish. Peel and grate rind of orange over fruit. Section orange, add. Drizzle with honey, add wine and enough water to cover.

Range

Bake at 350°F for 1 hour, until fruits are tender, stirring from time to time.

Microwave

Cook until fruits are tender, about 15 minutes, stirring halfway through cooking period.

Cooking Time Saved: about 45 minutes

Makes 8 servings.

218

CHERRIES JUBILEE

1 can (14½ ounces)
pitted bing cherries
1½ teaspoons cornstarch
1 tablespoon sugar

½ teaspoon cinnamon
¼ cup brandy or cognac
1 pint vanilla ice cream

Drain cherries, reserve liquid.

Range

Combine cornstarch with sugar and cinnamon in heavy saucepan, stir in cherry juice. Bring to boil over medium heat, cook until smooth and thickened, stirring constantly. Add cherries, heat through. Pour into serving dish. Warm brandy, ignite, pour over cherries.

Microwave

Combine cornstarch with sugar and cinnamon in 1½ quart serving dish. Stir in cherry juice. Cook 2 to 3 minutes, until thickened, stirring after 1½ minutes. Add cherries, heat through, about 2 minutes. Remove. Before serving, warm brandy in cup 20 seconds, ignite and pour over cherries.

*Spoon the flaming sauce over vanilla
ice cream. Makes 3 to 4 servings.*

FLAMING BANANAS

2 tablespoons butter or margarine
3 tablespoons brown sugar
2 bananas, peeled and split in half
1½ ounces banana liqueur (or other)

Range

Melt butter or margarine in small pan over low heat, add brown sugar and heat 1 minute, stirring constantly. Place bananas in baking dish, coat with syrup, bake at 350°F for 10 to 15 minutes. Heat liqueur, ignite, pour flaming over bananas, serve.

Microwave

Melt butter or margarine in shallow serving dish, about 30 seconds. Stir in brown sugar, heat 30 seconds. Add bananas, coat with syrup. Place liqueur in small glass in oven*with bananas, cook 40 seconds. Remove both. Ignite liqueur, pour flaming over bananas, serve.

*Do not ignite liqueur in microwave oven nor return dish to oven while it is still ablaze.

Cooking Time Saved: more than 10 minutes

Makes 2 servings.

CHOCOLATE MOCHA MOUSSE

4 ounces unsweetened
baking chocolate
⅔ cup sugar
½ cup brewed coffee
6 eggs, separated

2 tablespoons coffee liqueur
or Grand Marnier
2 tablespoons butter or
margarine (optional)

Range

In a double boiler over hot water,
melt chocolate with sugar and
coffee, stirring frequently. Remove
from heat.

Microwave

Combine chocolate, sugar and coffee
in a 2-quart bowl. Cook, uncovered,
2 minutes, until chocolate melts.

*Beat in egg yolks, one at a time. Cool. Stir in liqueur.
Beat egg whites until stiff but not dry. Fold into cooled chocolate
mixture. Spoon into individual sherbet glasses or a large serving bowl.
Chill 4 hours or overnight before serving. Makes 8 servings.*

*Note: If chocolate mixture is too stiff, or if a
richer texture is desired, stir in 2 tablespoons softened
butter or margarine after removing mixture from heat.*

CHOCOLATE FONDUE

1 package (6 ounces)
semi-sweet chocolate pieces
½ cup sour cream
2 tablespoons kirsch,
Mint liqueur or coffee liqueur
Strawberries, pineapple pieces,
apple wedges, cake cubes

Range

Combine chocolate pieces and sour
cream in a heavy saucepan. Melt
over low heat, stirring constantly,
until smooth, about 5 minutes.

Microwave

In serving bowl, heat chocolate with
sour cream about 1½ minutes. Stir
until smooth.

*Arrange fruits, cake cubes and long-handled fondue forks
on tray. Keep fondue warm. Guests spear fruit or cake on
forks, dip in chocolate. Makes 4 to 6 servings.*

CARAMEL CUSTARD

6 tablespoons sugar	¼ cup sugar
2 tablespoons water	1 teaspoon vanilla
2 eggs	2 cups milk, scalded
2 egg yolks	

Range

Heat 6 tablespoons sugar and 2 tablespoons water over low heat in a small heavy saucepan or skillet, turning and tipping pan constantly until mixture turns golden.

Microwave

Combine 6 tablespoons sugar and 2 tablespoons water in 1 pint measuring cup. Cook 4 to 5 minutes, stirring after 2 minutes, until mixture is just golden.

Immediately divide caramel syrup into 6 custard cups, turn to coat bottom. Beat eggs, egg yolks, ¼ cup sugar and vanilla together. Stir in hot milk. Divide into caramel-coated cups.

Range

Half fill a shallow baking pan with boiling water, arrange custard cups in water, bake at 350°F for 40 minutes, until set.

Microwave

Add 1 inch boiling water to 13-by 9-inch baking dish. Arrange custard cups in water. Cook 6 minutes, turn dish, cook 6 minutes longer, until custard is set.

Cooking Time Saved: 28 minutes

Chill, unmold onto serving dishes. Makes 6 servings.

EASY MOCHA DESSERT

1 envelope gelatin	2 cups whipped cream
1 cup cold coffee	or whipped topping
1 pint chocolate ice cream	Powdered instant coffee
	or chocolate curls

Range

Stir gelatin and cold coffee in a heavy saucepan over moderate heat until gelatin dissolves. Pour into a bowl.

Microwave

Combine gelatin and cold coffee in a 16-ounce measuring cup, cook 2 minutes, until gelatin dissolves.

Spoon ice cream into hot mixture a little at a time, stir until melted and smooth. Chill until on the point of setting, 15 minutes. Beat until light and frothy. Fold in whipped cream. Fill parfait glasses and garnish with coffee or chocolate curls. Chill until set. Makes 6 to 8 servings.

STEEPED DRIED FRUIT

8 ounces dried fruit
½ cup white wine
½ cup water

Range

Soak fruit 1 hour in wine and water in pan. Cover pan, simmer over low heat about 20 minutes, until fruit is tender. Add more liquid, as necessary.

Microwave

Soak fruit 1 hour in wine and water in glass bowl. Cover with wax paper, cook 4 minutes. Uncover, cook 2 minutes longer.

Cooking Time Saved: 14 minutes

The fruit will continue to soften in its juices as it stands in the refrigerator. Top with cream or sour cream, if desired. Makes 6 servings.

Tip: This method can be used to soften and restore very hard dried fruit.

STRAWBERRIES ROMANOFF

1 quart strawberries
½ cup heavy cream
½ pint vanilla ice cream
Juice of ½ lemon
3 tablespoons orange-flavored liqueur

Wash, hull and chill strawberries. Whip cream. Soften ice cream in small bowl (in microwave about 10 seconds, at room temperature about 20 minutes), whip with rotary beater until smooth. Fold in whipped cream, lemon juice and liqueur, fold in berries, pile into champagne goblets. Makes 4 servings.

PEACHES AND CREAM

2 pounds peaches	¼ cup sour cream
½ cup sugar	½ cup flour
¼ teaspoon ground cloves	¼ cup brown sugar
Dash salt	2 tablespoons butter
2 eggs, beaten	or margarine

*Plunge peaches into boiling water to loosen skins.
Peel and slice, arrange in a 9-inch pie plate. Sprinkle
with sugar, cloves and salt. Mix eggs with sour cream,
pour over peaches. Mix flour and brown sugar,
cut in butter or margarine to make coarse crumbs.*

Range	Microwave
Sprinkle crumbs on peaches, bake at 425°F for about 40 minutes, or until peaches are tender.	Cook, uncovered, 3 minutes, rotate plate ¼ turn. Cook 3 minutes, rotate plate ¼ turn. Sprinkle with crumbs, cook 4 minutes.

Cooking Time Saved: 30 minutes

PEACH SURPRISE

1 large ripe peach	1 teaspoon sugar
1 tablespoon chopped nuts	¼ teaspoon cinnamon
1 tablespoon raisins	1 tablespoon butter or margarine
1 tablespoon cookie crumbs	

*Plunge peach into boiling water to
loosen skin. Peel peach, cut in half,
remove seed. Fill with remaining ingredients.*

Range	Microwave
Arrange on small pan, add 2 tablespoons water, cover, bake at 350°F for about 20 minutes, until tender.	Arrange on serving plate, cook 2 minutes.

Cooking Time Saved: 18 minutes

Makes 1 serving.

STEWED PEACHES

2 pounds peaches
1 cup sugar
1½ cups boiling water
Grated rind and juice
from ½ lemon

Plunge peaches into boiling water to loosen skins.
Peel, cut in halves or slices, discard pits.

Range

Combine sugar and 1½ cups boiling water in 2-quart saucepan, simmer 5 minutes. Add grated lemon rind and peaches, simmer 10 minutes or until peaches are tender. Remove fruit to a serving bowl, boil syrup rapidly to reduce to desired consistency. Add lemon juice, pour over fruit, chill.

Microwave

Combine sugar and 1½ cups boiling water in serving bowl. Add lemon rind and peaches, cook 5 minutes, until fruit is tender. If desired, remove fruit and return liquid to microwave for a few minutes to reduce to desired consistency. Add lemon juice, pour over fruit, chill.

For variety, add a few cloves or a piece
of cinnamon stick with the lemon rind.
Discard before serving. Makes 6 servings.

MINUTE SOUFFLÉ

2 ounces
German sweet chocolate
1 tablespoon rum

1 tablespoon cornstarch
2 eggs, separated
Dash salt

Range

Melt chocolate in a cup placed in a pan of hot water. Stir rum with cornstarch, add to chocolate. Beat egg yolks until very light, add chocolate mixture. Beat egg whites stiff with salt, fold into chocolate mixture. Bake in a 12-ounce soufflé dish at 375°F for about 35 minutes, until well puffed.

Microwave

Melt chocolate in a cup, about 1½ minutes. Stir rum with cornstarch. Add to chocolate. Beat egg yolks until very light, add chocolate mixture. Beat egg whites stiff with salt, fold into chocolate mixture. Pour into 12-ounce soufflé dish, cook 1 minute, until well puffed.

Serve at once. Makes 1 or 2 servings.

PRALINE SOUFFLÉ

2 envelopes unflavored gelatin
⅔ cup boiling water
2 tablespoons dark rum,
  brandy or orange liqueur

4 eggs, separated
1 cup milk
2 cups praline powder (below)
3 cups heavy cream, whipped

*Tape a double-thick strip of aluminum foil around the
outside of a 6-cup soufflé dish, to make a collar that
stands 3 inches above rim of dish. Grease dish and foil
lightly, sprinkle with sugar. Place gelatin in a large
mixing bowl, add boiling water, and beat with rotary
beater until light and frothy. Beat in rum, egg yolks,
milk and 1¾ cups praline powder. Chill 15 minutes.
Meanwhile, beat egg whites until stiff. Fold whipped
cream into praline mixture. Fold in egg whites. Turn into
prepared soufflé dish. Sprinkle with ¼ cup praline
powder. Chill 4 hours or longer. Makes 8 to 10 servings.*

PRALINE POWDER

¼ cup water
1½ cups sugar
½ teaspoon cream of tartar
1 cup blanched almonds

Range

Combine water, sugar, cream of
tartar and almonds in heavy
saucepan. Cook, without stirring,
until mixture turns a deep brown.

Microwave

Combine water, sugar, cream of tartar
and almonds in a 1-quart casserole.
Cook 12 minutes, until mixture turns
a deep brown.

*Pour warm caramel and almond mixture onto a buttered baking
sheet, cool. Crack in small pieces and powder a little at a
time in an electric blender, or pound with a hammer between
sheets of wax paper. Praline will keep for months in a
tightly sealed jar in the refrigerator. Makes about 2 cups.*

STEWED RHUBARB

1 pound rhubarb
2 tablespoons water
Dash salt
½ cup sugar

*Wash and trim rhubarb, peel if stems
are tough. Cut into 1-inch lengths.*

Range

Combine rhubarb in a saucepan
with water and salt. Cook 10
minutes, covered. Add sugar,
simmer 5 minutes longer, until
rhubarb is just tender, but not soft.
Transfer to serving bowl.

Microwave

Add water, salt and sugar to rhubarb
in 6-cup glass casserole. Cover, cook 4
minutes. Stir, cover, cook 2 minutes
longer, until rhubarb is barely tender,
but not soft. Let stand 4 minutes.

*Taste and add more sugar, if desired.
Chill. Makes 6 to 8 servings.*

RHUBARB BETTY

3 cups rhubarb, in 1-inch pieces
2 cups toasted bread crumbs
1 cup sugar
Cinnamon, cloves
¼ cup butter or margarine

*Fill a 6-cup casserole with alternated layers of
rhubarb and bread crumbs, sprinkle with sugar, cinnamon
and cloves. Dot with butter or margarine.*

Range

Bake at 350°F for about 30 minutes,
until rhubarb is tender and top is
browned.

Microwave

Cover casserole, cook 5 minutes.
Turn casserole, remove cover, cook 5
minutes. Turn, cook 5 minutes, until
rhubarb is tender.

Cooking Time Saved: 15 minutes

*Serve with whipped cream or ice cream,
or custard sauce, if desired. Makes 4 servings.*

POACHED PEARS

6 fresh pears,
peeled, with stems
1 cup orange juice
Juice and grated rind
of 2 lemons

2 cinnamon sticks
Large piece ginger root
1 cup sugar
1 cup water, or to cover

Range

Lay pears on their sides in a large, shallow saucepan, add remaining ingredients. Stir to combine. Simmer, turning occasionally, about 20 minutes, until fruit is tender. Remove fruit from pan, continue to cook liquid until reduced by half, about 15 minutes.

Microwave

Lay pears on their sides in an 8-inch square baking dish, add remaining ingredients, stir to combine. Cook until tender about 12 minutes, turning fruit occasionally. Remove fruit from pan, continue to cook liquid until reduced by half, about 3 minutes.

Cooking Time saved: about 20 minutes

Chill fruit in liquid, serve cold. Cooking time depends on size and variety of pears used. Makes 6 servings.

INDIAN PUDDING

½ cup yellow corn meal
1 quart milk
½ teaspoon salt

½ cup molasses
½ teaspoon cinnamon
½ teaspoon nutmeg

Range

Add corn meal to ½ cup milk. Bring remaining milk to a boil in a heavy saucepan, add salt. Gradually stir in corn meal. Cook, stirring constantly, until thick, about 15 minutes. Add molasses and spices. Turn into buttered 2-quart baking dish. Bake at 350°F for 2 hours.

Microwave

Combine all ingredients in a 2-quart baking dish. Cook, covered, 10 minutes. Rotate dish ¼ turn, let stand 4 minutes, cook 10 minutes. Stir, let stand 4 minutes, cook 10 minutes longer. Let stand 10 minutes before serving.

Cooking Time Saved: 1 hour 30 minutes

Pudding is done when a knife inserted into center comes out clean. Serve warm or chilled. Makes 6 to 8 servings.

STEAMED CHOCOLATE PUDDING

2 tablespoons butter
or margarine
2 squares (2 ounces)
unsweetened chocolate
1 egg

1 cup sugar
1¾ cups flour
1 teaspoon salt
1 teaspoon baking powder
1 cup milk

Melt butter or margarine and chocolate over low heat (2 minutes in microwave). Beat egg with sugar, stir in chocolate. Toss flour with salt and baking powder, add alternately with milk.

Range
Fill greased 1-quart mold. Place mold in steamer or on rack in large pot over simmering water. Cover mold loosely with wax paper, cover steamer with lid. Steam 2 hours, until pudding is set.

Microwave
Fill greased 1-quart casserole, cover with wax paper, cook 6 minutes.

Cooking Time Saved: 1 hour 54 minutes.

Unmold, serve warm. Makes 8 servings.

PUDDING PUFFS

1 package instant pudding,
any flavor
2 cups milk
4 marshmallows

Prepare instant pudding as directed, fill 4 custard cups, chill thoroughly. Top each custard cup with a marshmallow.

Range
Set custard cups under broiler until marshmallows are puffed, about 6 to 8 minutes.

Microwave
Arrange custard cups on tray in microwave. Top each with a marshmallow, cook 30 seconds, until marshmallows are puffed.

Cooking Time Saved: about 5 minutes

Makes 4 servings.

RICE PUDDING

3 tablespoons rice, unwashed	¼ teaspoon salt
3 tablespoons sugar	1 teaspoon vanilla
1 quart milk	Cinnamon

Range

Combine rice, sugar, milk and salt in 6-cup baking dish. Bake at 325°F for about 2 hours, until rice is very soft, stirring every 15 minutes. Add vanilla, sprinkle with cinnamon, bake until a light golden crust forms, about 15 minutes longer.

Microwave

Combine all ingredients in 3-quart casserole, cook 45 minutes, stirring every 10 minutes, until rice is very soft. Add vanilla, sprinkle with cinnamon.

Cooking Time Saved: 1½ hours

Chill. Makes 4 servings.

POACHED ORANGES

6 oranges
1½ cups Sauterne
or other white wine
½ cup sugar
1 teaspoon cornstarch
1 tablespoon water

Sliver enough thinly peeled orange rind to make ¼ cup. Cover with boiling water, let stand. Peel fruit, discarding pith and membranes. Cut oranges into thick crosswise slices, reshape, fasten with wooden picks. Drain slivered orange rind.

Range

Bring wine, sugar and orange rind to a boil in a skillet, stirring until sugar dissolves. Simmer 10 minutes. Mix cornstarch with water, add to syrup, stir until sauce is clear and thickened. Add oranges, spoon sauce over fruit to glaze, simmer about 5 minutes, until heated through.

Microwave

Bring wine, sugar and orange rind to a boil in a covered 8-inch round cake dish, about 6 minutes. Mix cornstarch with water, add to syrup. Stir until sauce is clear and thickened. Arrange oranges in a ring around edge of pie plate, spoon sauce over fruit. Cover, cook 5 minutes. Let stand, covered 5 minutes, before serving.

Serve hot or cold. Makes 6 servings.

SAUCES
FOR
DESSERTS

HOT BLUEBERRY SAUCE

1½ cups frozen blueberries
¼ cup sugar
Pinch salt
⅛ teaspoon almond extract
2 teaspoons lemon juice

Range

Let frozen blueberries thaw slightly at room temperature. Combine with sugar and salt, crush coarsely with a fork. Bring to a boil in a heavy-bottomed small saucepan, simmer 5 minutes, stirring constantly. Add almond extract and lemon juice to taste.

Microwave

Mix berries, sugar and salt in 2-cup serving bowl. Cover, cook 5 minutes. Mash berries coarsely with a fork. Add almond extract and lemon juice to taste.

Makes about 1 cup sauce for plain cakes,
puddings or hot fruit desserts.

LEMON SAUCE

½ cup butter
or margarine
1 cup sugar
¼ cup water
Grated rind and
juice of 1 lemon
1 egg, beaten

Range

Combine butter or margarine, sugar, water, lemon rind and juice in heavy saucepan, bring to boil. Stir a little hot liquid into egg, return to pan and heat until thickened.

Microwave

Combine butter or margarine, sugar, water, lemon rind and juice in a glass serving dish. Heat 2 minutes, stir a little hot liquid into egg, return to pan, heat until thickened, about 1 minute.

Makes ⅓ cup sauce for plain cakes, puddings, fruit desserts. Serve hot or cold.

QUICK CARAMEL SAUCE

Range

Combine ½ pound caramels with ½ cup milk or cream in top of double boiler. Cook over boiling water, stirring frequently, until sauce is smooth.

Microwave

Combine ½ pound caramels with ½ cup milk or cream in a 1-quart casserole. Cook 3 minutes, until caramels melt. Stir to blend.

Makes 1 cup. Sauce for cakes, ice cream or custards.

Easy Caramel Frosting: Cream ½ cup butter or margarine. Add 1 pound sifted confectioners' sugar alternately with 1 cup cooled Quick Caramel Sauce and ½ teaspoon vanilla or rum-flavoring. Blend until frosting is smooth and creamy.

HOT FUDGE SAUCE

3 squares (3 ounces)
unsweetened chocolate
½ cup light cream or milk
¾ cup sugar

Dash salt
¼ cup butter or margarine
½ teaspoon vanilla flavoring

Range

Combine chocolate and cream in a small heavy saucepan, cook over low heat until chocolate melts, stirring often. Add sugar and salt, cook until sugar dissolves. Remove from heat.

Microwave

Combine chocolate and cream in a small serving bowl, cook uncovered, 3 minutes, until chocolate melts. Stir in sugar and salt, cook 1 minute longer.

Stir in butter or margarine and vanilla. Serve hot over ice cream. Makes about ½ cups.

CAKES
FOR
DESSERT

❧

CARROT CAKE

½ cup butter
or margarine
1 cup sugar
1 cup mashed cooked carrots
¼ cup orange juice
2 eggs, slightly beaten
2 cups flour

1 teaspoon baking soda
½ teaspoon nutmeg
1 teaspoon cinnamon
½ cup raisins
½ cup chopped nutmeats

Cream together butter or margarine and sugar.
Add carrots, orange juice and eggs; mix thoroughly.
Toss dry ingredients together and add gradually.
Stir in raisins and chopped nuts.

Range

Pour batter into 2 greased and
floured 8-inch round cake pans.
Bake at 350°F for 35 to 40 minutes.
Cool in pans 10 minutes before
removing to racks to finish cooling.

Microwave

Pour batter into two 8-inch round
cake pans lined with brown paper or
wax paper, cover top with paper
towel. Cook one layer at a time, 5
minutes. Rotate dish after 2½
minutes. Let stand in pans 5 minutes
before removing to racks to finish
cooling.

Cooking Time Saved: about 30
minutes

Frost with Cream Cheese Frosting (page 240).

BANANA LAYER CAKE

½ cup butter
or margarine
1½ cups sugar
2 eggs
1 teaspoon vanilla
½ teaspoon baking soda

¼ cup sour cream
2 cups flour
2 teaspoons baking powder
½ teaspoon salt
1½ cups mashed ripe bananas

Cream butter or margarine with sugar. Add eggs, one at a time, beating after each; add vanilla. Combine soda and sour cream, add to egg mixture. Toss together flour, baking powder and salt to mix, add alternately with bananas, blend well.

Range

Pour into 2 greased and floured 8-inch cake pans. Bake at 350°F, 30 to 35 minutes. Cool in pan 10 minutes, remove to racks.

Microwave

Cover bottom of two 8-inch glass layer cake dishes with brown paper or wax paper. Fill dishes, bake 1 layer at a time, about 6 minutes. Rotate dish ½ turn after 3 minutes. Cool in dish.

Cooking Time Saved: 12 to 18 minutes

ONE LAYER CHOCOLATE CAKE

1 cup flour
¾ teaspoon baking soda
¼ teaspoon salt
⅓ cup cocoa
⅓ cup butter or margarine

¾ cup sugar
2 eggs
1 teaspoon vanilla extract
⅓ cup buttermilk

Toss together flour, soda, salt and cocoa to mix. In large bowl, cream butter or margarine with sugar, beat in eggs and vanilla. Add dry ingredients alternately with buttermilk.

Range

Grease and flour an 8-inch round cake pan. Spread batter in pan, bake at 350°F for 35 to 40 minutes.

Microwave

Line an 8-inch glass layer cake dish with brown or wax paper. Spread batter in dish, cover with a paper towel. Cook 3 minutes, rotate pan ½ turn, cook 2 minutes longer.

Cooking Time Saved: about 35 minutes

GINGERBREAD

1¼ cups flour   ¼ cup sugar
¾ teaspoon baking soda   ¼ cup shortening
¼ teaspoon salt   1 egg
½ teaspoon cinnamon   ½ cup molasses
½ teaspoon ginger   ½ cup hot water
¼ teaspoon cloves

Measure all ingredients into mixing bowl, beat well.

Range

Turn batter into greased and floured 8-inch round cake pan. Bake at 350°F for 30 minutes.

Microwave

Turn batter into 8-inch round cake dish lined with brown or wax paper. Cook 6 minutes, rotating ¼ turn half-way through cooking.

Cooking Time Saved: about 25 minutes

Serve with whipped cream, applesauce or lemon sauce.

BRANDIED MINCEMEAT CAKE

1 package (18½ ounces)   2 eggs
spice cake mix   ¼ cup sugar
1 jar (1 pound 3 ounces) mincemeat   5 tablespoons water
4 tablespoons brandy

*To cake mix add mincemeat,
2 tablespoons brandy and eggs, beat well.*

Range

Turn into greased and floured 9-or 10-inch ring mold or bundt pan. Bake at 350°F for 1 hour 15 minutes, until cake tests done. Let stand on rack 5 minutes, unmold. Combine sugar and water in a small saucepan, bring to a boil, stir, boil 5 minutes.

Microwave

Turn batter into greased glass tube dish or glass bundt dish. Cook 5 minutes. Rotate dish ¼ turn, cook 5 minutes. Let stand 4 minutes, rotate dish ¼ turn, cook 5 minutes. Let stand 10 minutes. Unmold. Combine sugar and water in small bowl, cook 7 minutes.

Cooking Time Saved: 45 minutes

Add remaining 2 tablespoons brandy to syrup, pour over cake.

UPSIDE-DOWN CAKE

¼ cup melted butter or margarine
½ cup dark brown sugar
1 can (8 ounces)
sliced pineapple, drained
Maraschino cherries, walnut halves
¼ cup softened butter or margarine
¾ cup granulated sugar

1 teaspoon vanilla
2 eggs, beaten
1 cup flour
1½ teaspoons baking powder
½ teaspoon salt
½ cup milk

*Spread melted butter or margarine in an 8-inch layer
cake dish. (In the microwave, butter (or margarine) may be melted
directly in a glass layer cake dish, 1 minute). Sprinkle butter
with brown sugar. For microwave oven cook until sugar melts,
about 3 to 4 minutes. Arrange pineapple slices in a decorative
pattern on sugar, garnish with cherries and nuts. In large bowl,
cream softened butter or margarine (softening takes about 5 seconds in the microwave,
30 minutes or longer at room temperature)
with sugar until light and fluffy. Beat in vanilla and eggs.
Toss flour with baking powder and salt. Add to creamed mixture
alternately with milk, beating well after each addition.
Spread batter over fruit in cake dish.*

Range

Bake cake at 350°F for 30 to 35
minutes, until cake tests done.
Invert on serving platter
immediately.

Microwave

Cook 4 minutes, rotate dish ½ turn,
cook 4 minutes longer, until cake
tests done. Let stand 10 minutes.
Invert on serving platter.

Cooking Time Saved: about 25
minutes

APPLE UPSIDE-DOWN CAKE

*Substitute 2 apples, peeled and sliced, for
pineapple, cherries and nuts. Arrange fruit in
spiral pattern on brown sugar mixture in pan.
Sprinkle with cinnamon. Add batter, bake as directed.*

CHERRY UPSIDE-DOWN CAKE

*Substitute 1 can (16 ounces) sour pitted cherries,
drained, for pineapple. Substitute ½ teaspoon almond
extract for vanilla flavoring. Proceed as directed.*

SOUR CREAM STRAWBERRY SHORTCAKE

1 quart strawberries	1 egg
½ cup sugar	½ cup sour cream
2 cups biscuit mix	¼ cup water
¼ cup sugar	Sour cream or whipped cream for topping

*Wash, hull and slice strawberries, sprinkle with ½ cup sugar,
let stand 2 hours in refrigerator. Combine biscuit mix, ¼ cup sugar,
egg, sour cream and water. Knead briefly on a lightly floured board.
Roll out ½-inch thick. Cut into 3-inch circles or squares.*

Range	Microwave
Bake on ungreased baking sheet at 425°F for 10 to 15 minutes. Split cakes while still warm. .	Place shortcakes on wax paper, cook 2 minutes. Turn paper, cook 1 minute longer. Split cakes, toast, if desired. Cooking Time Saved: 7 to 12 minutes

*Fill and top with berries. Serve with sour cream or whipped cream, if desired.
Makes about 6 servings.*

PETITS FOURS

1 cup butter or margarine	2 cups flour
1 cup sugar	2 teaspoons baking powder
Juice and grated rind of ½ lemon	1 teaspoon baking soda
4 large eggs	1 teaspoon salt
	Nuts, candied violets or sliced berries, colored sugar for decoration

Cream butter or margarine, add sugar, cream until light and fluffy. Add lemon juice and rind. Beat in eggs, one at a time. Sift flour, baking powder, soda and salt over creamed mixture, fold in gently but thoroughly.

Range

Divide batter into 2 greased and floured 8-inch square baking pans. Bake at 350°F 20 to 25 minutes, until cake shrinks from the sides of the pan and a skewer inserted in the center comes out dry.

Microwave

Line the bottoms of two 8-inch square baking dishes with brown or wax paper. Divide batter into dishes. Cook, one cake at a time, 2 minutes. Rotate dish ¼ turn, cook 2 minutes longer or until a skewer inserted in the center comes out dry.

Cooking Time Saved: about 15 minutes

Cool cakes, cut into small 1- to 2-inch squares, diamonds, or circles. Place pieces on a rack over a pan. Sprinkle with 1 tablespoon rum or kirsch, if desired. Spoon icing (below) over tops and sides of cake pieces. Leftover icing may be stored in a covered jar, in the refrigerator. Decorate with nuts, candied violets or sliced berries and colored sugar to taste. Makes about 40 petits fours.

ICING FOR PETITS FOURS

1 pound confectioners' sugar	1 tablespoon rum, kirsch, or Grand Marnier
3 tablespoons corn syrup	Food coloring (optional)
3 tablespoons water	

Range

Combine ingredients except coloring in the top of a double boiler. Heat over simmering water until icing is of pouring consistencey. Add coloring to taste, and ice cakes immediately.

Microwave

Combine ingredients except coloring in a glass bowl. Heat in microwave 35 to 40 seconds or until icing is of pouring consistency. Add coloring to taste. If frosting becomes too thick, reheat 10 seconds in microwave.

Makes icing for about 40 petit fours.

EASY BUNDT CAKE

*Add to any yellow or white cake mix, 4 eggs,
1 cup liquid (wine, orange juice, milk, coffee
or water), ¼ cup oil, 1 package instant pudding
(a compatible flavor) and ½ cup chopped nuts.*

Range

Bake in a greased and floured tube pan, in 350°F oven, 1 hour.

Microwave

Bake in an ungreased glass tube pan, 12 to 14 minutes.

Cooking Time Saved: about 42 to 48 minutes

FROSTINGS
FOR
CAKES

BUTTER CREAM FROSTING

½ cup butter or
margarine, softened
1 box (1 pound)
confectioners' sugar, sifted
Dash salt
1 teaspoon vanilla
5 tablespoons milk

*Soften butter, 1 hour at room temperature, 15 seconds in
microwave. Cream thoroughly, gradually work in sugar and salt.
Add flavoring and milk to make a mixture of spreading
consistency. Beat until fluffy. To vary the butter cream frosting,
use orange juice, favorite liqueur or strong brewed coffee
instead of vanilla and milk, or add melted chocolate, to taste.*

CREAM CHEESE FROSTING

1 package (3 ounces) cream cheese
3 tablespoons orange juice
1 tablespoon grated orange rind
3 cups confectioners' sugar

*Soften cream cheese 10 seconds in microwave, 1 hour
at room temperature. Blend cream cheese with juice,
orange rind and confectioners' sugar. Use to frost two
8-inch layers or one 13- by 9-inch sheet cake.*

EASY CHOCOLATE FROSTING

1 package (6 ounces) chocolate chips
3 tablespoons milk or cream
2 tablespoons butter or margarine
1 cup confectioners' sugar

Range

Combine chocolate chips, milk and butter or margarine in saucepan. Stir over low heat until chocolate melts. Remove from heat.

Microwave

Place chocolate chips, milk and butter or margarine in small glass bowl. Melt in microwave 30 to 40 seconds, stirring twice

Beat in sugar until smooth. Add a few drops of water to bring to spreading consistency. Makes enough for a single 8- or 9-inch layer.

HUNGARIAN CHOCOLATE FROSTING

4 squares (1 ounce each) unsweetened chocolate
¼ cup hot water
2½ cups confectioners' sugar
1 egg
6 tablespoons butter or margarine, softened

Range

Melt chocolate over low heat in heavy pan, or over boiling water, stirring occasionally.

Microwave

Place chocolate in glass mixing bowl, cover, heat 3 minutes, until chocolate melts, stir.

Beat in remaining ingredients gradually. Beat until smooth. Makes 2½ cups.

241

WAIST WATCHERS
(OR HOW TO LIKE WHAT YOU EAT EVEN IF IT ISN'T FATTENING)

In this age of streamlined life styles and bodies to match, there is always someone you know (maybe you) who is on a diet. Waist watching does not have to be dull, boring or fast-like. Waist watching can be quite wonderful if you have some good recipes to get you through.

And that's what this section is all about.

In this section, as in all sections of the book, directions are given for both conventional and microwave cooking.

WAIST WATCHERS

VEGETABLES AND SAUCES

DESSERTS

SOUPS AND
APPETIZERS
AND SNACKS

ASPARAGUS SOUP

2 cups boiling water
2 chicken bouillon cubes
3 cups fresh or frozen asparagus, cut up
1 small onion, chopped

1 cup cottage cheese
½ cup skim milk
½ teaspoon cloves
Salt, white pepper

Range
In a heavy 2-quart saucepan, combine hot water, bouillon cubes, asparagus and onion. Cover, cook over moderate heat 15 minutes, until asparagus is very tender.

Microwave
In a 2-quart casserole, combine water, bouillon cubes, asparagus and onions. Cover, cook 6 minutes, until asparagus is tender.

Cooking Time Saved: 9 minutes

Cool soup. Force through a sieve or food mill with cottage cheese. Add skim milk and spices. Serve hot or chilled. Makes 4 servings.

HERBED BROTH

1 cup broth (beef, chicken, or vegetable)
1 tablespoon, chopped fresh parsley
1 tablespoon, chopped chives
Dash of thyme
Grated Cheddar, Swiss, or Parmesan cheese

Range
Combine all ingredients except cheese in a small saucepan, bring to a boil, simmer 5 minutes.

Microwave
Combine all ingredients except cheese in a soup bowl. Cook 3 minutes.

*Sprinkle with grated cheese if desired.
Makes 1 serving.*

LEMON YOGURT SOUP

2 egg yolks
Juice of ½ lemon
1 teaspoon cold water
½ cup chicken broth
Salt, white pepper
1 cup plain yogurt

Beat egg yolks until light. Beat in lemon juice and cold water.

Range	Microwave
Bring chicken broth to a boil in a heavy 1-quart saucepan. Remove from heat.	Cook chicken broth in a 2-cup glass measuring cup 2 minutes, until boiling.

Blend 2 tablespoons of hot chicken broth into egg mixture.
Cool broth and combine with egg mixture, seasonings to taste, add yogurt.
Serve well chilled. Makes 2 servings.

JELLIED LEMON CONSOMME

4 cups water   ¼ cup sherry
4 chicken bouillon cubes   1 lemon
1 envelope gelatin   Paprika

Range	Microwave
Bring ½ cup water to a boil, dissolve bouillon cubes. Add remaining water. Sprinkle gelatin on sherry in a cup, let stand 3 minutes. Place cup in a pan of hot water, stir over moderate heat until gelatin dissolves, about 6 minutes. Add to bouillon.	Put bouillon cubes, ½ cup water in cup. Put sherry and gelatin in another cup. Cook cups simultaneously 1 minute, stir to dissolve cubes and gelatin; combine, add remaining water.

Cut lemon in half. Squeeze juice from one half. Add to bouillon, chill until softly set. Stir with a fork, spoon into bouillon cups.
Cut remaining half of lemon into 6 thin slices, top each serving with a lemon slice, sprinkle with paprika. Makes 6 servings.

SPINACH EGG DROP SOUP

1 cup chicken broth
1 teaspoon soy sauce
¼ cup fresh spinach or escarole leaves, washed and trimmed
Dash ginger
1 egg white

Range	Microwave
Bring broth and soy sauce to boil in small saucepan. Add spinach and ginger, simmer 1 minute. Add egg white, stir gently until egg is set. Pour into soup bowl.	Heat broth and soy sauce in soup bowl 1½ minutes, until steaming. Add spinach and ginger, cook 1 minute. Add egg white, stir until set.

Makes 1 serving.

CRUSTLESS PIZZA

2 large ripe tomatoes, peeled and cut in ½-inch slices
2 cloves garlic, minced
1 small onion, cut in rings
¼ teaspoon each oregano and basil

Salt and pepper to taste
6 ounces low-fat mozzarella cheese, sliced
¼ cup black olives, cut in thin rounds (optional)
6 anchovy fillets (optional)

Arrange tomato slices in the bottom of an 8-inch square baking pan. Top with garlic and onion rings. Sprinkle with seasonings and top with slices of mozzarella cheese. If desired, top with olives and decorate with anchovy fillets.

Range	Microwave
Cook at 400°F for 20 minutes, until cheese is melted and tomatoes are cooked.	Cook, uncovered, for 5 minutes. Rotate dish ¼ turn, cook 2 to 3 minutes more, until cheese is melted and tomatoes are cooked.

Cooking Time Saved: 10 minutes

Cool slightly and cut into serving portions.
Makes 4 servings.

LOW-CALORIE SCRAMBLED EGGS

1 egg
1 egg white
1 tablespoon water or skim milk
Salt and pepper
1 teaspoon butter or margarine

Beat egg, egg white and water with seasonings.

Range
Heat butter or margarine in a small skillet. Pour egg mixture into skillet, cook, stirring with fork, until set, about 2 minutes. Turn onto serving plate.

Microwave
Grease a shallow plate with butter or margarine. Add egg mixture to plate, cook 30 seconds. Stir, cook 30 seconds longer. Stir. Cook 30 seconds or until set.

Makes 1 serving.

RICOTTA TOAST

1 thin slice whole wheat toast
¼ cup skim milk ricotta or dry cottage cheese

⅛ teaspoon cinnamon
1 teaspoon honey (optional)
¼ cup blueberries or sliced strawberries

Combine ricotta, cinnamon and honey, spread on toast. Top with berries.

Range
Cook under broiler until hot.

Microwave
Cook 45 seconds, until hot.

Makes 1 serving.

SPICY TOMATO COCKTAIL

1 cup tomato juice
1 teaspoon lemon or lime juice
¼ teaspoon celery salt

½ teaspoon horseradish or
3 drops hot pepper sauce
Dash Worcestershire sauce

Range
Combine ingredients in a 1-quart saucepan. Bring to a boil, cover, simmer over low heat 5 minutes. Pour into mug.

Microwave
Mix ingredients in serving glass or mug. Cook 3 minutes, until steaming hot.

Makes 1 serving.

ENTRÉES

FISH TURBANS FLORENTINE

1 package (10 ounces) frozen spinach
1 tablespoon oil
½ medium onion, minced
1 egg
¼ cup skim milk ricotta cheese

½ teaspoon sugar or sugar substitute
¼ teaspoon nutmeg
Salt, pepper to taste
4 fillets of white-fleshed fish
(6 to 8 ounces each)
½ cup clam juice or water

Defrost spinach (1 hour at room temperature or 4 minutes in the microwave). Drain thoroughly.

Range

In a heavy pan, heat oil, sauté onion until wilted. Add the drained spinach and stir over moderate heat until moisture evaporates. Remove pan from heat.

Microwave

Combine spinach, oil and onion in a 1-quart baking dish, cover, cook 3 minutes.

Combine spinach with egg, ricotta, sugar and seasoning. Put ¼ cup spinach mixture on each fish fillet, roll up, secure with wooden toothpicks. Arrange seam side down in a ring on a 9- or 10-inch pie plate. Cover with clam juice or water.

Range

Bake at 375°F for 12 minutes, basting occasionally, until fish is opaque and flakes readily with a fork.

Microwave

Cook 3 minutes, rotate plate ½ turn, baste fish with pan juices. Cook 3 minutes longer, until fish is opaque and flakes readily with a fork.

Makes 4 servings.

FISH FILLETS

4 green onions, sliced
2 cups sliced fresh mushrooms
2 tablespoons water
2 tablespoons lemon juice

Salt, pepper
1 pound fish fillets
1 tomato, cut in wedges

Range

In saucepan, cook green onions and mushrooms until tender in water seasoned with lemon juice, salt and pepper to taste. Fold fish fillets in thirds, place in shallow baking dish, add onions, mushrooms and their liquid, arrange tomato wedges in dish. Bake at 350°F for 15 minutes, until fish flakes easily with a fork.

Microwave

On a large serving platter, combine onions, mushrooms, water, lemon juice, and salt and pepper to taste. Cover, cook 5 minutes, or until vegetables are tender. Fold fish fillets in thirds, place on dish, spoon vegetables over fillets and cover with wax paper. Cook 2 minutes, add tomato wedges, cook 2 minutes longer, or until fish flakes easily with a fork.

Makes 2 to 3 servings.

FISH STEW

¾ cup chopped onions
½ cup chopped celery
2 cloves garlic
2 small tomatoes, quartered
1 cup tomato juice
2 cups clam juice or fish stock
¼ teaspoon cayenne

¼ teaspoon allspice
¼ teaspoon saffron
1 bay leaf
½ pound sea bass, cod or red snapper
½ cup sole, cubed
½ cup scallops
1 cup shelled mussels or oysters (fresh or canned)

Range

In a 3-quart stew pan combine all ingredients except sole, scallops and mussels, cover, simmer over low heat 45 minutes, remove bones. Puree the stock in a blender or force through a food mill. Adjust seasonings, add remaining ingredients, return to boil, simmer 2 minutes, until cooked.

Microwave

In a 3-quart covered casserole combine all ingredients except sole, scallops and mussels, cook 15 minutes, remove bones. Puree the stock in a blender or force it through a food mill. Adjust seasonings, add remaining ingredients, return to boil, cook 1 minute. Let stand 5 minutes before serving.

Cooking Time Saved: 30 minutes

Makes 4 servings.

STIR-FRIED BEAN SPROUTS AND TUNA

1 pound fresh bean sprouts, or
1 can (1 pound), drained
1 can (6 or 7 ounces)
water-packed tuna fish

1 tablespoon soy sauce
¼ cup chicken stock
1 teaspoon cornstarch
1 tablespoon sherry (optional)

Pour boiling water over fresh bean sprouts to cover, drain. Or drain canned sprouts.

Range

In a wok or skillet, stir sprouts and tuna over high heat. Mix soy sauce, chicken stock, cornstarch and sherry. Stir into wok or skillet. Cook until sauce is clear.

Microwave

Combine all ingredients in an 8-inch square glass baking dish, cover, cook 3 minutes. Stir, cover, cook 2 minutes, until sauce is clear.

Makes 3 to 4 servings.

MIZUTAKI

3 cups hot chicken broth
2 carrots, peeled and cut in strips
4 stalks celery, cut in strips
12 mushrooms, cut in half
2 cups fresh spinach, tightly packed

Salt, pepper, ginger to taste
1 whole chicken breast, cut in thin strips
8 medium large shrimp, peeled and deveined

Range

Bring chicken broth to a boil in a 3-quart saucepan. Add carrots and celery, cook 15 minutes. Add mushrooms, spinach and seasonings to taste, simmer 2 minutes. Add chicken and shrimp, cook 2 minutes.

Microwave

Combine all ingredients except spinach, chicken and shrimp in a 3-quart casserole. Cover, cook 8 minutes. Add remaining ingredients, cook about 2 minutes. Let stand, covered, 4 minutes.

Serve in soup bowls with forks or chop sticks and Mizutaki Sauce for dipping.
Makes 4 servings.

MIZUTAKI DIPPING SAUCE

¼ cup soy sauce
¼ cup lime or lemon juice

Blend soy sauce and lemon juice, serve as dipping sauce with Mizutaki.

LEMON CHICKEN

2 whole chicken breasts
1 lemon, peeled and seeded
½ slice dry white bread
2 tablespoons sherry

2 tablespoons sour cream
Worcestershire sauce
Salt, pepper, paprika

Split chicken breasts, discard skin and bones. Whirl lemon, bread, sherry, sour cream, Worcestershire sauce, salt and pepper in a blender. Arrange chicken breasts in an 8-inch square baking dish. Top with lemon mixture, sprinkle with paprika.

Range
Bake at 375°F for 40 minutes, until chicken is tender and the juices run clear when pierced with a fork.

Microwave
Cook, uncovered, 10 minutes, rotating dish ½ turn every 2 minutes, until chicken is tender and juices run clear when pierced with a fork. Let stand 5 minutes before serving.

Cooking Time Saved: 30 minutes

Makes 4 servings.

CHINESE STYLE CHICKEN LIVERS

1 pound chicken livers
¼ cup sherry
2 tablespoons soy sauce
2 tablespoons oil
½ cup bamboo shoots, sliced thin

½ cup sliced water chestnuts
1 chicken bouillon cube
½ cup water
1 teaspoon sugar
2 scallions, shredded

Wash and dry chicken livers, marinate in sherry and soy sauce for 5 minutes. Drain, reserve marinade.

Range
Heat oil in a wok or large skillet, add livers, cook, stirring, 2 minutes or until livers lose their pink color. Add marinade, bamboo shoots and water chestnuts. Cook, stirring, until hot. Add chicken bouillon cube, water and sugar, cook 2 minutes more. Transfer to serving dish.

Microwave
Cook livers in oil in a 9-inch serving dish 2 minutes, rotate dish ½ turn and stir. Cook 2 minutes longer. Add marinade, bamboo shoots and water chestnuts. Stir, cook 2 minutes. Add bouillon cube, water and sugar. Cook 2 minutes longer.

Before serving sprinkle with scallions.
Makes 3 to 4 servings.

LOW-CALORIE CHICKEN CACCIATORE

2 chicken breasts, split and skinned
1 teaspoon salt
¼ teaspoon pepper
1 clove garlic

1 onion, chopped
1 green pepper, slivered
1 can (1 pound) tomatoes
½ teaspoon mixed Italian herbs

Range

Arrange chicken breasts in heavy skillet, cover with remaining ingredients, bring to a boil. Lower heat, cover and simmer about 50 minutes, until chicken is tender. Adjust seasoning with more salt, pepper and herbs, to taste.

Microwave

Arrange chicken breasts in baking dish. Add remaining ingredients, cook, uncovered, until steaming hot, 10 minutes. Spoon sauce over chicken, rotate dish ½ turn. Cover, cook 10 minutes, until chicken is tender. Adjust seasoning, baste with sauce, let stand 5 minutes before serving.

Cooking Time Saved: 30 minutes

Makes 4 servings.

QUICK CURRY

2 teaspoons oil
1 medium cooking apple, peeled, cored and diced
1 medium onion, chopped
1 tablespoon curry powder

Salt, cayenne pepper to taste
½ cup chicken broth or water
½ cup yogurt
1 pound cooked turkey, chicken or veal, cut in slices

Range

In a heavy skillet heat oil, sauté apple and onion until soft, about 10 minutes. Sprinkle with curry powder, stir, cook 2 minutes. Add spices and chicken broth, cook 15 minutes over moderate heat. Stir in yogurt. Add cooked meat to sauce, cover and simmer until hot, transfer to serving platter.

Microwave

Cook apple and onion in oil in a 1-quart casserole, covered, 4 minutes, until onion is soft. Stir in curry powder, cover, cook 4 minutes. Add spices and chicken broth, cover, cook 3 minutes. Stir in yogurt. Arrange cooked meat on sauce, cover, cook 1 minute or until hot.

Cooking Time Saved: 16 minutes

Makes 3 to 4 servings.

BARBECUED TURKEY ROLL

1 white-meat turkey roll, 3 pounds
1 can (6 ounces) tomato puree
¼ cup lemon juice
2 tablespoons prepared mustard

2 tablespoons brown sugar or
equivalent sugar substitute
1 teaspoon instant minced onion
1 teaspoon garlic salt
Salt, pepper to taste

Defrost turkey roll (2 hours at room temperature or 8 minutes in microwave).
Mix remaining ingredients to make barbecue sauce.
Marinate turkey roll in sauce 1 hour at room temperature.

Range

Arrange turkey roll in a small roasting pan, add marinade. Cover, cook at 325°F for 1½ hours. Baste turkey with sauce, continue to roast uncovered until juices run clear when turkey is pierced with a fork, and the internal temperature reaches 175°F.

Microwave

Place turkey roll on a 9- or 10-inch pie dish, add sauce, cover loosely. Cook 10 minutes. Baste with drippings, cook 10 minutes more. Baste with drippings, let stand 5 minutes. Cook 10 minutes longer, until juices run clear when turkey is pierced with a fork, and internal temperature reaches 155°F. Let stand, covered, 10 minutes to finish cooking. Temperature will rise to 175°F.

Cooking Time Saved: about 1 hour

Makes 8 to 10 servings.

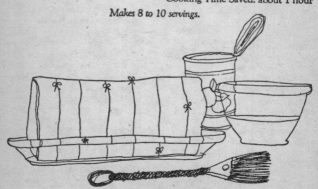

VEAL AND SPINACH JAPANESE

1 tablespoon oil
3 ounces thinly sliced boneless veal,
cut into strips
2 cups fresh spinach (tightly packed)
1 chicken bouillon cube
⅛ teaspoon ginger

2 drops hot pepper sauce
1 tablespoon soy sauce
¼ cup hot water
¼ cup water chestnuts,
sliced (optional)

Range

Heat oil in a heavy saucepan or
wok. Quickly stir-fry veal, about 1
minute. Add spinach and stir-fry
until just wilted. Stir in remaining
ingredients and cook until liquid
boils.

Microwave

Heat oil in a 1-quart casserole for 3 to
4 minutes. Stir in veal and spinach,
cook 2 minutes. Add remaining
ingredients, cook 2 minutes, until
liquid boils.

Makes 1 serving.

LIVER WITH ONIONS

2 small onions, sliced thin
½ cup hot beef broth
1 pound beef liver or chicken livers, sliced into bite-size pieces
½ teaspoon garlic powder

Range

Simmer onions and broth in a
2-quart saucepan, 5 minutes. Add
liver pieces and garlic. Cook, stirring
occasionally, just until liver loses its
pink color. Add more water if
necessary to prevent burning.

Microwave

Cook onions and broth in a covered
2-quart casserole, 5 minutes. Add
liver pieces and garlic powder, cook 2
minutes, stir, cook until liver loses its
pink color.

Be careful not to overcook. Makes 3 to 4 servings.

QUICK BEEF STEW

1 pound round steak	1 cup sliced mushrooms
1 tablespoon oil	1 cup sliced celery
1 clove garlic	1 teaspoon dry instant broth
½ bay leaf	Salt, pepper, paprika
½ cup red wine	

Have round steak cut ¼-inch thick; pound meat with a mallet or rolling pin to flatten, cut into uniform strips.

Range

Cook meat strips in oil over high heat just to brown. Add garlic clove stuck on a wooden toothpick for easy removal. Add remaining ingredients, bring to a boil. Cover, simmer about 30 minutes, until beef is tender.

Microwave

Preheat oil in 1½-quart casserole, 2 minutes. Add remaining ingredients. Cover, cook 3 minutes, stir, cook 3 minutes longer.

Cooking Time Saved: 24 minutes

Before serving discard garlic and bay leaf. Makes 3 to 4 servings.

BARBECUED BEEF

1 pound ground beef	1 cup tomato sauce
1 green pepper, chopped	2 tablespoons vinegar
1 medium onion, chopped	Salt, pepper, cayenne
2 cloves garlic, minced	Worcestershire to taste

Range

Brown beef in a heavy skillet, stirring with a fork. Drain off fat. Add remaining ingredients, bring to a boil. Cover, reduce heat, simmer 45 minutes. Adjust seasoning.

Microwave

Cook meat, covered, in 1½-quart casserole about 2 minutes, stir with fork, cook 1 to 2 minutes longer, until meat loses its pink color. Drain off fat. Add remaining ingredients and cook, uncovered, 15 minutes, stirring every 5 minutes during cooking time.

Cooking Time Saved: 30 minutes

Makes 4 servings.

STUFFED EGGPLANT

1 medium eggplant	½ teaspoon parsley
1 small onion, chopped	Salt, pepper
1 tomato, peeled and chopped	1 cup cooked chicken, cubed
2 cloves garlic, minced	1 tablespoon Parmesan cheese
½ teaspoon oregano	Paprika

Cut eggplant in half lengthwise.

Range

Arrange eggplant halves on a baking sheet, 1 inch apart, cook at 400°F for about 20 minutes, until flesh is very tender.

Microwave

Arrange eggplant halves on tray, 1 inch apart, cook 2 minutes, rotate dish ½ turn. Cook 2 to 3 minutes longer, until flesh is very tender.

Scoop out flesh, being careful not to damage the skin. Chop flesh with onion, tomato, garlic and seasonings to taste. Add chicken or ham. Fill eggplant shells, sprinkle with grated Parmesan cheese.

Range

Bake on a lightly oiled baking sheet, at 375°F for 20 minutes, until topping is browned.

Microwave

Arrange filled halves on an 8-inch pie plate, cover, cook 3 to 4 minutes, until topping is hot and melted.

Cooking Time Saved: about 35 minutes

Sprinkle with paprika before serving. Makes 2 servings.

MEATY HOT SLAW

1 medium head cabbage, shredded	2 cups slivered cooked chicken,
1 cup Low-Calorie Salad Dressing (page 265)	turkey, veal, ham or lamb

Range

Place shredded cabbage in a saucepan. Cover with hot Low Calorie Salad Dressing, add chicken or alternate choice, stir over moderate heat until slaw is piping hot.

Microwave

Combine shredded cabbage, hot Low Calorie Salad Dressing and chicken or alternate choice in a large glass serving bowl. Cook, uncovered, 2 minutes. Stir, cook 4 minutes, until slaw is piping hot.

Cooking Time Saved: 5 minutes

Makes 4 to 6 servings.

JAPANESE BEEF AND MUSHROOMS

1½ pounds flank steak
2 cups mushroom slices
1 tablespoon oil
¼ cup soy sauce
½ cup pineapple juice

2 cloves garlic, minced
½ teaspoon ginger
¼ teaspoon pepper
½ teaspoon dry mustard

Slice steak on the diagonal, across the grain, ¼-inch thick.

Range

In a heavy 1½-quart casserole heat oil and sauté mushroom slices until lightly browned. Add remaining ingredients, except meat, and bring to a boil. Add meat and simmer 2 minutes.

Microwave

Combine all ingredients except meat in a 1½-quart greased casserole. Cook 6 minutes. Stir in meat, cook 2 minutes. Stir and cook 2 minutes longer until meat loses its pink color.

Serve immediately. Makes 3 to 4 servings.

GREAT VEGETABLES AND SAUCES

LOW-CALORIE BROCCOLI MEDLEY

2 tablespoons water
1 package (10 ounces)
frozen broccoli spears
1 bay leaf, crumbled
Salt, pepper
4 small boiled onions
1 tomato, cut into wedges

Range

Combine broccoli, bay leaf and water in a 1-quart casserole with salt and pepper to taste. Cover, simmer 10 minutes. Add onions, stir. Top with tomato wedges. Cover, cook 5 minutes longer.

Microwave

Combine broccoli, bay leaf and water in a 1-quart casserole with salt and pepper to taste. Cover, cook 5 minutes. Stir, add onions, top with tomato wedges. Cover, cook 5 minutes.

Makes 4 servings.

BRAISED LETTUCE

1 large head iceberg lettuce
2 tablespoons butter or margarine
1 small onion, diced
6 cups boiling beef broth
Salt, pepper to taste

Cut iceberg lettuce in quarters.

Range

Heat butter or margarine in a deep 3-quart casserole or Dutch oven. Sauté onions until lightly browned. Add lettuce, continue cooking until outer leaves are wilted. Add hot beef broth to cover, adjust lid tightly, braise in a 350°F oven 45 minutes or until leaves are very tender.

Microwave

In a 3-quart casserole, melt butter or margarine. Add onions and cook, covered, until soft, about 4 minutes. Add lettuce and hot beef broth. Cover, cook 10 minutes, until lettuce is very tender.

Cooking Time Saved: about 35 minutes

Season with salt and pepper. Arrange lettuce on serving plate and moisten with braising liquid. Freeze enriched broth for future use in soups, stews or casseroles. Makes 4 servings.

EASY DILL AND MUSTARD PICKLED VEGETABLES

1 pound carrot sticks, cauliflower or celery
3 tablespoons vinegar
1 cup hot water
1 teaspoon dried dill

4 cloves garlic
1 teaspoon pickling spice
1 tablespoon salt
1 teaspoon dry mustard powder
1 teaspoon sugar or sugar substitute

Range

Cook vegetables in boiling water to cover, 10-12 minutes, until tender-crisp. Drain. Bring vinegar and hot water to a boil with remaining ingredients. Pack vegetables into hot sterilized jars. Cover with boiling vinegar mixture.

Microwave

Combine all ingredients in a 2-quart covered casserole. Cook until vegetables are tender-crisp. Pack vegetables into hot, sterilized jars. Cover with the boiling cooking liquid.

Seal. Refrigerate and let stand several days or a week before using. Makes 1 quart.

ZUCCHINI VICHYSSOISE

2 cups zucchini, unpeeled, sliced thin
¼ cup minced leeks or yellow onions
1 tablespoon oil, butter or margarine
Salt, white pepper

1 teaspoon lemon juice
1 cup skim milk
2 cups chicken broth
Chives, chopped (optional)

Range

In a heavy 2-quart casserole, sauté zucchini and leeks in oil, until wilted but not browned (about 12 minutes over moderate heat). Stir in remaining ingredients. Simmer, stirring occasionally, 25 minutes.

Microwave

Cook zucchini, onions and oil in a 2-quart covered casserole 8 minutes, stirring every 2 minutes, until wilted but not browned. Add remaining ingredients, cover, cook 10 minutes, stirring every 2 minutes.

Cooking Time Saved: 19 minutes

Cool, force through a food mill, or whirl in an electric blender. Refrigerate and serve well chilled. Garnish with chopped chives, if desired. Makes 4 servings.

LOW-CALORIE BARBECUE SAUCE

½ cup water
½ cup vinegar
1 tablespoon Worcestershire sauce
¼ teaspoon cayenne pepper
½ teaspoon dry mustard
Hot pepper sauce to taste

2 teaspoons sugar
1 clove garlic, minced
½ onion, minced
1 cup tomato juice
1 tablespoon cornstarch

Range

Combine ingredients in a saucepan, bring slowly to a boil, simmer 5 minutes, stirring often.

Microwave

Combine all ingredients except tomato juice and cornstarch in a 4-cup measuring cup. Cook 5 minutes, until steaming hot. Stir in tomato juice and cornstarch, cook 2 to 3 minutes, until thickened.

Use as a marinade or sauce for meats, fish and poultry. Makes 2 cups.

GREEN SAUCE FOR SEAFOOD

1 onion, minced
1 tablespoon oil
½ cup boiling water
¼ cup dry white wine
¼ teaspoon instant chicken bouillon

1 cup minced fresh parsley, or parsley mixed with dill, basil, chives
Pinches saffron powder and cayenne
Salt

Range

In saucepan, simmer onion in oil until soft, about 5 minutes. Add remaining ingredients, bring to a boil, reduce heat, simmer 5 minutes.

Microwave

Cook onion in oil in a serving bowl, 3 minutes. Add remaining ingredients, stir, cover, cook 2 minutes, until sauce is hot.

Cooking Time Saved: 5 minutes

Put through a sieve, or whirl in an electric blender. Refrigerate and serve cold with shellfish or other seafood. Makes 1 cup.

LOW-CALORIE HOLLANDAISE

1 cup water
2 teaspoons cornstarch
⅓ cup nonfat dry milk solids
2 egg yolks
½ teaspoon dry mustard
1 teaspoon salt
3 tablespoons lemon juice

Combine ingredients, except lemon juice, in an electric blender, cover, blend 10 seconds, until smooth. Or beat well.

Range

Pour mixture into the top of a double boiler. Cook over hot water, stirring constantly, until sauce is hot and thick.

Microwave

Pour mixture into deep 2-cup serving bowl or 2-cup glass measure. Cook 1½ minutes, stir, cook 1 to 2 minutes longer, until thickened.

Stir in lemon juice. Makes about 1½ cups.

LOW-CALORIE SALAD DRESSING

2 tablespoons cornstarch
1¼ cups water
½ cup cider vinegar
1 teaspoon celery seeds

1 teaspoon paprika
½ teaspoon dry mustard
½ teaspoon garlic salt

Range

In a saucepan, stir cornstarch with 2 tablespoons water until smooth. Gradually add remaining ingredients. Stir over moderate heat until dressing is thickened and smooth. Pour into a jar, cover.

Microwave

In a 2-cup jar, stir cornstarch with 2 tablespoons water until smooth. Add remaining ingredients, stir. Cook 6 minutes, stirring every 2 minutes, until sauce is thick and smooth. Cover with lid.

Store in refrigerator. Makes 2 cups dressing.

DESSERTS

SPIRIT OF '76

4 red apples
1 cup diet ginger ale
1 cup cottage cheese
1 cup fresh blueberries
(or Concord grapes or pitted canned plums)

Wash and core apples, cut in half. Place cut side down in a large baking dish, add ginger ale to pan.

Range

Bake at 350°F for about 30 minutes, until apples are tender, basting frequently with the cooking liquid.

Microwave

Cover with wax paper, cook 4 minutes, baste fruit with the cooking liquid, rotate dish ½ turn, cook 3 to 4 minutes longer, until apples are tender.

Cooking Time Saved: 22 minutes*

Chill apples in liquid, arrange on serving plate. Divide cottage cheese onto apple halves, top with blueberries. Makes 8 servings.

Note: Exact cooking time will depend on size and variety of apples.

MARMALADE SOUFFLÉ

2 egg whites
1 tablespoon sugar
½ tablespoon lemon juice
1½ tablespoons marmalade

Beat egg whites until frothy, gradually add sugar and lemon juice, and beat until very stiff. Fold in marmalade.

Range

Spoon mixture into the greased top of a small double boiler. Cover. Cook over hot water until soufflé **is well puffed, about 20 minutes.**

Microwave

Spoon mixture into two ungreased 6-ounce glass custard cups. Place cups in a dish of hot water. Cook 4 minutes, until soufflés are well puffed.

Cooking Time Saved: 16 minutes

Serve at once. Makes 2 servings.

POACHED PEACHES

4 medium peaches
1 can (12 ounces) diet raspberry or lemon-lime soda

Plunge peaches into boiling water to loosen skins. Peel, cut in half, discarding pits.

Range

Combine peach halves and diet soda in a 1½-quart saucepan, cover, simmer about 15 minutes, until peaches are tender.

Microwave

Combine peach halves and diet soda in a 1½-quart serving bowl. Cover, cook until peaches are tender, about 8 minutes. Stir halfway through cooking time.

Cooking Time Saved: about 7 minutes

Serve hot or cold. Makes 4 servings.

LOW-CALORIE COFFEE SPONGE

1 envelope unflavored gelatin
1¼ cups water
1 teaspoon instant coffee
4 tablespoons sugar

3 eggs, separated
½ cup yogurt
Dash of salt

Range

In the top of a double boiler over simmering water, combine gelatin, water, instant coffee, 2 tablespoons sugar, and egg yolks. Cook, stirring with a whisk, until gelatin is dissolved.

Microwave

Soften gelatin in water in a measuring cup. Add instant coffee and 2 tablespoons sugar, Cook 3 minutes, until gelatin dissolves. Beat egg yolks, warm with a little hot gelatin mixture, and combine.

Cool until syrupy. Stir in yogurt. Beat egg whites with salt until stiff, gradually beat in remaining sugar. Fold into coffee mixture. Refrigerate. Chill in a glass serving bowl or 4 individual goblets until set. Makes 4 servings.

LOW-CALORIE CHEESECAKE

2 envelopes unflavored gelatin
10 tablespoons sugar
¼ teaspoon salt
1½ cups skim milk
3 eggs, separated

3 cups creamed cottage cheese
1 teaspoon grated lemon rind
1 tablespoon lemon juice
1 teaspoon vanilla or 1 ounce dark rum

Range

Mix gelatin, 6 tablespoons sugar, salt, skim milk and egg yolks in the top of a double boiler. Place over boiling water and cook, stirring, until gelatin dissolves and mixture thickens slightly, about 6 minutes. Cool.

Microwave

Cook gelatin, 6 tablespoons sugar, salt and milk in a 2-quart covered casserole 4 minutes, until gelatin dissolves and mixture is hot. Stir egg yolks into hot mixture. Cool.

Beat cottage cheese in a mixer on high speed for 3 to 4 minutes. Beat in lemon rind, lemon juice and flavoring. Stir into cooled milk mixture. Beat egg whites until they hold their shape. Gradually add 4 tablespoons sugar, beat until very stiff. Fold into milk mixture. Pour into an 8-inch spring-form pan. Chill until firm, unmold. Makes 8 servings.

JUST FOR
THE FUN OF IT
(BREAD MAKING, CANDY MAKING,
INSTRUCTIONS ON DRYING FLOWERS
AND OTHER HAPPY STUFF)

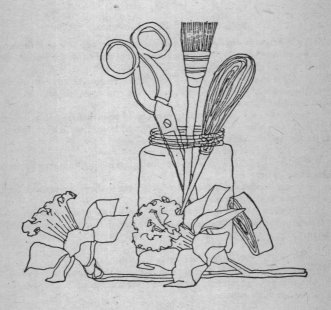

Cooking is no longer a chore; it is now a shared experience. And when we bake we do share the satisfaction of creation.

We have some interesting bread recipes that are made even simpler when you have a microwave oven. And we have some candy making recipes that are special fun for children.

We also have a hobby that comes fresh from the microwave oven: drying flowers. Many people do not know that flowers can be dried and preserved with microwaves.

Instructions on drying flowers

To dry flowers, first get the materials together. You will need flowers, scissors, silica gel (available at some florist shops and hardware stores), shoe boxes or small glass mixing bowls, wire (florist's wire is best), floral tape (it's available in different colors), glue or florist's adhesive spray, ice pick (or knitting needle or toothpick), delicate brush to remove silica gel, and plastic spray or artist's protective spray.

In choosing flowers select brightly colored ones that are half-open and firm.

Cut them when they are cool and dry, and keep them in a cool place or refrigerate until they are used.

First step in drying is to *embed the flowers*

• Pour silica gel in a shoe box or small glass mixing bowl to a depth of about two inches.

• Insert flowers right side up, spacing them so they do not touch each other or the sides of the container.

• Sift silica gel over the flowers until they are covered completely. Use a toothpick to separate the petals and make sure they retain their original shape.

Next *heat the flowers*

• Place the container in the oven and set the timer.

• Remove from oven after heating and leave the flowers in the silica gel containers overnight. (If flowers do not seem completely dry, place in oven for one more minute.)

To *remove the flowers*

• Tip the container gently so the silica gel crystals begin to flow off the flowers slowly.

• As the flowers become exposed carefully slide two fingers under the flowers and lift out. Shake each flower carefully to remove any crystals that stick.

To *add stems*

• Carefully push the wire stem into the heaviest part at the base of the flower.

• Add florist's tape to further bind the flower to the stem.

• Use plastic spray or artist's protective spray to help keep the moisture out of the flower.

Flower Drying Times	Microwave minutes
Carnations:	1 minute
Asters, calendulas, daffodils, dogwood, grape hyacinths, pansies, poppies, scillia, violets and violas:	2½ minutes
African daisies, clematis, chrysanthemums; coral bells, dianthus, marigold, peonies, roses, salvia, tulips:	3 minutes
Delphinium (larkspur), zinnia:	4 to 5 minutes
Dahlia, iris, tithonia (Mexican sunflower):	5 to 7 minutes

JUST FOR
THE FUN OF IT

COOKIES AND CANDIES

JAMS AND RELISHES

PIES

LEMON CHEESE PIE

8 ounces cream cheese	Unbaked 9-inch graham cracker crust
¼ cup lemon juice	1 cup sour cream
2 eggs, beaten	1 teaspoon grated lemon rind
½ cup sugar	1 tablespoon sugar

Soften cream cheese (30 seconds in microwave, 1 hour at room temperature). Blend with lemon juice until smooth. Add eggs and ½ cup sugar; beat until fluffy. Pour into graham cracker crust (page 281).

Range
Bake at 350°F for 30 minutes, until filling is set. Combine sour cream, lemon rind and sugar, spread over pie, bake 10 minutes longer.

Microwave
Cook 6 minutes, until filling is just set, stirring twice during cooking without disturbing the crust. Combine sour cream, lemon rind and sugar, spread over pie, cook 2 minutes longer.

Cooking Time Saved: 32 minutes

Cool before serving.

MOCHA PIE

1 cup sugar
1 tablespoon instant coffee
¼ cup cornstarch
¼ cup cocoa
Dash salt

2 cups milk
2 eggs, beaten
1 teaspoon vanilla
2 tablespoons butter or margarine
Baked 9-inch pie shell

*Combine sugar, instant coffee, cornstarch, cocoa and salt.
Gradually add milk, stir until smooth.*

Range

Bring mixture to a boil in a
saucepan over medium heat, stirring
constantly. Cook, stirring, until
thick. Stir a little of the hot sauce
into the beaten eggs, return egg
mixture to pan, blend over heat 1
minute. Remove pan from heat, add
vanilla and butter or margarine, stir.

Microwave

Cook mixture in mixing bowl, 6
minutes, stirring every 2 minutes. Stir
a little of the hot sauce into the
beaten eggs, return egg mixture to
bowl. Cook 1½ minutes, stirring at
halfway point. Add vanilla and butter
or margarine, stir.

Cool, stirring occasionally. Pour into baked pie shell, chill until firm.

PECAN PIE

3 eggs, beaten
¾ cup dark corn syrup
¼ teaspoon salt
¾ cup sugar

⅓ cup melted butter or margarine
1 teaspoon vanilla
1 cup pecan halves
Unbaked 9-inch pie shell

Combine filling ingredients, mix well.

Range

Fill pie shell, bake at 375°F for
40 to 50 minutes until filling is set.

Microwave

Prick pie shell with a fork, cook 5
minutes. Cool. Add filling, cook 9
minutes, until set.

Cooking Time Saved: 35 minutes

PEANUT BUTTER AND HONEY PIE

1 envelope unflavored gelatin
¾ cup cold water
3 eggs, separated
½ cup honey
½ teaspoon salt

½ cup peanut butter
1 teaspoon vanilla extract
Pinch salt
Baked 9-inch pie shell
Chocolate curls

Soften gelatin in ½ cup water. Beat egg yolks until thick and lemon colored, add honey and salt, blend well. Stir in gelatin.

Range

Cook in the top of a double boiler over boiling water, stirring constantly, until smooth and thick, about 5 minutes.

Microwave

Cook 2 minutes in bowl, stir well, cook a few seconds longer, if necessary, to thicken.

Cool. Add remaining ¼ cup water to peanut butter, beat until smooth. Stir in vanilla and yolk mixture. Chill until thickened, but not firm. Beat egg whites with salt until stiff but not dry. Fold into yolk mixture. Fill baked pie shell, chill until firm. Decorate with chocolate curls.

STRAWBERRY PIE

3 pints strawberries
1 cup sugar
3 tablespoons cornstarch
⅓ cup water or wine
Baked 9-inch pie shell

Wash and hull berries. Mash enough berries to make 1 cup pulp. Combine sugar and cornstarch, stir in water or wine, add mashed berries, whirl in blender to puree.

Range

In saucepan, cook over moderate heat, stirring constantly, until sauce is thick and smooth.

Microwave

Cook 5 minutes, in a 1-quart bowl, stirring 3 times until sauce is thick and smooth.

Cool sauce, stirring occasionally. Arrange whole berries in pie shell, pour cooked berry mixture over fruit. Chill.

PUMPKIN PIE

2 eggs
1 can (1 pound) pumpkin
½ cup brown sugar
Dash salt
1 teaspoon cinnamon

½ teaspoon ginger
¼ teaspoon ground cloves
1 can (13 ounces) evaporated milk
Baked 9-inch pie shell
with high fluted rim

Beat eggs, stir in pumpkin, blend well. Mix sugar, salt and spices, add. Add milk, stir until smooth.

Range

Pour pumpkin mixture into a greased 9-inch pie plate, bake at 350°F for about 45 minutes, until custard is set.

Microwave

Pour pumpkin mixture into 9-inch glass pie plate, cook 12 minutes, stirring every 3 minutes. Cook 3 minutes longer.

Cooking Time Saved: about 30 minutes.

Loosen filling from sides of pan with a sharp knife, slip into baked crust.

PIE CRUSTS

PIE CRUST

1 cup flour
½ teaspoon salt
⅓ cup hydrogenated shortening
3 tablespoons ice water

Toss flour and salt together. Cut in shortening with a pastry blender or 2 knives. Sprinkle with water, 1 tablespoon at a time. Toss with a fork to mix. Work into a firm ball, with a fork or your hands. Roll out between sheets of wax paper into a round about 1½ inches larger than an inverted 9-inch pie plate. Ease dough into plate without stretching. Trim edge evenly, fold under, press firmly against pie plate. Trimmings may be used to anchor pastry against plate. Prick well with a fork.

Range
Bake at 425°F for 10 to 15 minutes, until crisp and browned to taste.

Microwave
Cook 2 minutes, prick again. Cook 2 minutes, rotate dish and prick again. Cook 2 to 3 minutes, until crisp.

COOKIE CRUMB PIE CRUST

⅓ cup melted butter or margarine
1½ cups cookie crumbs (vanilla wafers,
   chocolate cookies, gingersnaps, macaroons, etc.)

Range

Melt butter or margarine in a small pan, stir in cookie crumbs. Press against bottom and sides of a 9-inch pie plate. Bake at 375°F for 8 to 10 minutes, until set.

Microwave

Melt butter or margarine in a 9-inch pie plate, stir in crumbs, press against bottom and sides of plate. Cook 3 minutes, rotating the plate halfway through cooking period.

Cool before filling.

Tip: To make crumbs, put cookies in a paper bag, crush with a rolling pin. Or whirl cookies in a blender.

NUTTED PIE CRUST

1¼ cups flour
¼ cup sugar
½ teaspoon salt
½ teaspoon each cinnamon and allspice

½ cup butter or margarine
1 teaspoon grated lemon rind
¼ cup finely grated almonds
   or other nuts
1 egg, beaten

Toss flour, sugar, salt and spices to mix. Work in butter or margarine to make a crumbly mixture. Add lemon rind, nuts and beaten egg, blend to make a firm dough. Press against the bottom and sides of a 9-inch pie plate.

Range

Bake at 425°F for 35 to 40 minutes, until crisp.

Microwave

Cook 5 minutes, rotating plate ¼ turn 3 times during cooking.

Cooking Time Saved: about 35 minutes

Cool. Use for any prepared pie filling.

RICH PIE SHELL

1½ cups flour ½ cup butter or margarine
1 tablespoon sugar 2 egg yolks
½ teaspoon salt 1 tablespoon water

*Toss flour, sugar and salt to mix. Cut butter or margarine into small pieces,
work into flour mixture with a pastry blender or two knives.*
*Add egg yolks and water, blend to make a firm dough. Pat evenly into a 9-inch pie plate
to cover bottom and sides.*

Range
Bake at 400°F for about 15 minutes,
until crisp and golden.

Microwave
Cook shell 6 minutes, until crisp.

Cooking Time Saved: about 9
minutes

*Fill with chiffon mixtures or with cooked fruit, or use in any recipe
calling for a baked pie shell.*

WHOLE WHEAT PIE CRUST

1 cup whole wheat flour
1 tablespoon sugar
½ teaspoon salt
⅓ cup oil
2 tablespoons milk

*Toss flour, sugar and salt. Add oil and milk, mix with a fork. Form
into a ball, roll out between sheets of wax paper into a round 1 inch
larger than 9-inch pie plate. Fit into pie plate, flute edges. Prick bottom
and sides of crust with fork.*

Range
Bake at 425°F for 15 to 20 minutes,
until well browned.

Microwave
Bake 4 minutes, until crisp.

Cooking Time Saved: about 15
minutes

Cool. Use for any prepared pie filling.

GRAHAM CRACKER PIE CRUST

¼ cup butter or margarine, cut in 4 pieces
¼ cup sugar
¼ cup finely chopped nuts (optional)
1⅓ cups graham cracker crumbs

Range

Melt butter or margarine over low heat, add with sugar and nuts to graham cracker crumbs in bowl, mix thoroughly. Press against bottom and sides of a 9- or 10-inch pie plate. Chill. Or bake at 350°F for about 10 minutes.

Microwave

Melt butter or margarine in a 9- or 10-inch glass pie plate 45 seconds. Add crumbs, sugar and nuts, mix thoroughly and press against bottom and sides of plate. Chill. Or cook 2 minutes, turning dish once.

Cool before filling.

BREADS
AND ROLLS

BRIOCHE

¼ cup milk
1 cup butter or margarine
½ cup sugar
½ teaspoon salt
1½ teaspoons grated lemon rind

2 envelopes yeast
¼ cup very warm water
6 beaten eggs
4½ to 5 cups flour

Heat milk and butter or margarine to boiling point (2 minutes in microwave, or over medium heat on range). Add sugar, salt, and grated lemon rind, cool to lukewarm. Sprinkle yeast over warm water, let stand 5 minutes. Combine with cooled milk mixture. Add beaten eggs. Add 3 cups flour, beat thoroughly. Add remaining flour to make a soft dough that can be handled, beat until mixture is smooth. Cover with a damp towel, let rise until double in bulk (reduce rising time by heating in microwave 30 seconds at beginning of rising period). Stir down, cover tightly and chill. To make small brioches, pinch off a piece of dough ⅓ the size of large custard cups, roll into a ball, place in greased cup. Cut a cross in the top of ball and insert a second, smaller ball of dough. Cover, let rise in a warm place until doubled in bulk.

Range
Bake at 400°F for 12 to 15 minutes, until browned.

Microwave
Cook, 6 at a time, 3 minutes. Transfer to 425°F oven and bake 5 minutes, until browned, if desired.

Makes about 24 brioches.

BELIEVE-IT-OR-NOT BAGELS

1 envelope dry yeast	4 to 4½ cups flour
1½ cups very warm water	Coarse salt, poppy or sesame seeds
3 tablespoons sugar	(optional)
1 tablespoon salt	1 egg, beaten

Sprinkle yeast over warm water, stir to dissolve. Add sugar, salt and enough flour to make a soft dough. Turn out onto lightly floured surface, knead until smooth and elastic, about 10 minutes.

Range

Cover, let rise about 15 minutes, punch down, divide dough into 12 equal portions, shape each into a strip about 8 inches long. Bring ends together to form a ring, pinch to secure. Let rise 30 minutes. Bring 1 gallon water to a boil, boil a few bagels at a time, about 8 minutes. Remove to a towel to drain. Sprinkle with coarse salt, poppy or sesame seeds, if desired. Transfer to ungreased baking sheet, bake at 375°F for 30 to 35 minutes, until browned.

Microwave

Cover, heat in microwave 30 seconds, let rise 10 minutes. Punch down, divide dough into 12 equal portions, shape each into a strip about 8 inches long. Bring ends together to form a ring, pinch to secure. Heat in microwave 30 seconds, let rise 10 minutes. Cook in a baking dish in 1 inch boiling water, 4 bagels at a time, 3 minutes. Remove to a towel to drain. Sprinkle with coarse salt, poppy or sesame seeds, if desired. Cover tray with paper towel. Cook bagels on tray, 4 at a time, 3 minutes. Brown on ungreased baking sheet in conventional oven set at 425°F about 10 minutes.

Serve hot. Makes 1 dozen.

SPOON BREAD

½ cup yellow corn meal
1 teaspoon salt
1½ cups milk
1 teaspoon sugar

1 tablespoon butter or margarine
2 eggs, beaten
1 teaspoon baking powder

Range

Combine corn meal and salt in medium saucepan. Add milk and sugar. Cook over medium heat, stirring, until mixture is thick and smooth, about 5 minutes. Cool slightly, beat in butter or margarine, eggs and baking powder. Pour batter into greased 1-quart casserole. Bake at 375°F for about 25 minutes, until set.

Microwave

Combine corn meal and salt in 1½-quart casserole. Stir in milk and sugar. Cook, uncovered, until mixture is thick and smooth, about 5 minutes. Cool slightly. Beat in butter or margarine, eggs and baking powder. Cook until set, about 5 minutes. Let stand a few minutes.

Cooking Time Saved: 20 minutes

Makes 4 to 6 servings.

APPLE NUT BREAD

½ cup butter or margarine
1 cup sugar
2 eggs
1 teaspoon vanilla
2 tablespoons water
2 cups flour

1 teaspoon baking powder
1 teaspoon baking soda
½ teaspoon salt
1 cup chopped nuts
1 cup chopped apple

Cream butter or margarine with sugar, beat in eggs, combining well. Add vanilla and water, beat until smooth. Toss together flour, baking powder, soda, salt, nuts and apples. Fold in.

Range

Bake in greased 9- by 5-inch loaf pan at 325°F for about 1 hour.

Microwave

Cook in 9- by 5-inch glass loaf pan lined with brown paper, 5-6 minutes, or until done in center. Rotate ½ turn, cook 5 minutes longer. If desired brown in 425°F oven, about 10 minutes.

Cooking Time Saved: 50 minutes

Cool before slicing.

BUTTERMILK CORN BREAD

1⅓ cups corn meal
½ teaspoon salt
⅓ cup flour
1 cup buttermilk
1 teaspoon baking powder
1 egg
1 teaspoon baking soda
2 tablespoons melted bacon drippings
1 tablespoon sugar
or oil

Toss dry ingredients to mix. Combine buttermilk and egg, add all at once to dry ingredients, stir until smooth. Stir in bacon drippings.

Range

Bake at 400°F for 25 minutes in a greased 8-inch square pan, until browned.

Microwave

Cook in ungreased 8-inch square dish 5 minutes, rotating dish ½ turn at the halfway point. Brown under browning unit or broiler, if desired.

Cooking Time Saved: about 20 minutes.

PITA BREAD

5 to 6 cups flour
1 tablespoon sugar
2 teaspoons salt
1 envelope dry yeast
2 cups very warm water

Mix 2 cups flour, sugar, salt and yeast in a large bowl. Gradually add water, beat until smooth. Add 1 cup flour and beat until smooth. Add enough additional flour to make a soft dough. Beat well. Turn out on lightly floured board; knead until smooth and elastic, about 10 minutes. Place in a greased bowl, turning dough to grease top. Cover and let rise in warm place until doubled in bulk, about 1 hour. (Speed rising by placing dough in microwave for 30 seconds at beginning of rising period.) Punch dough down; turn out onto lightly floured board. Cover, let rest 30 minutes. Divide dough into 12 equal pieces, shape each into a ball. On a lightly floured board, roll out each ball into a 5-inch circle.

Range

Bake on a preheated cookie sheet, on lowest rack of 450°F oven about 5 minutes. Brown tops under broiler.

Microwave

Cook 3 at a time on microwave tray, 2 minutes. At serving time, brown tops and bottoms under browning unit or broiler.

ENGLISH MUFFINS

1 package dry yeast
¼ cup very warm water
¾ cup milk
2 tablespoons butter or margarine

1 teaspoon salt to 3½ cups flour
(part hard-wheat bread flour,
if available)
Corn meal

Dissolve yeast in warm water. Scald milk, add butter or margarine and salt, cool to lukewarm, add to yeast. Add 2 cups flour, beat until smooth, add 1 cup or more flour to make a stiff dough. Knead until smooth on lightly floured board, about 10 minutes. Turn dough in greased bowl, cover with damp towel. (To speed rising, first place in microwave 30 to 40 seconds.) Let rise in warm place until double. Punch down, roll out ½-inch thick on surface dusted lightly with corn meal. Cut into 3-inch rounds, sprinkle with more corn meal. Let rise in warm place until double.

Range
Lightly grease a griddle or large, heavy frying pan. Brown muffins 7 to 10 minutes on each side over medium heat. Split and toast cut side, serve hot.

Microwave
Place 4 muffins at a time on wax paper, cook 2 minutes, turn over and cook 1 minute longer. Split and toast on both sides, serve hot.

Makes 8 muffins.

CINNAMON ROLLS

1 cup biscuit mix
⅓ cup milk
2 tablespoons soft butter or margarine

3 tablespoons sugar
1 tablespoon cinnamon
2 tablespoons raisins or chopped nuts

Combine biscuit mix with milk, knead briefly. Pat into a 7-inch square. Spread with butter or margarine, sprinkle with 2 tablespoons sugar, 2 teaspoons cinnamon and raisins or nuts. Roll up, seal edges. Cut into 6 slices.

Range
Set each slice, cut side up, in greased muffin cup. Sprinkle each with remaining sugar and cinnamon. Bake at 400°F for 15 to 20 minutes.

Microwave
Set each slice, cut side up, into a custard cup, sprinkle each with remaining sugar and cinnamon. Place in a circle in microwave, cook 2½ minutes, until set.

Cooking Time Saved: about 15 minutes

286

THREE GRAIN BREAD

2 envelopes yeast	2 teaspoons salt
½ cup very warm water	¼ cup oil
3 cups rolled oats	¼ cup molasses
1 cup yellow corn meal	1½ cups warm milk
3 cups whole wheat flour	2 eggs, lightly beaten

Dissolve yeast in warm water, let stand about 5 minutes.
Combine oats, corn meal and flour in large mixing bowl.
Stir in salt, oil and molasses. Add yeast. Stir in milk and
eggs, beat until smooth. Turn out on a lightly floured board, knead until smooth
and satiny, adding more flour, if necessary. Grease bowl, turn dough in bowl
to coat all sides. Cover and let rise in warm place
until doubled in bulk, about 1 hour.
(Reduce rising time by first heating in microwave 30 seconds.)
Punch down, knead briefly and divide in half. Shape into 2 loaves.

Range

Place in 2 greased 8- by 4-inch loaf pans. Let rise until doubled in bulk, about 1 hour. Bake at 350°F for 50 to 60 minutes, until loaves sound hollow when tapped.

Microwave

Place in 2 greased 8- by 4-inch glass loaf pans. Let rise until doubled in bulk. Cook, one at a time, 8 minutes. Brown in 450°F oven 10 minutes if desired.

Cooking Time Saved: 40 to 50 minutes

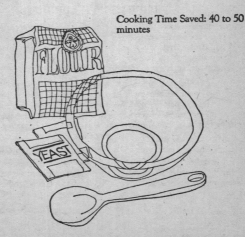

WHOLE WHEAT BREAD

1 envelope dry yeast
¼ cup very warm water
2 cups milk
1 tablespoon salt

2 tablespoons butter or margarine
¼ cup light molasses
6 cups whole wheat flour

Dissolve yeast in water, add milk, salt, butter or margarine, molasses and half the flour. Beat well, work in remaining flour. Knead well, adding more flour if necessary, to make a dough that does not stick to the hands. Place in oiled bowl, roll to oil top, cover with damp towel. Let rise until double in bulk. (To speed rising, heat dough in microwave 30 seconds at beginning of rising period.) Punch down, shape into 2 loaves.

Range

Bake in greased 8- by 4-inch loaf pans at 350°F for about 45 minutes, until loaves sound hollow when tapped.

Microwave

Cooked in ungreased 8- by 4-inch glass loaf pans one at a time, about 6 to 8 minutes, rotating ¼ turn halfway through cooking, until firm. If desired, brown under browning unit or in hot oven.
Cooking Time Saved: about 30 minutes

SWEET POTATO BREAD

1 envelope yeast
¼ cup very warm water
½ cup shortening
⅓ cup sugar
1½ cups cooked, mashed sweet potatoes

⅓ cup milk or cream
2 eggs, beaten
1 teaspoon salt
5 cups flour

Dissolve yeast in water. Cream shortening and sugar. Beat in sweet potatoes, milk, eggs and salt. Combine with yeast. Beat in part of flour. Work in remaining flour and knead 5 minutes. Cover, let rise in warm place until doubled. (Speed rising by placing dough in microwave 30 seconds at beginning of rising period.) Punch down, shape into 2 loaves.

Range

Bake in 2 greased 8- by 4-inch loaf pans at 350°F for about 30 minutes, until loaves sound hollow when tapped.

Microwave

Cooked in ungreased 8- by 4-inch glass loaf pans, about 8 minutes, 1 loaf at a time. Brown in 425°F oven 10 minutes, if desired.

Cooking Time Saved: 12 or 22 minutes

COOKIES
AND CANDIES

ALMOND CRESCENTS

1 cup almonds, finely grated
1¼ cups flour
¼ cup confectioners' sugar
½ cup butter or margarine
1 egg yolk

Combine almonds, flour and sugar. Work in butter or margarine and egg yolk with hands until well blended. Chill. Pinch off pieces of dough the size of walnuts, shape into crescents.

Range
Bake on greased cookie sheets at 325°F for about 20 minutes.

Microwave
Place 8 cookies at a time on wax paper on tray, cook about 2 minutes.

Cooking Time Saved: about 15 minutes

Makes 2 dozen.

BANANA BOATS

Bananas
Chocolate chips
Miniature marshmallows
Salted peanuts

Peel banana skins back, leave skins attached at base. Split each banana lengthwise to make a pocket. Fill pocket with chocolate chips, marshmallows and peanuts. Replace skins, fasten with wooden picks.

Range
Bake bananas on a shallow baking pan at 325°F for about 15 minutes, until bananas are tender.

Microwave
Place bananas on serving plate, cook 2 banana boats about 4 minutes, 4 about 8 minutes.

BROWNIES

¾ cup flour
½ teaspoon baking powder
½ teaspoon salt
2 squares (2 ounces) unsweetened chocolate
½ cup butter or margarine

1 cup sugar
2 eggs
1 teaspoon vanilla
½ cup broken walnut or pecan meats

Toss flour, baking powder and salt to mix. Set aside.

Range
Melt chocolate and butter or margarine in saucepan, pour into mixing bowl. Stir in sugar. Add eggs, beat well. Stir in dry ingredients and vanilla. Spread in greased and floured 8-inch square baking dish. Sprinkle with chopped nuts. Bake at 350°F for 30 to 35 minutes.

Microwave
Melt chocolate and butter or margarine in mixing bowl, about 1½ minutes. Stir in sugar. Add eggs, beat well. Stir in dry ingredients and vanilla. Spread in ungreased 8-inch square baking dish. Sprinkle with chopped nuts. Cook 3 minutes, rotate pan ¼ turn. Cook 3 minutes longer.

Cooking Time Saved: about 25 minutes

Cool slightly, cut into 2-inch squares. Makes 16 brownies.

CHOCOLATE NUT CLUSTERS

1 package (6 ounces)
semi-sweet chocolate morsels
¼ cup light corn syrup
2 teaspoons vanilla

Pinch salt
1½ cups peanuts or other nuts
½ cup raisins (optional)
2 tablespoons confectioners' sugar

Range
Combine chocolate morsels and syrup in heavy pan, stir over low heat until chocolate melts.

Microwave
Combine chocolate morsels and syrup in glass bowl, cook 3 minutes, until chocolate melts.

Add vanilla, salt, nuts, raisins and confectioners' sugar, stir until well blended. Drop from a teaspoon onto a buttered baking sheet or wax paper. Chill until firm. Makes about 40 clusters.

CHOCOLATE FROSTED FRUITS

Fruit: Banana halves, orange or apple wedges, peach or pear quarters
1 package (6 ounces) semi-sweet chocolate morsels

Freeze fruit in refrigerator trays 1 hour.

Range
Melt chocolate in small pan over hot water, stirring constantly.

Microwave
Melt chocolate in bowl 5 minutes, stir.

Dip frozen fruit into melted chocolate to coat, drain excess. Wrap in foil, return to freezer, store until wanted. Makes about 8 large frosted fruits.

S'MORES

4 graham crackers
2 marshmallows
1 bar sweet chocolate (about 1 ounce)

Range
Divide chocolate bar in half, cover 2 graham crackers. Spear marshmallows on forks, toast over high heat until soft. Arrange on chocolate, top with graham crackers.

Microwave
Divide chocolate bar in half, cover 2 graham crackers. Top each with a marshmallow and second cracker. Cook on serving plate, 30 seconds, until marshmallows are soft.

Makes 2 S'mores.

FUDGE

½ pound marshmallows
(4 cups miniature or 32 large)
¼ cup butter or margarine
⅔ cup evaporated milk
1½ cups sugar

¼ teaspoon salt
1 package (12 ounces) chocolate chips
1 teaspoon vanilla
½ cup chopped nuts

Range

Combine marshmallows, butter or margarine, milk, sugar and salt in large, heavy, saucepan. Cook, stirring, until mixture comes to full boil. Boil 5 minutes over medium heat, stirring constantly.

Microwave

Combine marshmallows, butter or margarine, milk, sugar and salt in 3-quart casserole. Cook until mixture boils, 8 minutes, stir. Cook 3 minutes longer.

Remove from heat, add chocolate chips. Beat until chocolate melts, add vanilla and nuts. Pour into buttered 9-inch square pan. Cool until firm, cut into squares. Makes 2½ pounds.

FLUFFY MARSHMALLOWS

1 envelope unflavored gelatin
⅓ cup cold water
½ cup sugar

⅔ cup light corn syrup
½ teaspoon vanilla
Confectioners' sugar

Range

Sprinkle gelatin on cold water in top of double boiler. Place pan over boiling water. Cook, stirring until gelatin dissolves. Add sugar, stir until dissolved. Transfer to large mixing bowl, add corn syrup, vanilla and gelatin.

Microwave

Sprinkle gelatin over cold water in large mixing bowl. Cook in microwave until gelatin dissolves, about 45 seconds. Add sugar and heat briefly, until sugar dissolves. Add corn syrup and vanilla.

Beat with electric mixer until mixture is very thick and marshmallow-like, about 15 minutes. Turn into 8-inch square pan generously coated with confectioners' sugar. Let stand at room temperature until set, about 1 hour. Invert on board generously sprinkled with confectioners' sugar, cut into 1-inch squares with knife dipped in cold water. Coat with confectioners' sugar. Makes 64.

FLORENTINES

½ cup heavy cream
3 tablespoons butter or margarine
½ cup sugar
⅓ cup flour

Dash salt
½ cup finely chopped
candied orange peel
1½ cups finely chopped almonds
1 package (6 ounces) chocolate chips

Range

Combine cream, butter or margarine and sugar in saucepan, bring to a boil. Remove from heat, stir in flour, salt, orange peel and almonds. Drop from teaspoon onto greased and floured cookie sheet. Bake at 350°F for about 10 minutes. Cool on cookie sheet a few minutes, remove to rack. Melt chocolate over low heat, spread on cooled cookies.

Microwave

Bring cream, butter or margarine and sugar to a boil in glass casserole, about 1½ minutes. Stir in flour, salt, orange peel and almonds. Drop from teaspoon in a ring onto wax paper. Cook 8 cookies at a time, 5 to 7 minutes. Cool on paper. Melt chocolate in small bowl 3 minutes, spread on cooled cookies.

Makes about 2 dozen.

PEANUT BRITTLE

2 tablespoons butter or margarine
¼ cup sugar
¼ cup molasses

½ cup dark corn syrup
1½ cups peanuts
⅛ teaspoon baking soda

Range

Combine butter or margarine, sugar, molasses and corn syrup in heavy saucepan or skillet. Cook over medium heat, stirring, until well blended. Add peanuts, bring to a boil, and cook to soft crack stage (280°F). A little dripped into cold water will separate into hard (not brittle) threads.

Microwave

Combine butter or margarine, sugar, molasses and corn syrup in 3-quart casserole. Cook until sugar dissolves, about 4 to 5 minutes. Add peanuts, bring to boil, cook to soft crack stage (280°F) about 6 to 7 minutes. A little dripped into cold water will separate into hard (not brittle) threads.

Stir in soda. Pour onto buttered baking sheet to cool and harden. Remove candy, break into irregular pieces. Makes about ¾ pound.

FRUIT SQUARES

1 cup flour	1 teaspoon baking powder
¼ cup white sugar	1 teaspoon vanilla
½ cup butter or margarine	Pinch salt
¾ cup brown sugar	½ cup chopped nuts
2 eggs	½ cup flaked coconut
2 tablespoons flour	½ cup mixed dried or
	candied fruits, chopped

Make crust: combine 1 cup flour, the white sugar and butter or margarine, pat into 8-inch square pan. Mix remaining ingredients to make topping.

Range	Microwave
Bake crust at 350°F for about 20 minutes, until light brown. Spread fruit mixture on crust and bake 15 minutes longer.	Cook crust 5 minutes, until set. Spread fruit mixture on crust, cook 6 minutes longer.
	Cooking Time Saved: 24 minutes

Cut into 2-inch squares. Makes 16.

JELLY-FILLED STRIPS

1½ cups flour	½ cup butter or margarine
2 tablespoons sugar	1 egg
½ teaspoon salt	1 cup jelly or preserves

Combine flour, sugar and salt. Cut in butter or margarine until mixture is crumbly. Add egg and form into a ball. Chill about 15 minutes. Divide dough in half, roll or pat each half into a 6-by12-inch rectangle. Spread one rectangle with jelly, top with other rectangle.

Range	Microwave
Bake on lightly greased cookie sheets at 375°F for about 15 minutes.	Place in oven on wax paper or on glass utility dish, bake 3 minutes.
	Cooking Time Saved: about 12 minutes

Cool slightly and cut into bars. Makes 20.

SCOTCH SHORTBREAD

½ cup butter or margarine
1¼ cups flour
⅓ cup sugar
Pinch salt

Soften butter or margarine (½ to 1 hour at room temperature, 15 seconds in microwave).
Mix flour, sugar and salt, work in butter or margarine with spoon or
hands to make a firm dough. Pat evenly in an ungreased 9-inch pie plate.
With a sharp knife mark 16 wedges. Prick well.

Range	Microwave
Bake at 350°F. for about 25 minutes, until firm but not colored.	Cook about 2 minutes, rotate plate ½ turn, cook 2 minutes longer. Let stand until firm.

Cooking Time Saved: 21 minutes

Separate wedges with a knife. Makes 16.

SUGAR COOKIES

¾ cup butter or margarine
1 cup sugar
2 eggs, beaten
1 teaspoon vanilla

2⅔ cups flour
2 teaspoons baking powder
½ teaspoon salt

Soften butter or margarine (½ hour to 1 hour at room temperature, 15 seconds in
microwave). Cream butter or margarine, gradually add sugar, cream until fluffy.
Beat in eggs and vanilla. Toss flour, baking powder and salt to mix.
Add to creamed mixture, combine well. Chill dough 1 hour, until firm.
Roll out ¼-inch thick. Cut into shapes with cookie cutter.

Range	Microwave
Bake cookies on ungreased baking sheet at 375°F for about 10 minutes. Remove from pan at once.	Arrange 8 cookies in a ring on wax paper on microwave tray. Cook 2 minutes. Let stand until firm, remove from paper.

Makes 3 to 4 dozen cookies, depending on size of cutters.

OATMEAL REFRIGERATOR COOKIES

½ cup butter or margarine	1 teaspoon grated lemon rind
½ cup white sugar	¾ cup flour
½ cup brown sugar	½ teaspoon baking soda
1 egg, beaten	½ teaspoon salt
½ teaspoon vanilla	1½ cups rolled oats

Soften butter or margarine (about 15 seconds in microwave, ½ to 1 hour at room temperature). Cream butter or margarine, gradually add white and brown sugar, cream until light and fluffy. Beat in egg, vanilla and lemon rind. Toss flour, baking soda and salt to mix. Add to creamed mixture, blend well. Add oats, blend. Shape dough into a roll 2 inches in diameter. Wrap in waxed paper, chill thoroughly.

Range
Cut chilled cookie dough into quarter-inch slices, bake on a greased baking sheet at 400°F for 6 to 8 minutes. Remove from pan. Place on rack to cool.

Microwave
Cut 8 quarter-inch slices from chilled cookie dough. Arrange in a ring on wax paper on microwave tray, cook 3 minutes. Rotate wax paper ½ turn halfway through cooking time.

This amount of dough makes 3 dozen cookies; dough may be stored in the refrigerator and the cookies freshly baked as required.

JAMS
AND RELISHES

LEMON CURD

6 tablespoons butter
¼ cup granulated sugar
2 teaspoons grated lemon rind
¼ cup lemon juice
3 eggs, beaten

Range

Put butter into top of double boiler, add sugar, lemon rind and juice. Strain eggs into pan. Stir constantly over moderate heat until thick. Do not boil.

Microwave

Cut butter into 4 pieces, soften in 1-quart casserole or bowl 10 seconds. Stir in lemon rind and juice. Strain eggs into casserole, blend well. Cover with wax paper, cook 2 minutes 45 seconds, stirring every 30 seconds, until mixture is thick.

Cooking Time Saved: about 12 minutes

Pour into a jar and cool to thicken further. Store in a cool place. Makes 1½ cups.

CRANBERRY SAUCE

1 pound cranberries (1 quart)
2 cups sugar
2 cups boiling water
Pinch salt
Grated rind of ½ orange

Pick over cranberries, discard stems, wash.

Range

Boil sugar and water 5 minutes. Add cranberries, salt, and orange rind, return to a boil, cook 5 minutes longer until cranberries pop open. Pour into serving dish, chill.

Microwave

Combine ingredients in 2-quart casserole, cover, cook 8 minutes, until cranberries pop open. Chill before serving.

Makes 1 quart.

CANDIED CRANBERRY RELISH

1 pound cranberries
1½ cups sugar
Pinch salt
½ teaspoon powdered cloves

Pick over cranberries, discard stems, wash.

Range

Stir cranberries with remaining ingredients in a 2-quart baking dish. Bake at 300°F for about 1 hour, until berries are tender, stirring often.

Microwave

Combine ingredients in a 2-quart glass casserole. Cook, stirring occasionally, until berries are tender, 15 to 20 minutes.

Cooking Time Saved: 40 minutes

Chill. Serve as a relish with poultry or meat.
Makes 2½ cups.

MARMALADE

1 orange	Water
1 grapefruit	Sugar
1 lemon	

Peel fruit thinly, leaving white inner skin intact. Cut peels into thin strips, cover with boiling water, boil 5 minutes (in microwave or range). Drain water, add fresh water, boil again 5 minutes, drain. Trim off white membranes and cut fruit into very thin slices. Discard seeds. Add slices to peel, measure.

Range

In large kettle, add 2 cups water to each cup of fruit, boil rapidly, uncovered, 40 minutes. Measure, add 1 cup sugar for each cup fruit mixture. Boil rapidly until thick and amber in color (about 1 hour), stirring frequently.

Microwave

In 3-quart bowl, add 1 cup water to each cup of fruit, cook 20 minutes. Measure, add 1 cup sugar for each cup fruit mixture. Cook 25 minutes, until thick and amber in color, stirring occasionally.

Cooking Time Saved: about 1 hour

To Test, pour syrup from the side of a spoon. When the last drops come together and fall in a sheet, the mixture has reached the jellying stage. Cool 5 minutes. Pour into hot, sterilized jars and cover with a layer of paraffin immediately.
Makes 4 jars, 6-ounces each.

WATERMELON PICKLE

2 pounds watermelon rind	2 cups sugar (range)
Boiling water	1 cup sugar (microwave)
2 tablespoons salt	Juice of 1 lemon
2 cups cider vinegar (range)	2 sticks cinnamon
1 cup cider vinegar (microwave)	6 whole cloves

Peel and discard the green skin from the watermelon rind; leave a thin rim of pink on the inner side of the rind. Cut into 1½-inch pieces.

Range

Cover watermelon rind in a large saucepan with boiling water, add salt, cover, bring to a boil. Cook 30 minutes, until tender. Drain and rinse rind. Mix 2 cups each vinegar and sugar, lemon juice and spices in saucepan, bring to a boil, boil 5 minutes. Add rind, simmer 20 minutes, until rind is transparent and syrup is thick.

Microwave

Cover watermelon rind in a 4-quart casserole with boiling water, add salt, cover, bring to a boil. Cook 15 minutes, until tender. Drain and rinse rind, return to casserole. Add 1 cup each vinegar and sugar, lemon juice and spices. Stir, cook 5 minutes, stir. Cover, cook 20 minutes, until rind is transparent and syrup is thick.

Pack rind into 4 or 5 sterile half-pint jars, cover with hot syrup. Makes 5½ pints.

INDEX

307